Letts

Revise
GCSE

Geography

Jol  Bilham-Boult

Contents

Spec	Unit	Title	% Full GCSE	Time	Decision Making Examination (Using pre-release resources. Themes will change annually.)	Controlled Assessment (All tasks set by boards 2 years before submission. Tasks will change each year. Adapt fieldwork tasks to the local context.)	Available Jan–June	Date of First Assessment
AQA A	1	Physical Geography	37.5	1hr 30				June 2010
	2	Human Geography	37.5	1hr 30			June	June 2010
	3	Local fieldwork Investigation	25	6hr (write-up)		1 question at a local scale, f/w compulsory. Q chosen from 11 task statements provided by the Board.	June	June 2010
AQA B	1	Managing places in the 21st Century	25	1hr			Both	Jan 2010
	2	Hostile world	25	1hr			Both	June 2010
	3	Investigating the shrinking world	25	1hr			June	June 2010
	4	Local Investigation (incl. fieldwork)	15	4hr (write-up)		Choose 1 task from 4 set by Board. Tasks based on Units 1 & 3.		
		Geographical Issue Investigation	10	2hr (write-up)		1 investigation task from a choice of 2 set by the Board. Tasks based on: • Energy in the 21st Century • Water – a precious resource	June	June 2010
EDEXCEL A	1	Geographical skills & challenges	25	1hr			Both	June 2010
	2	The natural environment	25	1hr			Both	June 2010
	3	The human environment	25	1hr			Both	June 2010
	4	Investigating geography	25			8 themes are listed in the specification. The Board will identify 1 task for each theme. Candidates to select 1 as a fieldwork investigation.	June	June 2010
EDEXCEL B	1	Dynamic planet	25	1hr			Both	June 2010
	2	People & the planet	25	1hr			Both	June 2010
	3	Making geographical decisions	25	1hr	The Board will identify the theme 2 years before the examination.		June	June 2010
	4	Researching geography	25			4 themes are listed in the specification. The Board will identify 2 tasks for each theme. Candidates to select 1 as a fieldwork investigation.	June	June 2010

your GCSE course

Board	Code	Unit title	%	Duration	Details	Timing	Date
OCR A	A671	Extreme environments	25	1hr			
	A672	You as a global citizen (2 pieces of work, one must include fieldwork)	25	1hr 30	2 tasks set by the Board.		
	A673	Similarities and differences	25	1hr			
	A674	Issues in our fast-changing world	25		Resource booklet will be issued in late April.	June	June 2011
OCR B	B561	Sustainable decision making	25	1hr	Title will be based on 1 of the 4 Key Themes.	Both	June 2010
	B562	Geographical enquiry (2 pieces of work) • Fieldwork focus task	15		4 tasks set by the Board. Tasks based on the 4 Themes, 1 task per theme, except for Rivers & Coasts which will have 1 each.		
		• Geographical investigation	10		9 themes listed in the Specification. Board will set 2 tasks per theme annually. Candidates to select 1 for investigation.	Both	June 2010
	B563	Key geographical themes. 4 Themes, 3 assessed annually (excludes theme covered in unit B561). Themes will rotate each year **as set out in the specification.**	50	1hr 30		June	June 2011
WJEC A	1	Core geography	40	1hr 45		June	June 2010
	2	Options geography	35	1hr 45		June	June 2011
	3	Geographical enquiry (2 pieces of work) • Fieldwork enquiry (10%) • Problem solving / decision making exercise (15%)	25		The Board will publish a list of tasks based on each of the core & optional themes. Single tasks may be used to address both pieces of work, alternatively 2 different tasks can be selected.	June	June 2011
WJEC B	1	Challenges & interactions in geography	30	1hr		Both	June 2010
	2	Development & problem solving in geography	45	2hr		Both	June 2010
	4	Geographical enquiry (2 pieces of work): • Enquiry based on fieldwork	15		The board will publish a list of tasks which will cover all 3 themes: • Select 1 task for the **fieldwork enquiry** • Select 1 task for the **issue** addressing different key questions to the enquiry. Write up the report following the **'framework for delivering the task'** as published in the specification.	June	June 2011
		• Issue based on research	10				
CCEA	1	Understanding our natural world	37.5	1hr 30		June	June 2010
	2	Living in our world	37.5	30		June	June 2010
	3	Fieldwork report	37.5		List of 4 generic titles from across the themes	June	June 2011

Preparing for the examination

Planning your study

The final **three months** before taking your GCSE examination are very important in preparing for the exam and enabling you to achieve your best grade. However, success can be assisted by an organised approach throughout the course.

- After completing a topic in school or college, go through the topic again in your **Revise GCSE Geography Study Guide**. Copy out the main points again on a sheet of paper or use a highlighter pen to emphasise them.
- A couple of days later try to write out these key points from memory. Check differences between what you wrote originally and what you wrote later.
- If you have written your notes on a piece of paper, keep this for revision.
- Try some questions in the book and check your answers.
- Decide whether you have fully mastered the topic and write down any weaknesses you think you have.

Preparing a revision programme

In the last three months before the final examination go through the list of topics in your Examination Board's specification. Go through and identify which topics you feel you need to concentrate on. It is a temptation at this time to spend valuable revision time on the things you already know and can do. It makes you feel good but does not move you forward.

When you feel you have mastered all the topics, spend time trying past questions. Each time check your answers with the answers given. In the final couple of weeks go back to your summary sheets (or the sections you have highlighted in the book).

How this book will help you

Revise GCSE Geography Study Guide will help you because:

- It contains the **essential content** for your GCSE course without the extra material that will not be examined.
- It contains **progress checks** to help confirm your understanding.
- It gives **advice from examiners** on how to improve your answers.
- The summary table will give you a **quick reference** to the requirements for your examination.
- Examiner's hints and highlighted key points will draw your attention to important things you might otherwise miss.
- It contains important **case studies** to supplement those used in your course and these will help you gain higher marks.

Six ways to improve your grade

Preparation is essential
– the following suggestions should point you in the right direction.

❶ Planning your time

Make sure you **know how many questions** you have to answer and if there are any rules about which ones are compulsory and which ones you need to choose to answer. **Plan how much time** you have for each question. Keep to time – do not answer too quickly or too slowly as both can lead to lost marks.

❷ Read the question carefully

Many students fail to answer the actual question set. They might they misread the question or tried to answer a similar question to one they have seen before. **Read the question once right through and then again more slowly.** Some students underline or highlight key words in the question as they read it through. Questions at GCSE contain a lot of information. Command words are usually the first words in a question. They are very important because they tell you exactly what the examiner wants you to do. When you read the question for the first time underline the command word, e.g. **describe**, **explain**, **compare**.

❸ Give enough detail

If part of a question is worth **three marks** you should make at least **three separate points** or develop one point fully. Be careful that you do not make the same point three times. Approximately 25% of the marks on your final examination papers are awarded for questions requiring longer answers. Practise writing 8 to 20 lines of text to answer a question worth 8 to 20 marks.

❹ Quality of Written Communication (QWC)

Some marks on GCSE papers are given for the quality of your written communication. This includes correct sentence structures, correct sequencing of events and use of geographical words. Read through and correct your answer before moving onto the next part. Remember, you must finish the paper.

❺ Using geographical terms correctly

There is an important geographical vocabulary you should use. Try to **use the correct geographical terms** in your answers and spell them correctly. The use of the right terms in the correct place is important in showing your understanding of the topic. Use the right term when labelling diagrams. As you revise, make a list of geographical terms you meet and check that you understand the meaning of these words.

❻ Case studies are important

Many answers gain higher marks when you **use a case study of a real place to illustrate the points you are making.** Make time in your revision to learn relevant case studies carefully, include local place names and if possible draw a sketch map.

1 Rocks and landscape

The following topics are covered in this chapter:

- **The physical landscape**
- **The quarrying industry**

1.1 The physical landscape

LEARNING SUMMARY

After studying this section you should be able to understand:

- how to describe and explain a physical landscape
- the nature and formation of igneous, sedimentary and metamorphic rocks
- the way in which the 'recent' history of the earth has been subdivided into a geological timescale
- the different types of weathering
- the roles of rocks and weathering in three different landscapes

Describing a physical landscape

AQA A	✓
AQA B	✓
EDEXCEL A	✓
EDEXCEL B	✓
OCR A	✓
OCR B	✓
WJEC A	✓
WJEC B	✓
CCEA	✓

*Practise reading the contours on a map. Look at the key. What is the contour interval?

**If contours are close together, the slope is steep.

***A V-shaped valley has V-shaped contours pointing upstream.

A **landscape** consists of a group of **landforms** that need to be described.

Landscapes can be described in the field with reference to a map, and by drawing and labelling a field sketch (see Figure 1.1).

A landscape can also be described from a photograph.

When describing a landscape, the following points need to be considered:

- *The **height** (**altitude**) in metres of a number of prominent points or areas.
- **Relief** – the general shape of the land and the differences in height between the lower and higher areas.
- **The **slope of the land** – steep, gentle or flat.
- The **shape of the upland areas** – jagged, craggy or smooth.
- ***The **shape of the valleys** – flat-floored, U-shaped, V-shaped and gorges.
- The nature of the **surface** of different areas – rock outcrops, loose rock fragments or soil-covered.
- The **presence of water** – lakes, sea, rivers (meanders) and waterfalls.
- The **vegetation** – moorland, forest, woods, grass and marshes.
- Any **human impact**, e.g. quarries.
- **Personal attitude and feelings**, e.g. attractive, awesome, desolate, boring, exciting.

Explaining how a landscape has been formed

Describing a landscape is only the first stage towards **explaining** the formation of a landscape and the variety of landforms that are found there.

To explain a landscape, you need to take the following ideas into account:

- The types and structure of the rocks.
- How different rocks vary in their resistance to...
  - weathering processes
  - the physical processes of erosion, transportation and deposition, which result from the work of rivers, seas, ice and tectonic forces.
- How, in the past, when the climate was much colder or warmer, weathering and physical processes were different from those that shape the landscape today.

> **You may be asked to draw and label (annotate) a diagram to explain a landform or process.**

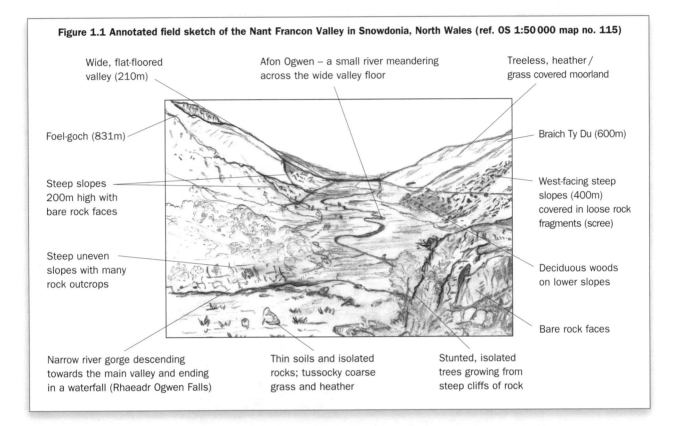

Figure 1.1 Annotated field sketch of the Nant Francon Valley in Snowdonia, North Wales (ref. OS 1:50 000 map no. 115)

Wide, flat-floored valley (210m)

Afon Ogwen – a small river meandering across the wide valley floor

Treeless, heather / grass covered moorland

Foel-goch (831m)

Braich Ty Du (600m)

Steep slopes 200m high with bare rock faces

West-facing steep slopes (400m) covered in loose rock fragments (scree)

Steep uneven slopes with many rock outcrops

Deciduous woods on lower slopes

Bare rock faces

Narrow river gorge descending towards the main valley and ending in a waterfall (Rhaeadr Ogwen Falls)

Thin soils and isolated rocks; tussocky coarse grass and heather

Stunted, isolated trees growing from steep cliffs of rock

PROGRESS CHECK

1. Suggest some labels that could be added to Figure 1.1 to explain why the valley has steep sides and a flat floor.

1. Accept any suitable labels, e.g. a glacial trough or U-shaped valley; truncated spurs; hanging valley and waterfall; misfit stream.

The formation of rocks

AQA A	✓
AQA B	✓
EDEXCEL A	✓
EDEXCEL B	✓
OCR A	✓
OCR B	✓
WJEC A	✓
WJEC B	✓
CCEA	✓

Rocks can be divided into three types based on their formation: **igneous**, **sedimentary** and **metamorphic**.

Igneous rocks

Igneous rocks form from the molten interior of the Earth. They can be divided into two types:

- **Volcanic** rocks form when molten material, such as lava, is thrown out onto the surface of the Earth and cools quickly (e.g. basalt rock).
- **Intrusive** rocks, such as **granite**, form when large masses of molten material are forced up into the crust and cool slowly under great pressure deep underground.

There are several features of **granite**:
- Minerals within the molten rock cool slowly to form large crystals of quartz, mica and feldspar.
- Joints, cracks and weaknesses develop as the rock comes closer to the Earth's surface, and pressure is released.
- It is **impermeable**.
- It is a hard, resistant rock that forms upland areas, e.g. Dartmoor, the Cairngorm Mountains in Scotland and the dramatic cliffs at Land's End in Cornwall.
- It is an important building stone, for example, granite from four different parts of the country has been used in Trafalgar Square in London.
- Weathered granite produces **kaolin**, which is used in china, paper and toothpaste.

Many other rocks are used as building stone – discover some in your area.

> **KEY POINT**
>
> An **impermeable** rock allows very little water to pass through it. Most rainwater stays on the surface and runs off.
>
> A **permeable** rock allows water to...
> - penetrate into the rock through the pore spaces – **porous** rock
> - pass along joints and bedding planes – **pervious** rock.

Understand these terms clearly and use them in your answers.

Sedimentary rocks

Sedimentary rocks form when rock that has been eroded by rivers, ice or the sea is transported away and **deposited**. Limestone, chalk, sandstone and clay are all types of sedimentary rock.

Figure 1.2 Sedimentary rock

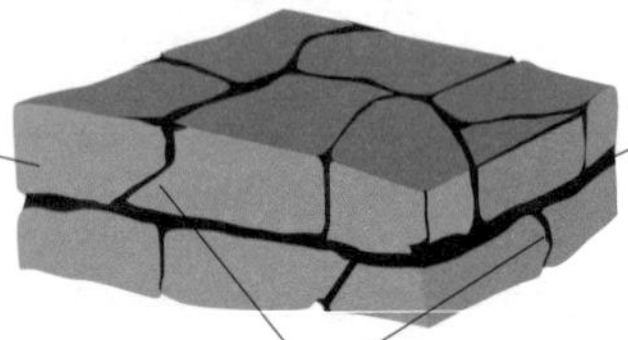

Deposited in layers or **beds** of rock of varying thickness

Beds are separated by horizontal **bedding planes**

Vertical joints (cracks / weaknesses) form in some rocks as they dry out and contract

Carboniferous limestone is a hard, grey rock composed of calcium carbonate:
- It has prominent bedding planes and many joints.
- It is very **permeable** (**pervious**) with little surface drainage.
- It forms upland areas such as the **Yorkshire Dales**.
- It is used as a building stone, and in steel making and cement.

Chalk is a white or grey rock with many fine pore spaces:
- It has many bedding planes and joints.
- It is very **permeable** (**porous**) with little surface drainage.
- It is used in cement making.
- Large amounts of underground water are stored in the pore spaces in the rock called an **aquifer**. This is an important source of domestic water.
- It forms hills such as the **North and South Downs** and the **Chilterns**.

Clay is formed from very fine particles of rock:
- It is impermeable with lots of surface drainage (marshes, rivers and streams).
- Many river valleys are eroded into clay, e.g. Oxford Clay Vale from Oxford to Peterborough.
- It is used for brick-making and pottery.

Metamorphic rocks

Metamorphic rocks form when rocks such as sedimentary rocks are altered by pressure or heat in the crust deep below the Earth's surface:

- Clay rocks can change to become **slate** (e.g. found in north Wales).
- Limestone can change to become **marble** (e.g. found on the Isle of Skye, north-west Scotland).

The geological timescale

AQA A	✓
AQA B	✓
EDEXCEL A	✓
EDEXCEL B	✓
OCR A	✓
OCR B	✓
WJEC A	✓
WJEC B	✓
CCEA	✓

Geology is the study of the Earth. It is thought that the Earth was **formed** about 4600 million years ago, but geologists mostly focus on the last 600 million years. Through the study of rocks, structures, processes and fossils they have established a **geological timescale**. This provides us with a common set of names and a timescale, which helps when describing and understanding different landscapes.

> Knowledge of the timescale and the occurrence of specific events may be useful in developing a good answer in the exam.

Figure 1.3 Simplified geological timescale

Era	Date (million years before present) *Not to scale*	Period	Some important events in the British Isles and Europe
Cenozoic		Quaternary	Holcene – post glacial <0.01 million years
	2.6	Quaternary	Pleistocene – major ice ages separated by warm interglacial periods
	23	Neogene	• Formation of the Alps (see p. 100 Figure 8.8) • Folding of the chalk in S. England will become the North and South Downs
	65	Palaeogene	• Skye granites • Violent volcanic activity in Scotland and N. Ireland – lava floods across the landscape and deposits basalt rocks that form Fingal's Cave and the Giant's Causeway
Mesozoic	145	Cretaceous	Deposition of chalk
	199	Jurassic	
	251	Triassic	
Palaeozoic	299	Permian	Dartmoor granites
	359	Carboniferous	Deposition of carboniferous limestone
	416	Devonian	
	443	Silurian	Cairngorm granites
	488	Ordovician	
	542	Cambrian	
	>542	Pre-Cambrian	

Weathering – the process of rock disintegration

AQA A	✓
AQA B	✓
EDEXCEL A	✓
EDEXCEL B	✓
OCR A	✓
OCR B	✓
WJEC A	✓
WJEC B	✓
CCEA	✓

*You need to understand clearly the difference between weathering and erosion.

> **KEY POINT**
>
> Rocks at or near the surface of the Earth are broken up or decomposed *in situ* by weathering processes.

*Rock that has been weathered or broken into fragments is more easily eroded by rivers, ice or the sea and transported away.

There are three types of weathering: **physical**, **chemical** and **biological**.

Physical (mechanical) weathering

Physical weathering can occur by **freeze-thaw** or **frost shattering**.

Figure 1.4 Stages in a freeze-thaw cycle

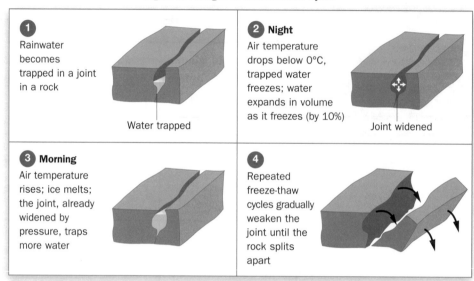

1 Rainwater becomes trapped in a joint in a rock

Water trapped

2 Night Air temperature drops below 0°C, trapped water freezes; water expands in volume as it freezes (by 10%)

Joint widened

3 Morning Air temperature rises; ice melts; the joint, already widened by pressure, traps more water

4 Repeated freeze-thaw cycles gradually weaken the joint until the rock splits apart

Figure 1.5 Weathering and mass wasting, e.g. Wastwater screes (Lake District)

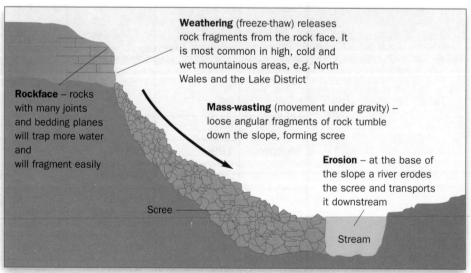

Weathering (freeze-thaw) releases rock fragments from the rock face. It is most common in high, cold and wet mountainous areas, e.g. North Wales and the Lake District

Rockface – rocks with many joints and bedding planes will trap more water and will fragment easily

Mass-wasting (movement under gravity) – loose angular fragments of rock tumble down the slope, forming scree

Erosion – at the base of the slope a river erodes the scree and transports it downstream

Scree

Stream

Physical weathering can also occur by **pressure release**.

Rocks, such as granite, cool deep in the Earth's crust, under very high pressures. When exposed at the surface, as on Dartmoor, the pressure is released and many horizontal and vertical joints and weaknesses develop in the rock (see Figures 1.8 and 1.12).

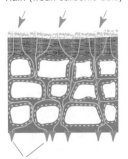

Figure 1.6 limestone section

Rain (weak carbonic acid)

Calcium bicarbonate
carried away in solution

**Figure 1.7
limestone pavement**

Grykes (deep
widened joints)

Clints (upstanding
blocks)

**Figure 1.8 A and B Granite
disintegration (hydrolysis)**

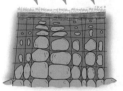

A Rain (weak carbonic acid)

B A granite tor (today)

Chemical weathering

Rainwater passing through the atmosphere absorbs carbon dioxide and becomes a weak carbonic acid. The acid reacts with minerals in the rock causing decomposition.

Limestone solution (carbonation):
- Limestone is made up largely of calcium carbonate, which is insoluble.
- Weak acidic water, passing through the joints, reacts with calcium carbonate converting it to calcium bicarbonate, which is soluble and is carried away in solution (see Figure 1.6). (Chemical reactions were faster during periods in the past when the climate was warmer than it is today, see Figure 4.1.)
- Joints and bedding planes are slowly widened.
- If the soil is removed, a surface is left of upstanding blocks (**clints**), which are separated by wide joints (**grykes**). This is called a **limestone pavement** (see Figure 1.7).

Granite disintegration (hydrolosis):
- Granite is partly composed of the mineral **feldspar**.
- Weak acidic water passing along joints and weaknesses reacts with the hydrogen ions in the feldspar, which decomposes into clay (kaolin).
- Chemical reactions were faster during periods in the past when the climate was warmer than it is today (see Figures 4.1 and 6.26).
- Loose, disintegrated rock is left surrounding unweathered blocks of granite.
- If the weathered material is eroded and washed away, a pile of granite blocks will be left – a **tor** (see Figure 1.8B). Tors are found on higher parts of the Cairngorm Mountains and Dartmoor, e.g. Combestone Tor (see Figure 1.11).

Biological weathering:
- The roots of plants and trees growing in joints and crevices on a rock face expand with age, forcing the rock apart.
- Rotting vegetation creates humic acid, which adds to the processes of chemical weathering.

PROGRESS CHECK

1. Slate and marble are what type of rock?
2. In which geological period was chalk deposited?
3. Rocks at or near the surface of the Earth are broken up or decomposed *in situ* by which three processes?

3. Physical, chemical and biological weathering
2. Cretaceous
1. Metamorphic

Landscapes – three case studies

AQA A	✓
AQA B	✗
EDEXCEL A	✓
EDEXCEL B	✗
OCR A	✓
OCR B	✗
WJEC A	✗
WJEC B	✗
CCEA	✗

Landforms in carboniferous limestone areas

The following are **surface** landforms caused **by solution**:
- **Limestone pavements** are beds of limestone that have been exposed to give flat areas of rock. Solution has widened the grykes, and clints are left upstanding (see Figure. 1.7).
- **Swallow holes (potholes)** are enlarged joints, which allow surface streams to take underground routes that follow bedding planes and joints in the limestone.
- **Limestone gorges** are deep, steep-sided valleys, often occupied by a stream, which may be the result of a cavern roof collapsing.

- **Limestone scars** are exposed beds of horizontal limestone on valley sides, frequently with areas of scree below them due to freeze-thaw weathering.
- **Resurgences** are places where streams re-emerge from an underground course, to flow on the surface again. Often this is at the junction of limestone with impermeable rock below.

Ensure you can describe the process of limestone solution (see p. 13).

The following are underground landforms caused **by solution and deposition**:
- **Caverns and caves** are the result of widened bedding planes that have often been further enlarged by roof collapse, e.g. Ingleborough Cave System (see Figure 1.9).
- **Stalactites and stalagmites** are caused by water seeping and dripping from joints in the roof of a cavern. The water re-deposits calcium carbonate, which develops as features that grow down from the roof (stalactites) and up from the floor (stalagmites).

Case study 1: Carboniferous limestone (karst) scenery

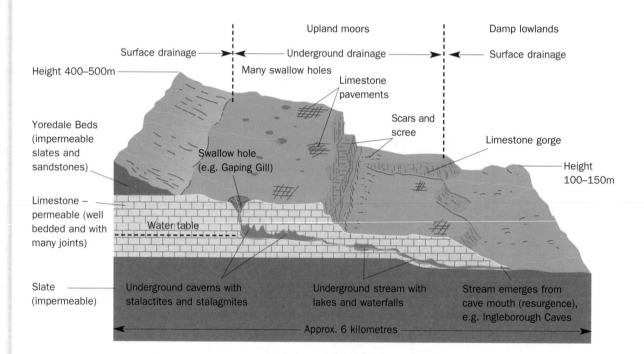

Figure 1.9 Gaping Gill. Block diagram of the limestone area around Ingleborough, Yorkshire Dales National Park (based on OS 1:50 000 map no. 98)

The land has different uses and economic activities.

Upland moors:
- High rainfall – cold winters (altitude).
- Isolated farms; very few villages.
- Thin soils and poor rough pasture provides extensive summer grazing for sheep.
- Popular walking area for hikers.

Damp lowlands:
- Small farms with rights to moorland grazing.
- Small fields and woods – mixed farming.
- Small villages, e.g. Clapham.
- Main road (A65T) and railway provide access to popular tourist area.
- Good scenery with tourist visits to underground caverns.

Case study 2: Chalk and clay vale landscapes

This area can be found on OS map (1:50 000, map no. 198) – practise your map reading of contours.

Figure 1.10 Block diagram of the South Downs and Clay Vale (North of Brighton, East Sussex). (Part of a newly declared National Park, 2009)

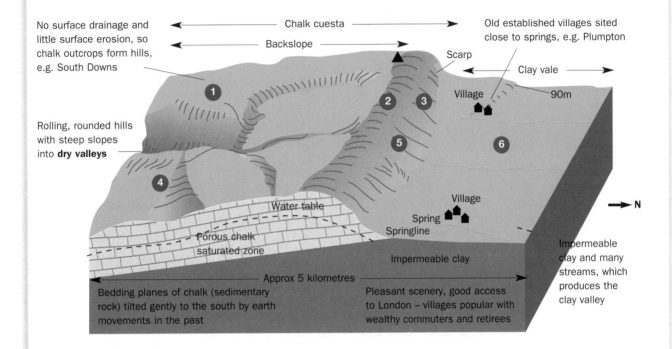

No surface drainage and little surface erosion, so chalk outcrops form hills, e.g. South Downs

Rolling, rounded hills with steep slopes into **dry valleys**

Chalk cuesta

Backslope

Scarp

Old established villages sited close to springs, e.g. Plumpton

Clay vale

Village

90m

Water table

Village

Spring
Springline

Porous chalk
saturated zone

Impermeable clay

N

Impermeable clay and many streams, which produces the clay valley

Approx 5 kilometres

Bedding planes of chalk (sedimentary rock) tilted gently to the south by earth movements in the past

Pleasant scenery, good access to London – villages popular with wealthy commuters and retirees

1 Large arable fields (grain) with few hedges. Some ancient woodlands preserved.

2 High ridge at top of scarp, e.g. Ditchling Beacon (248m) – route of long distance footpath (South Downs Way).

3 Scarp face – a good site for quarry and cement works.

4 Little settlement, isolated farms in valley bottoms.

5 Sheep grazing on very steep slopes – rare chalk grasslands preserved.

6 Damp clay soils, mixed farming, many small fields and woods – diversification into livery stables.

Be prepared to explain how different rock types affect the landscape. Use specific examples with place names to develop your answer.

KEY POINT

Ensure you can describe and explain all of the following terms. (You should be prepared to use these terms when describing a photograph, map or diagram of a chalk area.)

- **Surface landforms**: cuesta, backslope, scarp, dry valleys, rounded landscape, clay vales and springs.
- **Underground features**: porous rock, saturated zone, water table and impermeable clay.

Case study 3: Granite landscapes – Dartmoor, Devon (Dartmoor National Park)

Figure 1.11 Annotated map of the Dart Valley and surrounding moors (adapted from OS 1:50 000 map no. 191 and 202)
Dartmeet and Combestone Tor – popular tourist spots in the National Park – wild, remote scenery – excellent walking country – (DofE) (evidence from OS map (not shown): 6 car parks, public toilets & telephone, long distance footpath, camping barns, pony trekking (diversification))

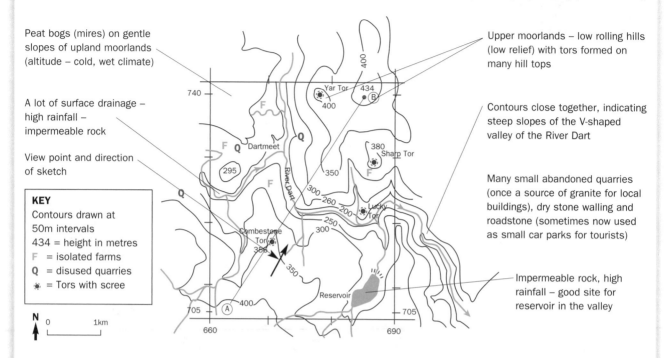

Peat bogs (mires) on gentle slopes of upland moorlands (altitude – cold, wet climate)

A lot of surface drainage – high rainfall – impermeable rock

View point and direction of sketch

KEY
Contours drawn at 50m intervals
434 = height in metres
F = isolated farms
Q = disused quarries
✳ = Tors with scree

N
0   1km

Upper moorlands – low rolling hills (low relief) with tors formed on many hill tops

Contours close together, indicating steep slopes of the V-shaped valley of the River Dart

Many small abandoned quarries (once a source of granite for local buildings), dry stone walling and roadstone (sometimes now used as small car parks for tourists)

Impermeable rock, high rainfall – good site for reservoir in the valley

Figure 1.12 Field sketch of Combestone Tor and Dartmeet (see Figure 1.11)

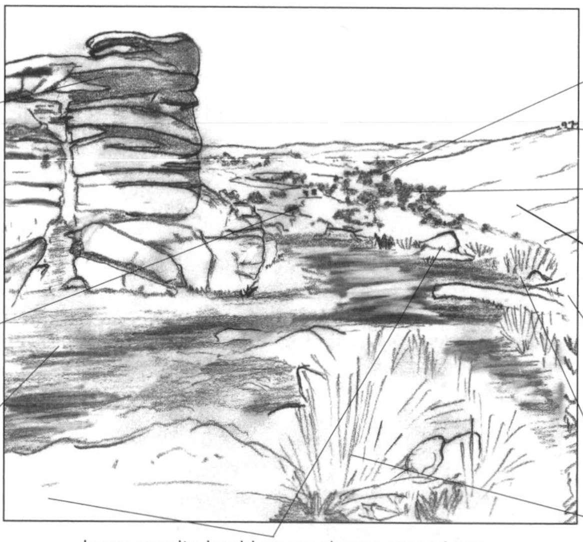

Combestone Tor (356m) – rounded granite blocks standing about 10m above the surrounding grassy hilltop. Popular tourist attraction with good views over Dart valley and surrounding moors

Isolated sheep farms in more sheltered valleys, surrounded by small grass fields for spring grazing (barns for shelter during winter) and rights to graze sheep on open moorlands in summer

Grassy slopes – thin soils easily eroded along tourist footpaths

Large granite boulders on slopes around tor – weathered boulders forming scree (see Figure 1.5)

Dartmeet (stream confluence). A popular picnic spot for families

Yar Tor (400m)

Woodland in sheltered valley

Treeless open moorland, coarse grass and bracken. Extensive summer sheep pastures

River Dart valley – deep V-shaped form

Juncus grass (reeds) indicating poor drainage on impermeable granite

PROGRESS CHECK

1. Draw a cross-section from A to B (marked on Figure 1.11). Use a vertical scale of 4mm : 50m.
2. Label the different parts of the section using ideas from the map and field sketch, Figure 1.12.
3. Explain **two** of the features you have identified.

1. **If you need help, a sketch cross-section has been started on p.190 question 3.**
2. **The following labels should be included:** two tors (one named); River Dart; V-shaped valley; Gentle moorland slopes.
3. Accept a labelled diagram that explains the formation of a tor (see Figure 1.8) and a V-shaped valley (see Figure 2.8).

1.2 The quarrying industry

LEARNING SUMMARY

After studying this section you should be able to understand:

- the importance of the quarrying industry
- issues related to the quarrying industry
- how quarries can be a future resource

Quarrying – a contemporary issue

AQA A	✓
AQA B	✗
EDEXCEL A	✗
EDEXCEL B	✗
OCR A	✗
OCR B	✗
OCR C	✗
WJEC	✗
CCEA	✗

Fact file

Quarrying is a **primary** industry; there are over 1500 quarries in the UK. Surface extraction of **coal** is generally referred to as **open-cast mining**. Surface extraction of **clay** is generally referred to as **clay pits**.

Aggregates is a term used for all quarry products in any form (e.g. sand, gravel or crushed rock). The most important aggregates are limestone (including chalk), sand, gravel and granite.

The table below shows how aggregates are used in the UK.

> Recognising issues and trends from tables and graphs is an important skill. How important are roads and housing compared to other uses?

Use	% Aggregates
Roads	32%
Housing	25%
Other public works	16%
Factories and warehouses	13%
Offices and shops	14%

Quarrying is an important part of the UK economy:
- The sale of aggregates is worth over £3000 000 000 per year.
- About 30 000 people are directly employed, with many other people employed in linked industries (e.g. ready-mixed concrete).
- Significant local taxes come from the quarry companies.

The government requires local councils to agree sufficient planning proposals to maintain an adequate supply of aggregate for the next ten years (called the **landbank**).

Proposals for new quarries or extensions to existing sites require planning permission from the local council. Public concern has increased over the years and proposals are often opposed by...
- national bodies, e.g. CPRE (Council for the Protection of Rural England) and Friends of the Earth
- local councils and residents.

Demand for aggregates

The greatest demand for aggregates is from the construction industry:

- Major projects, such as the Channel Tunnel, use up to 10 million tonnes.
- 125 000 tonnes are used in constructing 1 kilometre of a new motorway.
- Building an average house uses 50–60 tonnes.

Demand doubled from 150 million tonnes in 1975 to 300 million tonnes in 1998. Some experts think it might double again in a much shorter timescale.

The table below shows some arguments for and against quarrying.

Arguments for quarrying	Arguments against quarrying

• Provides essential products to the economy:
  – limestone for cement and lime for fertiliser
  – clay for bricks
  – slate for roofing
  – sand and gravel for the construction industry
• Local employment and income
• Income for local councils (taxes)
	• Causes dust pollution from blasting operations, quarry machinery, crushing and sorting plants
	• Visual pollution from spoil heaps and large ugly buildings
	• Scenic pollution – ugly scars on hillsides can be seen from long distances
	• Noise pollution from blasting and lorry traffic
	• Heavy lorries cause vibrations and damage to buildings in villages, and cause damage and congestion along narrow country lanes

Figure 1.13 A cartoon used by CPRE to illustrate some of the issues of quarrying and its effects on the environment

Use the cartoon to describe and explain some of the issues connected with quarrying. Is there any bias shown in the cartoon? Give the cartoon a title.

Alternative strategies to opening new quarries

Some alternative strategies to opening new quarries are listed below:

- Reduce the rate of road building.
- Ensure new buildings are built to last longer.
- Recycle alternative materials, e.g. powdered glass for aggregate.
- Re-use materials from derelict buildings and when replacing old road surfaces.

Reduce, recycle, reuse – are these strategies a more sustainable way forward?

Quarries – a future resource?

Quarries are not permanent – the resources can become either exhausted or too expensive to exploit. When this happens quarry companies have to submit plans for the restoration of the site to the local council and have them approved. The costs of restoration are paid for by the company, which may also have to maintain the site for up to five years.

Some examples of the use of former quarries include the following:

- **Nature reserves and conservation sites** – natural regeneration and landscaping under the management of the local Wildlife Trust or the RSPB can provide a range of habitats and preserve rare plants or important geological features, e.g. Bardon Hill Quarry in Leicestershire.
- **Amenities** in National Parks, e.g. small quarries close to popular beauty spots may be used as car parks (see Figure 1.11 – Dartmoor).
- Sand and gravel pits can be restored to farmland.
- **Landfill** – controlled management of waste disposal including household waste, e.g. Calvert landfill site in Buckinghamshire.
- **Urban infill** – quarries close to urban areas can be developed for industrial estates, retail parks or housing estates. Such use will reduce the demand for developing greenfield sites, e.g. Lakeside Retail Park in Essex.
- **Recreation** – flooded quarries can provide sites for water sports, such as sailing, windsurfing, fishing and jet-skiing, e.g. Cotswold Water Park, near Cirencester.

> Can you link these different methods of restoration to examples in your region? How successful have they been? Are they sustainable?

Case study: a quarry

Use the Internet or other resources to research a site where there are proposals to open a new quarry or extend an existing one. One example is Bintree Wood in Norfolk, but you should try to find an example in your local area.

- Build a fact file detailing the proposals.
- List the reasons given by the quarry company (a stakeholder) as to why their new proposals are needed – try to group them as **short term** and **long term**.
- Are there any groups (stakeholders) opposing the proposals? List their reasons under the following headings: **Economic**, **Social** and **Environmental**.
- Do you support the proposals or reject them? Make a decision **giving your reasons**.
- Give reasons why some stakeholders will support your decision. Which stakeholders might disagree? Give your reasons.

> Be prepared, with specific details, to answer a question starting 'For a case study of a quarry you have studied...'.

PROGRESS CHECK

1. Complete the following sentences using the list of terms provided.
   **primary   secondary   limestone   warehouses   aggregates
   sand   housing   granite   housing   shops   roads   slate**
   Quarrying is a .... industry. .... is the name given for all quarry products, the most important of which include .... and .... The two most important uses of quarry products are for building .... and ....

2. a) Give one economic reason for quarrying.
   b) Give one environmental and one social reason against quarrying.

1. primary; aggregates: limestone/granite, granite/limestone; roads/housing, housing/roads.
2. a) **Accept any one of:** Important products for the construction industry; Local employment; Tax revenue for local councils. b) **Accept any one of:** Environmental: Ugly scars in the landscape; Dust pollution killing vegetation around the quarry; Noise from blasting. **Accept any one of:** Social: Heavy lorries passing through villages; Noise and dust pollution spoiling outdoor activities in local settlements.

2 River landscapes and hydrology

The following topics are covered in this chapter:

- River landscapes
- River management

2.1 River landscapes

LEARNING SUMMARY

After studying this section you should be able to understand:

- how a drainage basin functions as a system and is part of the hydrological cycle
- the factors affecting the hydrological cycle
- how rivers erode, transport and deposit material
- that river processes vary between upland and lowland areas
- the characteristic landforms associated with upland and lowland river valleys

The drainage basin and the hydrological cycle

AQA A	✓
AQA B	✗
EDEXCEL A	✓
EDEXCEL B	✓
OCR A	✗
OCR B	✓
WJEC A	✗
WJEC B	✓
CCEA	✓

The **drainage basin** is the area of land drained by a river and its tributaries. It is defined from other basins by its **watershed**.

Figure 2.1 The drainage basin of the River Adur, Sussex (based on OS 1:50 000 map no. 198)

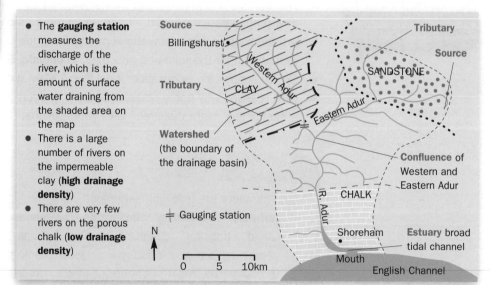

- The **gauging station** measures the discharge of the river, which is the amount of surface water draining from the shaded area on the map
- There is a large number of rivers on the impermeable clay (**high drainage density**)
- There are very few rivers on the porous chalk (**low drainage density**)

The hydrological cycle

> **KEY POINT**
>
> The **hydrological cycle** (or water cycle) is the continuous movement of water between the sea, the atmosphere and the land. It is a closed system, i.e. no water is lost or gained.

The drainage basin forms part of the hydrological cycle.

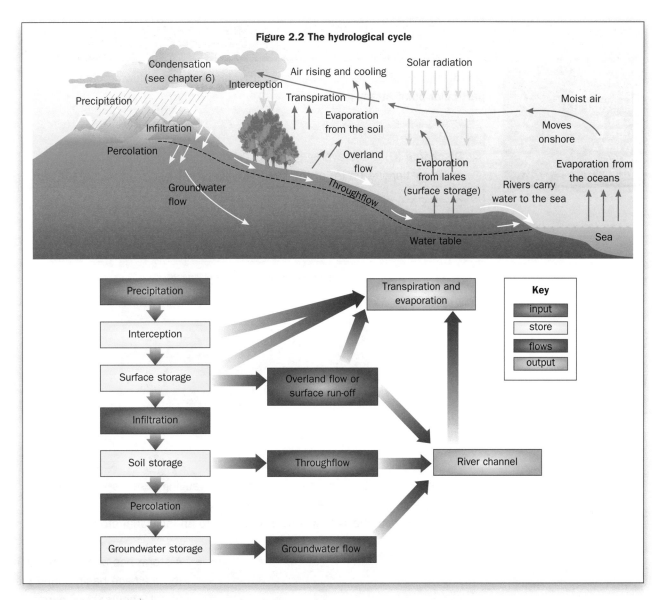

Figure 2.2 The hydrological cycle

Factors affecting the hydrological cycle

If rains fail it will affect the rest of the cycle (see Figure 6.23).

Climate:
- Large amounts of rain or snowmelt over a period of time will cause saturation of soils and an increase in overland flow.
- Violent storms cause an increase in overland flow.
- Hot summer weather and light showers cause increased transpiration and evaporation.

Think of ways in which human activity (e.g. urbanisation, farming, deforestation) might affect some factors.

Vegetation:
- Woodlands and forest, particularly in summer, intercept more rainfall.
- Vegetation will increase transpiration (plants lose moisture, normally through the leaves).
- There will be decreased **infiltration** (the movement of moisture from the surface into the soil or rock).

Slopes – steep slopes encourage overland flow and decreased infiltration.

Soils – deep, permeable soils increase infiltration and throughflow.

Rock type:
- Impermeable rocks increase overland flow.
- Porous rocks increase groundwater storage and flow.

River discharge and hydrographs

AQA A	✓
AQA B	✗
EDEXCEL A	✓
EDEXCEL B	✓
OCR A	✗
OCR B	✓
WJEC A	✗
WJEC B	✓
CCEA	✓

The **discharge** of a river is the **amount or volume of water** flowing past a **particular point** at any given time.

> **KEY POINT**
>
> **Discharge** (Q) is the average velocity (V) of the river multiplied by the cross-sectional area (A) of the river.
>
> $Q = V \times A = (m/sec \times m^2/sec) = m^3/sec$
> (i.e. cubic metres per second or **cumecs**)

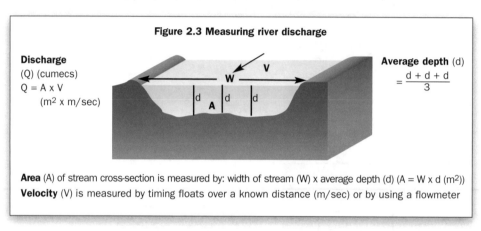

Figure 2.3 Measuring river discharge

Discharge
(Q) (cumecs)
Q = A x V
   (m² x m/sec)

Average depth (d)
$= \dfrac{d + d + d}{3}$

Area (A) of stream cross-section is measured by: width of stream (W) x average depth (d) (A = W x d (m²))
Velocity (V) is measured by timing floats over a known distance (m/sec) or by using a flowmeter

Official measurements of discharge are taken at gauging stations along the river. The changes in discharge over a period of time are recorded on a **hydrograph**. A **flood hydrograph** shows how a river responds to an individual storm.

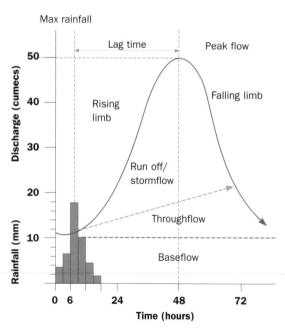

Figure 2.4 Flood hydrograph

> You may be provided with a storm hydrograph in an exam and asked to 'describe what happens to discharge' and 'calculate the lag time'.

- A storm has been recorded in the drainage basin during the first 12 hours; maximum rainfall was at **6 hours**.
- The rising limb shows discharge slowly increasing as rainfall close to the gauging station finds its way into the river by overland flow.
- Discharge increases more rapidly after 24 hours, as rain that fell throughout the drainage basin flows down the river.
- A peak discharge of 50 cumecs is recorded at **48 hours**.
- The **lag time** is 42 hours (48 – 6 = 42).

> **KEY POINT**
>
> **Lag time** is the time difference between maximum rainfall and peak flow.
> Lag time is important – rivers with a short lag time are more likely to flood.

Factors affecting lag time and peak flow

Climate can be a factor due to the amount and intensity of rainfall and snowmelt.

The river basin can be a factor due to the vegetation, slopes, soil and rock type.

Human activity can **decrease** lag time by...
- draining more fields by underground drainage pipes
- removing woodland and forests (deforestation)
- building more houses and roads
- straightening river channels and artificially raising the height of river banks (levées).

Human activity can **increase** lag time by...
- planting more woodlands and forest
- building dams to store and control discharge
- extracting water for industrial and domestic use
- allowing flood water to be temporarily stored on the floodplain or in 'washes' during the winter.

A **decrease in lag time** can increase the likelihood of flooding.

> The reasons why human activity affects lag time is a topic that often appears in exam questions. Make sure you can explain why each factor will affect lag time. Use the correct terms from figure 2.2.

River profiles and processes

AQA A	✓
AQA B	✗
EDEXCEL A	✓
EDEXCEL B	✓
OCR A	✗
OCR B	✓
WJEC A	✓
WJEC B	✓
CCEA	✓

River profiles

Most rivers flow from their source to the sea. Some rivers in arid deserts may not reach the sea, but flow into landlocked basins / lakes. (Can you think of an example of this?)

The slope that the river follows is called the **long profile**.

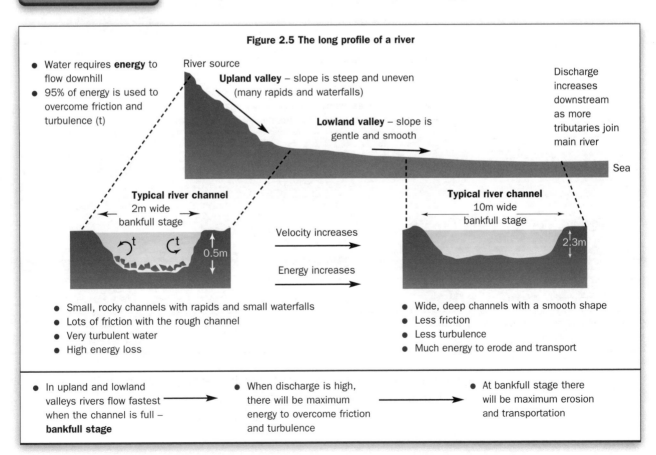

Figure 2.5 The long profile of a river

- Water requires **energy** to flow downhill
- 95% of energy is used to overcome friction and turbulence (t)

River source

Upland valley – slope is steep and uneven (many rapids and waterfalls)

Lowland valley – slope is gentle and smooth

Discharge increases downstream as more tributaries join main river

Sea

Typical river channel
2m wide
bankfull stage
0.5m

Velocity increases

Energy increases

Typical river channel
10m wide
bankfull stage
2–3m

- Small, rocky channels with rapids and small waterfalls
- Lots of friction with the rough channel
- Very turbulent water
- High energy loss

- Wide, deep channels with a smooth shape
- Less friction
- Less turbulence
- Much energy to erode and transport

- In upland and lowland valleys rivers flow fastest when the channel is full – **bankfull stage**

- When discharge is high, there will be maximum energy to overcome friction and turbulence

- At bankfull stage there will be maximum erosion and transportation

River processes

> **KEY POINT**
>
> **River energy** is the energy required for a river to flow downhill, to **erode** and **transport** material. Loss of energy causes a river to **deposit** material.

> Learn these terms carefully and use them when explaining how rivers erode.

Erosion is the wearing away of the banks and bed of the river channel. Erosion can be caused by the following:

- **Abrasion** or **corrasion** – sediments carried along rub and abrade the channel sides and bed; pebbles swirled in cavities in the bed can drill downwards, forming circular **potholes**.
- **Attrition** – transported rocks collide, break up and become smaller and more rounded downstream.
- **Hydraulic action** – the immense weight and force of the flowing water removes material from the bed and sides of the channel.
- **Corrosion** – water reacts with minerals (chemicals) in the rocks, and the minerals are carried away in solution. Corrosion is an important process where rivers pass over areas of limestone and chalk.

Transportation is the movement of eroded sediments (boulders, sand and mud) downstream. Sediments are transported in four ways:

- Traction
- Suspension
- Saltation
- Solution

> **KEY POINT**
>
> A river's load is the amount of sediment being transported.

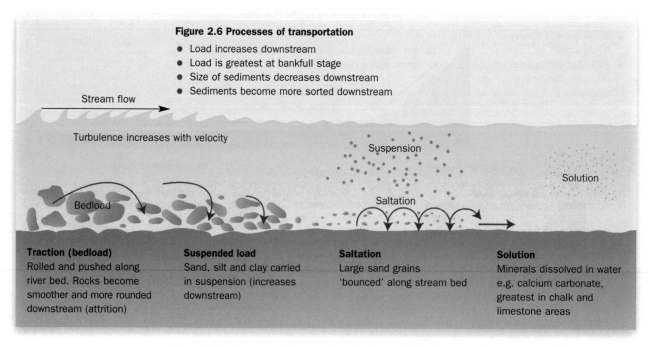

Figure 2.6 Processes of transportation
- Load increases downstream
- Load is greatest at bankfull stage
- Size of sediments decreases downstream
- Sediments become more sorted downstream

Stream flow

Turbulence increases with velocity

Suspension

Solution

Saltation

Bedload

Traction (bedload)	Suspended load	Saltation	Solution
Rolled and pushed along river bed. Rocks become smoother and more rounded downstream (attrition)	Sand, silt and clay carried in suspension (increases downstream)	Large sand grains 'bounced' along stream bed	Minerals dissolved in water e.g. calcium carbonate, greatest in chalk and limestone areas

Deposition occurs when a river lacks sufficient energy to transport the load it is carrying. Often this is when the river loses velocity and can happen...

- on entering a lake or the sea (e.g. an estuary)
- on the inside of a bend or meander.

Figure 2.7 Rivers deposit their load on entering a lake

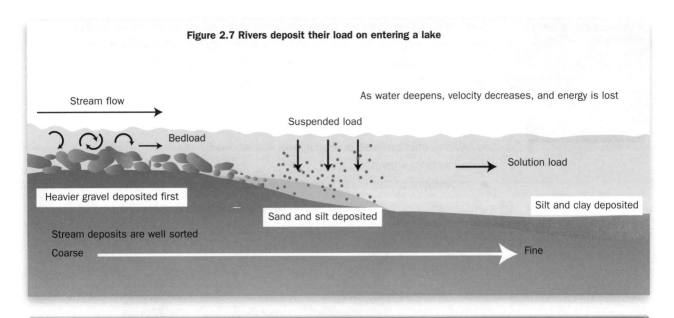

Stream flow

As water deepens, velocity decreases, and energy is lost

Suspended load

Bedload

Solution load

Heavier gravel deposited first

Sand and silt deposited

Silt and clay deposited

Stream deposits are well sorted

Coarse ——————————————————————→ Fine

River landforms

AQA A	✓
AQA B	✗
EDEXCEL A	✓
EDEXCEL B	✓
OCR A	✓
OCR B	✓
WJEC A	✓
WJEC B	✓
CCEA	✓

River landforms in an upland area

Many rivers have their source and headwaters in upland areas, for example, the Rivers Severn and Dee rise in upland Wales.

Upland areas in the UK often have impermeable rocks, high precipitation with heavy snowfalls, steep slopes and thin soils with sparse vegetation.

Rivers in upland areas have the following characteristics (see Figure 2.5):
- Steep, uneven courses with many small waterfalls (long profile).
- Narrow, rocky channels with no flood plain.
- Short lag times (overland flow important).
- Sudden increases in discharge.
- Very turbulent.
- Can transport boulders, rolling them along the bed by traction.
- Mainly erode downwards – **vertical erosion**.

> How do the characteristics of an upland area help to explain why rivers have short lag times in upland areas?

> Remember, many upland areas have been glaciated and the shape of the main valley has changed to a U-shape (see chapter 4, p.47-48).

River valleys in upland areas are often **V-shaped with interlocking spurs**, for example, the River Dart Valley in Dartmoor (see p.16, Figure 1.11).

Figure 2.8 The formation of V-shaped valleys and interlocking spurs

V-shaped valley
(cross-section of an upland valley)

Interlocking spurs
(view down valley)

River erodes downwards by abrasion / corrasion

- As the valley deepens the sides become too steep and unstable
- Rock tumbles and slides into the valley bottom (mass wasting) (see Figure 1.5)
- Loose rock is carried away by the stream
- The valley widens to a V-shape

Harder beds of rock may cause 'cliffs' on the valleyside

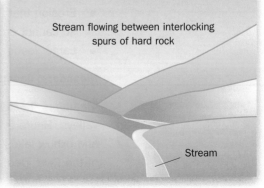

Stream flowing between interlocking spurs of hard rock

Stream

Spectacular waterfalls, e.g. Niagara Falls and Victoria Falls, are popular tourist venues. You may need to develop a case study of one of them.

Waterfalls and **gorges** are common landforms. Where rivers cross beds of harder and softer rocks, a waterfall may form together with a deep, steep-sided gorge. For example, Cauldron Snout and High Force on the River Tees (N. Pennines) are formed where the river crosses a hard band of rock called the 'Whin Sill' (see OS 1:50 000 map no. 91).

Waterfalls may also be the result of...

- glacial erosion (see p.48, Figures 4.4 and 4.5)
- a fall in sea level
- movement of the Earth's crust (e.g. fault lines).

Figure 2.9 Formation of waterfalls and gorges

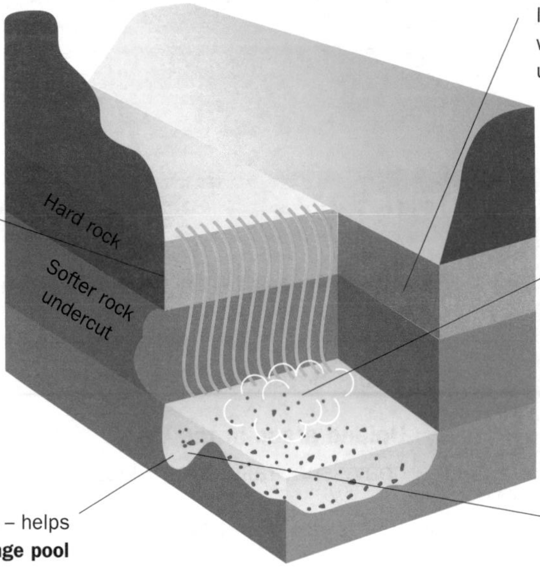
Overhanging rock eventually collapses – waterfall moves upstream (e.g. Niagara Falls moves upstream by approx. 1m/year)
Steep-sided **gorge** left behind as waterfall retreats upstream
Hard rock
Softer rock undercut
Very turbulent water
Hydraulic pressure – helps create a deep **plunge pool**
Rocks in the plunge pool swirl around and erode it deeper (abrasion)

Use process terms to make your explanations clearer.

River landforms in a lowland area

Rivers such as the Severn and Dee flow through wide, lowland valleys before reaching the sea.

Lowland areas in the UK, compared with the uplands, have less resistant rocks, lower precipitation, deeper soils and more vegetation.

How do the characteristics of a lowland area, listed here, help to explain why rivers have long lag times in lowland areas?

Rivers in lowland areas often have the following characteristics (see Figure 2.5):

- Low gradients and gentle long profiles.
- Wide, deep, smooth channels.
- Long lag times.
- Large discharges (from the whole drainage basin) particularly at bankfull stage.
- Strong currents (velocity).
- Low friction and turbulence.
- Erosion that is mostly from side-to-side – **lateral erosion** (close to sea level so cannot erode vertically).
- Large 'loads' of fine sediment transported by saltation and suspension.

Meanders, floodplains and oxbow lakes

Be prepared for a question asking: 'With the aid of diagrams, explain the formation of an oxbow lake'.

Meanders, **floodplains** and **oxbow lakes** are common landforms in lowland river valleys. Figure 2.10 shows the stages in the formation of meanders, floodplains and oxbow lakes. Figure 2.11 shows examples of these landforms in the valley of the River Dee.

Figure 2.10 Formation of meanders, floodplains and oxbow lakes

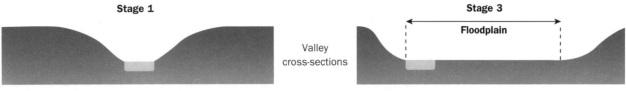

Stage 1

Stage 3

Floodplain

Valley cross-sections

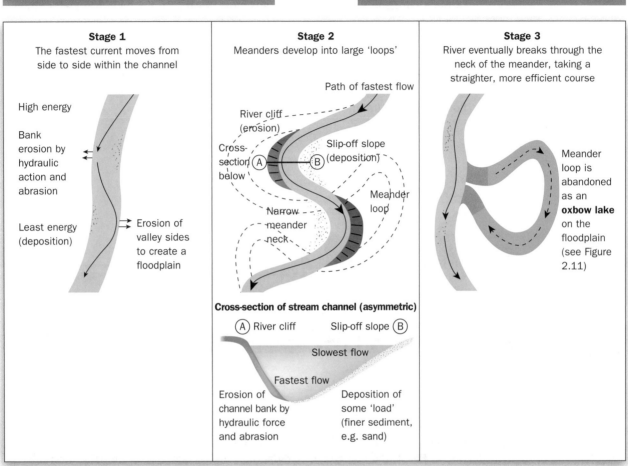

Stage 1
The fastest current moves from side to side within the channel

High energy

Bank erosion by hydraulic action and abrasion

Least energy (deposition)

Erosion of valley sides to create a floodplain

Stage 2
Meanders develop into large 'loops'

Path of fastest flow

River cliff (erosion)

Cross-section below

(A) (B)

Slip-off slope (deposition)

Meander loop

Narrow meander neck

Cross-section of stream channel (asymmetric)

(A) River cliff   Slip-off slope (B)

Slowest flow

Fastest flow

Erosion of channel bank by hydraulic force and abrasion

Deposition of some 'load' (finer sediment, e.g. sand)

Stage 3
River eventually breaks through the neck of the meander, taking a straighter, more efficient course

Meander loop is abandoned as an **oxbow lake** on the floodplain (see Figure 2.11)

Figure 2.11 Map of River Dee (Afon Dyfrdwy) showing floodplain, meanders and oxbow lakes (based on OS 1:50000 map no. 117)

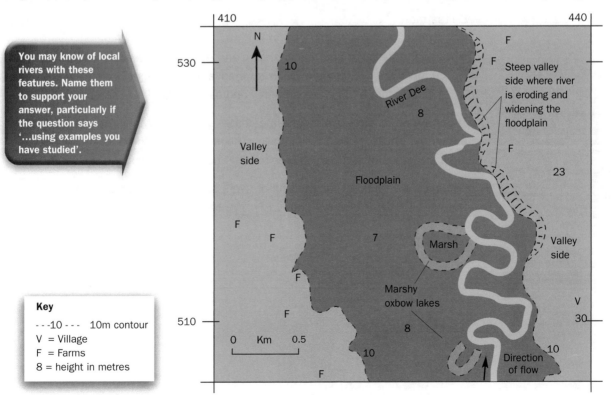

You may know of local rivers with these features. Name them to support your answer, particularly if the question says '...using examples you have studied'.

Key

- ---10--- 10m contour
- V = Village
- F = Farms
- 8 = height in metres

River Dee

Steep valley side where river is eroding and widening the floodplain

Valley side

Floodplain

Marsh

Marshy oxbow lakes

Valley side

Direction of flow

0   Km   0.5

Floodplains and Levées

At times of very high discharge, rivers may overflow their banks and spread out across the **floodplain**. Floodplains are natural 'stores' of water until the floodwaters go down.

At bankfull stage the river carries maximum 'load'. On flooding, the water slows suddenly, energy is lost, and deposition takes place. Coarse sediments (sand) are deposited immediately on the river banks, and form natural **levées**.

Finer sediment (silt and clay) forms deposits across the floodplain called **alluvium**. Alluvium is very fertile. In the lower Nile valley in Egypt, farmers rely on annual floods to bring fresh supplies of alluvium to their land.

Figure 2.12 Floodplains and levées

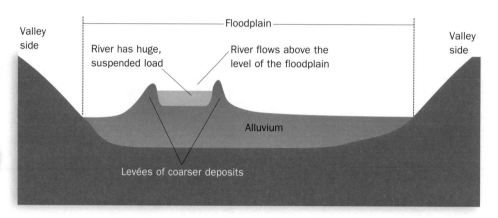

> Along the River Rhone (Switzerland) and the Mississippi (USA), levées have been built to contain flood waters. Are there any dangers from this policy?

Deltas and Estuaries

Deltas and **estuaries** are landforms found where rivers reach the sea.

Deltas form at the mouths of many of the world's larger rivers, for example the Nile in Egypt, the Ganges in Bangladesh, the Mississippi in the USA, and the Mekong in Vietnam (see case study, page 33 Figure 2.14).

Deltas form where...
- rivers carry huge 'loads' of fine sediments
- a river enters the sea, loses energy and deposits its load, and the tidal currents are not strong enough to remove the sediment
- a river enters a lake, loses energy and deposits its load (see Figure 2.7).

There are no large deltas around the coasts of the UK. Many rivers have **estuaries**, which are broad river valleys flooded daily by the tide. At low tide, large expanses of saltmarshes, sandflats and mud are exposed.

> Questions will often ask you to link estuaries to the location of large ports (e.g. Humber / Hull) and to industries such as oil refineries (Dee estuary / Connah's Quay). What do you think are the advantages of these industries being sited at these locations?

Estuaries are found at the mouths of rivers such as the Thames, Severn and Dee (see OS 1:50 000 map no. 117). The Humber is an estuary.

PROGRESS CHECK

1. What is the area drained by a river and its tributaries called?
2. What is the flow of water downhill just below the surface called?
3. What are the units of river discharge measured in?
4. On a hydrograph, what is the name given to the time difference between maximum rainfall and peak discharge?
5. What is the name given to the movement of sediment along a streambed by short hops and jumps?
6. What name is given to an abandoned 'loop' of a river, found on a floodplain?
7. What is the name given to wide river valleys such as the Humber that are flooded daily by the tide?

1. Drainage basin 2. Throughflow 3. Cumecs (m³/sec) 4. Lag time 5. Saltation 6. Oxbow lake 7. Estuaries

2.2 River management

LEARNING SUMMARY	**After studying this section you should understand:**
	• the variety of factors that are responsible for flooding
	• that flooding is a complex issue to manage

Managing floods

AQA A	✓
AQA B	✗
EDEXCEL A	✓
EDEXCEL B	✓
OCR A	✗
OCR B	✓
WJEC A	✓
WJEC B	✓
CCEA	✓

KEY POINT

Flooding occurs when the discharge of a river is too great for its channel to hold. Water will flow over the banks and occupy the floodplain.

Floods can have huge social and economic costs, but they can also be beneficial, e.g. creating fertile soils. Large numbers of people all around the world live in low lying areas that suffer from regular flooding.

Causes of flooding

Most flooding is a combination of climatic factors, drainage basin factors and human activity.

Climate factors:
• Heavy rainfall is less likely to infiltrate and will reach the river quickly by overland flow.
• Excessive rainfall saturates the ground, preventing infiltration (widespread flooding in the UK during summer 2007 was the result of the wettest summer since records began in 1766).
• Rapid snowmelt contributed to the 1995 Rhine floods in Germany and the Netherlands.

Drainage basin factors – impermeable rock, thin soils, steep slopes and saturated ground.

> Scientists report that heavy winter rainfall and extreme river flows have increased in the last 30–40 years, making flooding more likely.

> Research the causes of the Boscastle flood in 2004 or the Derwent floods in 1999. Use the headings 'climate factors, drainage basin factors and human activity' to organise your case study.

Human activity:

- Deforestation reduces interception and transpiration.
- Urbanisation and modern farming practices increase overland flow.

Impacts of flooding

The May–July period in the UK 2007 was the wettest for 250 years.

The following are some of the impacts from the floods in the UK summer 2007:

- People were **evacuated** from their homes (in Hull, 8600 homes were flooded and many people had not returned 12 months later).
- Buildings and property were **damaged**. There were high insurance costs (claims of about £3 billion).
- Animals were trapped and crops were ruined (many thousands of hectares of grain crops were lost).
- Public utilities were **disrupted** – electricity, gas, water supplies (flooding in Gloucestershire left 140,000 homes without water for over 2 weeks).
- Transport and communications flooded (the M1 was closed for 40 hours, threatened by a reservoir dam failing).
- It had an economic impact on shops, offices and industry (Meadowhall shopping centre closed for a week and 300 schools were damaged in Yorkshire and Humberside).
- Political pressures were put on government (funding doubled from 2000 to 2008).

Impacts in less economically developed countries (**LEDCs**) are likely to be more severe than in more economically developed countries (**MEDCs**).

Political causes:

- Governments cannot afford to invest in costly flood prevention schemes. It is estimated that schemes in Bangladesh will cost over £1 billion over a period of 30 years (Bangladesh already has a large international debt).
- Governments give higher priority to investing in industry and exports (in order to raise their GNP) than in flood prevention schemes.
- Schemes funded by the World Bank provide only long-term solutions. Aid agencies are only able to support schemes to improve farming, schools and hospitals, which will improve survival rates rather than schemes to prevent flooding.
- Poor communications and medical services mean help is slow to arrive.

Social causes:

- Dense populations are attracted to the fertile soils on floodplains and deltas where subsistence agriculture (see page 156) provides them with food (e.g. Mekong Delta) and these areas are likely to suffer annual floods.
- Living at subsistence level, a flood can destroy crops and livestock, causing food shortages, starvation and disease.
- Flood warning systems are poorly developed and many people do not have telephone, radio or television.

Flood control

Hard strategies:

- **Dams** can store and control river discharge (dams are used to control tributaries of the Mississippi, e.g. River Missouri).
- **Levées and retaining walls** – by raising the height of river banks, water can be contained. (November 2000, the flood walls in York contained record river levels and saved many homes from flooding.)

- **Straightening meanders** – increases speed of flow and reduces the length of the river (the length of the Mississippi has been shortened by over 240km).
- **Flood relief channels** – provides additional channels alongside existing course of river (the Maidenhead, Windsor and Eton Relief Channel removed 5500 homes from the threat of Thames floodwater).

Soft strategies:

Many experts believe soft strategies are the sustainable way forward.

- **Washlands or spillways** – in times of high discharge sluice-gates are opened and water is allowed to flood adjacent areas. (Washlands have been in use along the Great Ouse in Cambridgeshire for many centuries; a new washland (WWF) in South Yorkshire saved many homes in Doncaster from flooding in 2007).
- **Afforestation** (the planting of woods and forests) – increases interception and reduces run-off (e.g. Tennessee river valley, a tributary of the Mississippi).
- **Planning regulations** – reject development proposals on floodplains so that they can still be allowed to flood. Between 1970 and 1990 in the UK, 2 million homes were built on floodplains, 200 000 are planned along the Thames Gateway).
- **Flood warning systems** – in September 2000, the Environment Agency (UK) issued flood warning codes to be broadcast on the radio and television, and produced flood plan checklists.

Managing flood control (UK)

The severe and costly flooding in summer 2007 highlighted several factors:

- That the responsibility for flood control, particularly in urban areas, was spread over too many organisations (e.g. Environment Agency, local councils, water companies, private land owners).
- There was the need for a more coordinated approach under a single organisation, e.g. the Environment Agency.

Climate change may be causing more floods and flooding in areas where there has not been any before. This can put many schools, and police, ambulance and fire stations at risk.

To obtain planning permission, a flood control scheme must satisfy three criteria:

- Engineers must consider the scheme viable.
- It must be sustainable and environmentally sound.
- It must be economically viable (cost-benefit analysis).

KEY POINT

Cost-benefit analysis assesses whether the benefits gained from building flood controls (e.g. less damage to property and crops, disruption of services and quality of life) outweigh the costs of construction.

PROGRESS CHECK

1. Where have more than 2 million houses been built, which are now liable to flooding?
2. What was the main climatic cause of the UK floods in 2007?
3. Which of the following are 'soft' strategies in controlling floods?
   a) Dams b) Afforestation c) Washlands

3. Afforestation and washlands
2. Very heavy rainfall. The May–June period in 2007 was the wettest for 250 years.
1. On floodplains

MEDC case study: Mississippi floods, August 1993

In 2007 the flooding of New Orleans was mostly the result of a tidal surge caused by hurricane Katrina.

Causes:

- There had been continuous rainfall from April to July; soils were saturated with rapid run-off.
- Heavy thunderstorms in June throughout the upper drainage basins of the Missouri and Mississippi produced over twice the normal rainfall.
- Huge drainage basins (30% of the USA); large rivers meeting at confluences, e.g. St. Louis, combined to give record discharges.
- Silt had raised the bed of the channel; levées had been raised. The river flowed above the level of the surrounding floodplain.
- Record discharges caused levées to collapse and the river eroded huge gaps in the banks and flooded the low-lying floodplains.
- Growth of large urban populations demanded higher flood defences and caused rapid run-off.

Figure 2.13 The drainage basin of the Mississippi

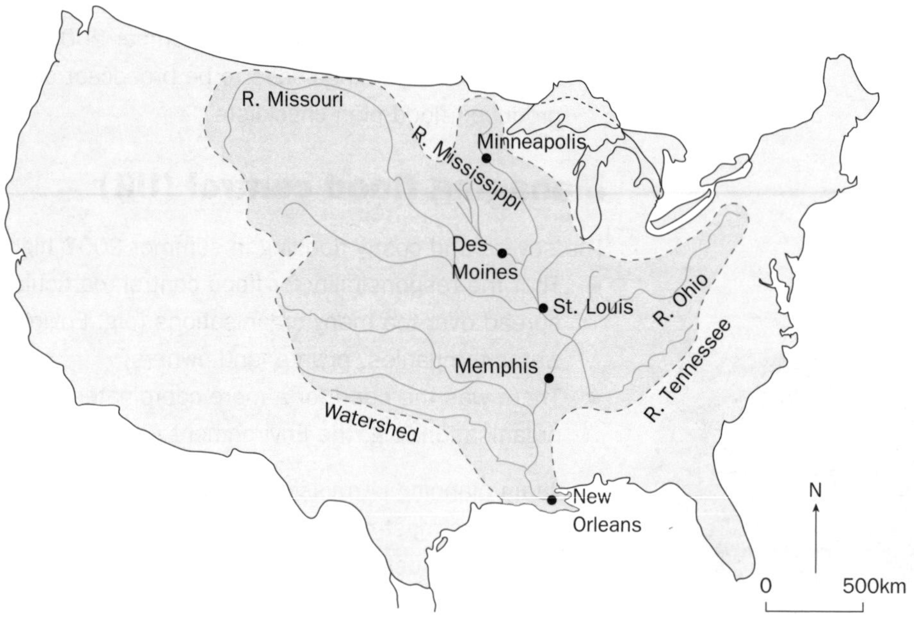

Impacts:

- Severe flooding occurred from Minneapolis to Memphis (8 million hectares).
- 47 people died, 74 000 were evacuated and 45 000 homes were affected.
- Des Moines and St. Louis lost electricity and water supplies.
- Sewage contaminated water supplies over large areas.
- Crops of grain and soya beans, valued at $6.5 billion, were ruined.
- Communications were disrupted.
- Total cost was estimated at $11 billion.

Outcomes:

- The Government declared a state of emergency; military aid supplemented local emergency services; states received large amounts of federal aid.
- 'Hard' defences were soon repaired and raised to hold more water in the river – more spillways and washes have been designated to store surplus water in the short term.
- Most people had insurance policies to meet the costs of destruction.

LEDC case study: Mekong Delta (Vietnam) floods, 2000

Figure 2.14 The drainage basin of the Mekong river

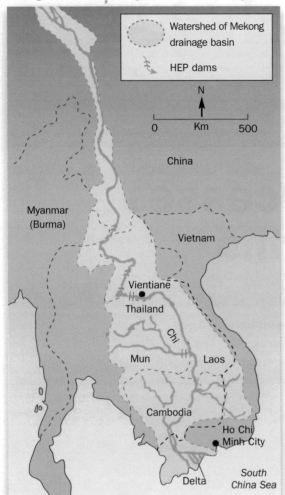

Record flood levels covered large areas of the delta and extended almost to the capital city, Ho Chi Minh.

Fact file: Mekong River
- Length 4200km
- Source in China 5000m above sea level
- HEP potential high
- 'Lifeblood' for up to 50 million people: fish supplies, irrigation of rice fields and orchards, important waterway.

Causes:
- The mountainous, steep-sided valleys in Laos and Cambodia received heavy rainfall.
- The monsoon rainfall (wet and dry seasons) was above average for the previous three years, so the ground was very saturated from the rainfall.
- Much of the rainfall fell in very intense storms.
- Rural communities in Laos and Cambodia depend on the river and forest for building materials, food and medicines; many are shifting cultivators.
- Population growth and illegal logging is causing deforestation.
- Concrete-lined riverbanks are increasing in urban areas such as Vientiane, the capital of Laos.
- Dam building in Laos and China is causing deforestation.
- Dense rural population living in the delta is causing overgrazing and soil erosion.

> Make a simple table to compare impacts and outcomes with a MEDC case study, e.g. Mississippi.

Impacts:
- 350 people dead; mostly young children.
- Many hundreds of thousands forced to leave their homes in June to occupy small muddy banks. They were unable to return to their villages until December.
- Three successive years of flooding left no reserve food supplies; people had to rely entirely on relief workers to bring food.
- New high-yielding rice strains are unable to withstand long floods; the year's rice crop was lost.
- A plague of golden water snails threatened all surviving crops.
- There were life-threatening diseases from contaminated water.

> Note the additional problems of international co-operation when a river passes through six countries.

Outcomes:
- The government extended small loans so that families can build houses on stilts. It has also distributed thousands of small boats so that families can continue to fish for food during floods.
- The government implemented a successful policy restricting families to two children only; population growth reduced.
- Dams in Laos will help control floods but will also reduce the amount of silt carried down by the river. Delta farmers rely on fresh fertile silt to replenish their land. The lack of silt will cause the delta to shrink in size and become lower – threatening worse flooding.

3 Coastal landscapes

The following topics are covered in this chapter:

- **Coastal processes and landforms**
- **Coastal management**

3.1 Coastal processes and landforms

LEARNING SUMMARY

After studying this section you should be able to understand:

- how waves form and the different types of wave
- the processes of erosion, transportation and deposition
- the landforms associated with erosion and deposition

> **KEY POINT**
>
> The **coast** is the interface or narrow zone where the sea, land and atmosphere meet.

Coasts are shaped by the processes of **erosion**, **transportation** and **deposition**. The forces most responsible for these processes are **waves**, **tides** and **currents**.

Coasts can change shape rapidly (i.e. during a single storm) but most landforms are the result of long-term changes. The nature of the rocks forming the coast will affect its shape and form.

Formation of waves

AQA A	✓
AQA B	✓
EDEXCEL A	✓
EDEXCEL B	✓
OCR A	✗
OCR B	✓
WJEC A	✓
WJEC B	✓
CCEA	✓

Waves result from the wind blowing over the surface of the sea. (N.B. This is not how a tsunami is formed, see chapter 8, p.111.)

The largest waves have the most energy. Wave size depends on...

- the **strength** of the wind
- the **duration** of the wind
- the **fetch**.

> **KEY POINT**
>
> The **fetch** is the distance the wind has travelled over the sea before reaching the coast.

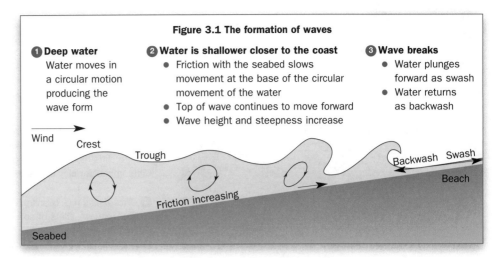

Figure 3.1 The formation of waves

① Deep water
Water moves in a circular motion producing the wave form

② Water is shallower closer to the coast
- Friction with the seabed slows movement at the base of the circular movement of the water
- Top of wave continues to move forward
- Wave height and steepness increase

③ Wave breaks
- Water plunges forward as swash
- Water returns as backwash

Wind · Crest · Trough · Backwash · Swash · Beach · Friction increasing · Seabed

At Land's End in Cornwall, waves with the highest energy come from the southwest (Atlantic Ocean):

- Frequent storms over the Atlantic produce gale force winds.
- Winds blowing from the south-west are the **prevailing winds**.
- Winds from the south-west have a fetch of many thousands of miles.

Types of waves

Figure 3.2 Types of waves

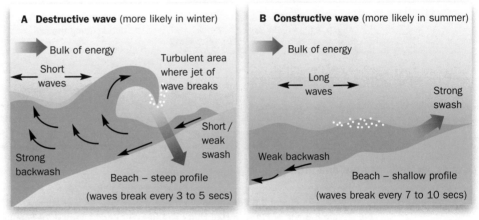

A Destructive wave (more likely in winter)

Bulk of energy · Short waves · Turbulent area where jet of wave breaks · Short / weak swash · Strong backwash · Beach – steep profile (waves break every 3 to 5 secs)

B Constructive wave (more likely in summer)

Bulk of energy · Long waves · Strong swash · Weak backwash · Beach – shallow profile (waves break every 7 to 10 secs)

Tides

At **high tide** the water will be deepest offshore and larger waves with more energy can reach the beach or cliff. Storm waves at high tide have the highest energy of all and these waves are responsible for most of the erosion and transportation.

Processes and landforms of erosion

AQA A	✓
AQA B	✓
EDEXCEL A	✓
EDEXCEL B	✓
OCR A	✗
OCR B	✓
WJEC A	✓
WJEC B	✓
CCEA	✓

Note the similar terms used in river erosion.

Processes of erosion

Waves can erode in four different ways:
- **Hydraulic action**: the pressure of the wave hitting a cliff traps and compresses air into joints and cracks, weakening the rock and breaking it up.
- **Abrasion (corrasion)**: waves hurl rocks against the cliff and swirl sand backwards and forwards, wearing the rock away.
- **Attrition**: rocks and sand rub against each other, making them smaller and more rounded.
- **Corrosion (solution)**: salt water corrodes minerals in many types of rock, causing rocks to break up.

> Link the examples you have studied, providing detail such as place names and rock types.

Landforms of erosion

Headlands and bays

Figure. 3.3 Formation of headlands and bays (see Figure 3.6)

Wave energy concentrated on headlands forming steep cliffs

Waves

As the bay forms it becomes more sheltered, sand and shingle are deposited to form beaches

Headland

Bay

Headland

Harder / resistant rock is eroded more slowly, e.g. granite, chalk and limestone

Weaker / less resistant rock is eroded more quickly, e.g. clay and sands

Cliffs and wave-cut platforms

Figure 3.4 Stages in the cycle of cliff retreat and the formation of a wave-cut platform

Granite cliffs mostly retreat at under 1 metre per 100 years. Cliffs in boulder clay can retreat up to 5+ metres per year.

❹ Cliffs of hard rock (granite) become weakened by weathering (freeze-thaw). Cliffs of soft rock (e.g. boulder clay in N. Norfolk) are saturated by rainwater and become unstable

❺ As they are undercut, the cliffs eventually collapse or slide into the sea (mass movement) and retreat. Waves remove the cliff falls and the cycle begins again (more quickly for cliffs in boulder clay)

❶ High energy waves erode a wave-cut notch, undercutting the cliff

High tide

Low tide

❸ Loose rocks fall from cliff face – abrasion

❷ Wave-cut notch – erosion along bedding planes and joints

❻ Wave cut platform – a gently sloping rock surface exposed at low tide extends as cliff is eroded (retreats)

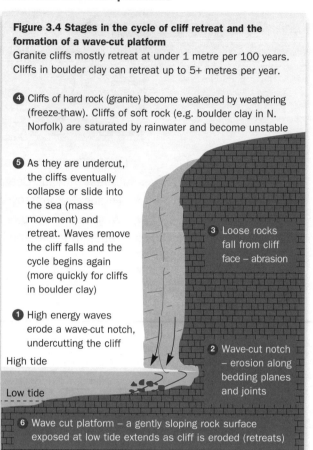

Caves, arches, stacks and stumps

Figure 3.5 Formation of caves, arches, stacks and stumps, e.g. Figure 3.6 Isle of Purbeck (Old Harry and His Wife) and Figure 3.14 Flamborough Head

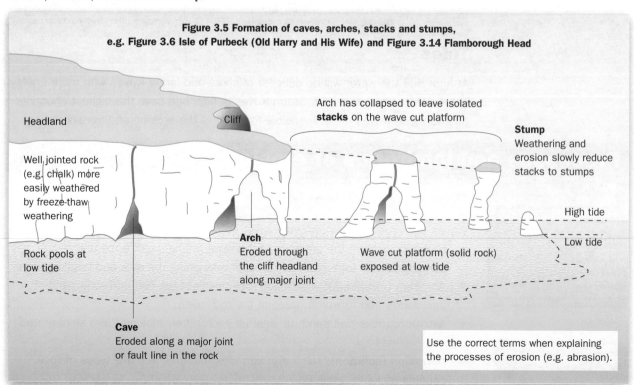

Headland

Cliff

Arch has collapsed to leave isolated **stacks** on the wave cut platform

Stump Weathering and erosion slowly reduce stacks to stumps

Well jointed rock (e.g. chalk) more easily weathered by freeze-thaw weathering

Rock pools at low tide

Arch Eroded through the cliff headland along major joint

Wave cut platform (solid rock) exposed at low tide

High tide

Low tide

Cave Eroded along a major joint or fault line in the rock

> Use the correct terms when explaining the processes of erosion (e.g. abrasion).

Case study: Coastal landforms, geology and processes along the Dorset coast

> **KEY POINT**
>
> Coastlines with prominent headlands and bays often form where the geological beds are at right angles to the coast – a **discordant** coast. Where the coastline and beds are parallel, the coast is much straighter – a **concordant** coast.

Figure 3.6 Coastal landforms, geology and processes along the Dorset coast (OS 1:50000 maps 194 and 195)

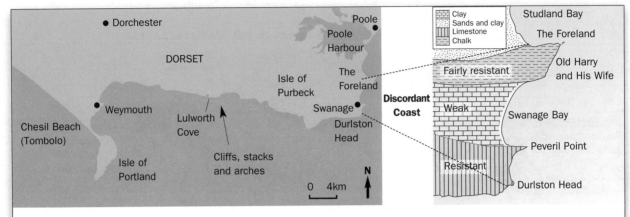

- Pronounced headlands of limestone and chalk.
- Wide bays where the softer clays have been more easily eroded.
- Sandy beaches are found in the shallow and sheltered waters of the bays.
- Stacks and stumps are found off the headlands (Old Harry).

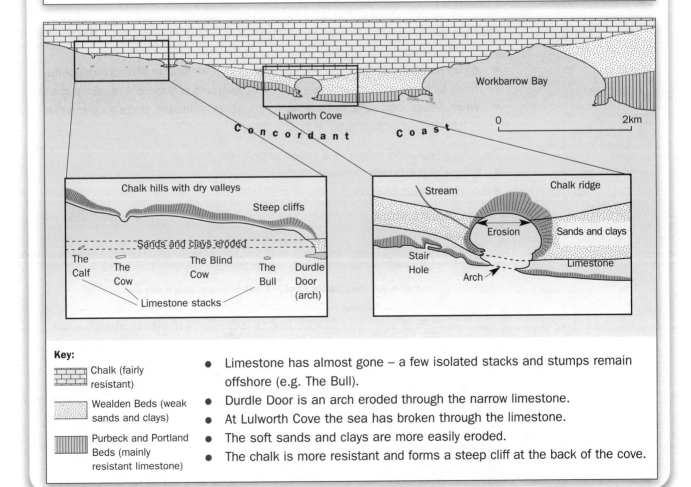

Key:

- Chalk (fairly resistant)
- Wealden Beds (weak sands and clays)
- Purbeck and Portland Beds (mainly resistant limestone)

- Limestone has almost gone – a few isolated stacks and stumps remain offshore (e.g. The Bull).
- Durdle Door is an arch eroded through the narrow limestone.
- At Lulworth Cove the sea has broken through the limestone.
- The soft sands and clays are more easily eroded.
- The chalk is more resistant and forms a steep cliff at the back of the cove.

Landforms of transportation and deposition

AQA A	✓
AQA B	✓
EDEXCEL A	✓
EDEXCEL B	✓
OCR A	✗
OCR B	✓
WJEC A	✓
WJEC B	✓
CCEA	✓

Processes of transportation

Waves transport...
- rocks and sediments eroded from the cliffs
- sediments carried down to the sea by rivers.

Sediments are moved up and down the beach (swash and backwash), see Figure 3.1. Sediments are moved along the beach by **longshore drift**.

Figure 3.7 Longshore drift (see Figures 3.9–3.11)

Dominant waves come from the direction of maximum fetch and the strongest or prevailing winds.

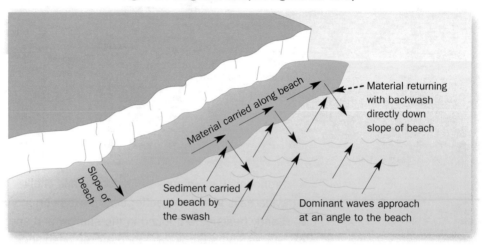

Landforms of deposition

Beaches are the most common landforms that result from deposition. Beaches are formed of sand and shingle. They form in the following conditions:
- When sufficient sediment is available from cliff erosion or offshore deposits.
- When longshore drift maintains a constant movement of sediment along the coast.
- When waves lack sufficient energy to transport sediment, because the water is too shallow or sheltered, e.g. in a bay.

The size, shape and height of a beach depend on the...
- nature of the beach material
- dominant type of wave.

> **KEY POINT**
>
> **Tidal range** is the difference in the height of the sea between high and low tide.

Figure 3.8 The differences of beaches in shape, height and size

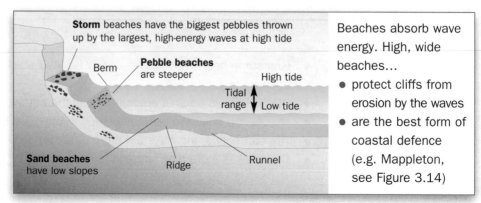

Figure 3.9 Spit formation at Orford Ness, Suffolk (OS 1:50000 maps 156 and 169)

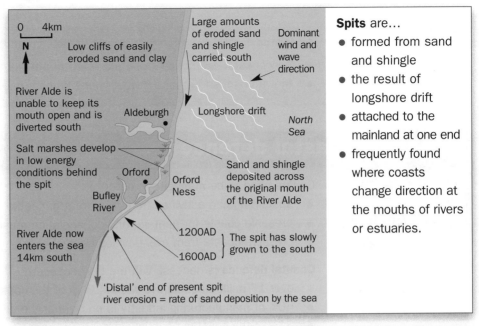

Low cliffs of easily eroded sand and clay

Large amounts of eroded sand and shingle carried south

Dominant wind and wave direction

Longshore drift

North Sea

River Alde is unable to keep its mouth open and is diverted south

Aldeburgh

Salt marshes develop in low energy conditions behind the spit

Orford

Orford Ness

Bufley River

Sand and shingle deposited across the original mouth of the River Alde

River Alde now enters the sea 14km south

1200AD
1600AD } The spit has slowly grown to the south

'Distal' end of present spit
river erosion = rate of sand deposition by the sea

0   4km
N

Spits are...
- formed from sand and shingle
- the result of longshore drift
- attached to the mainland at one end
- frequently found where coasts change direction at the mouths of rivers or estuaries.

Figure 3.10 Chesil Beach, Dorset (OS 1:50000 map 194)

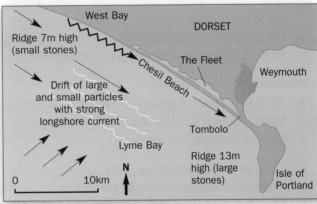

West Bay

DORSET

Ridge 7m high (small stones)

Chesil Beach

The Fleet

Weymouth

Drift of large and small particles with strong longshore current

Lyme Bay

Tombolo

Ridge 13m high (large stones)

Isle of Portland

0   10km
N

Tombolos are similar to spits, but they link the mainland to an offshore island, for example at Chesil Beach in Dorset.

Figure 3.11 Sand bar at Slapton Ley, Devon (OS 1:50000 map 202)

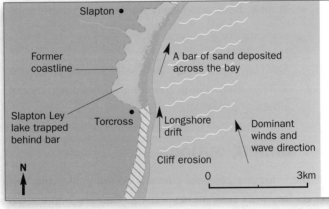

Slapton

Former coastline

A bar of sand deposited across the bay

Slapton Ley lake trapped behind bar

Torcross

Longshore drift

Dominant winds and wave direction

Cliff erosion

N

0   3km

Bars are similar to spits, but they form right across a bay, from headland to headland.

PROGRESS CHECK

1. What name is given to the distance the wind has travelled over the sea?
2. Which type of wave has a short swash and a strong backwash?
3. Name the process of erosion when wave pressure breaks up rocks.
4. Draw a labelled diagram to show the formation of caves, arches, stacks and stumps.
5. What is the most common landform produced by deposition?
6. Orford Ness is an example of which type of landform? Describe briefly how it was formed.

1. Fetch 2. Destructive 3. Hydraulic pressure 4. See page 36 5. Beach 6. It is a spit. Dominant winds from the NE cause longshore drift. Large amounts of sand are transported from north to south. A spit has formed across the old mouth of the River Alde, forcing the river to be diverted south.

3.2 Coastal management

LEARNING SUMMARY	After studying this section you should be able to understand:
	• how coastal defences can be managed to prevent flooding
	• that tourism and other activities along a coast have to be managed

Managing coastal defences

AQA A	✓
AQA B	✓
EDEXCEL A	✓
EDEXCEL B	✓
OCR A	✗
OCR B	✓
WJEC A	✓
WJEC B	✓
CCEA	✓

Coasts need to be **managed** in order to...
- sustain human activities from the threat of coastal erosion
- preserve coasts for heritage and conservation reasons
- preserve coasts from over-development.

Coastal defence is necessary in the UK because...
- over 17 million people live within 10km of the coast
- 40% of manufacturing industry is on or near the coast
- 31% of the coastline has investments in roads, buildings and recreation facilities
- the pressure to develop coastal sites for housing and industry, including tourism, leisure and retirement, is likely to increase.

Responsibility lies mainly with...
- **the Environment Agency** (national government agency – all coasts)
- **Defra** (national government agency – all coasts)
- **District Councils** (local coasts).

To obtain **planning permission**, schemes must satisfy three basic criteria:
- Engineers must consider the scheme to be viable.
- It must be environmentally sound.
- It must be economically viable (cost-benefit analysis).

> **KEY POINT**
>
> Cost-benefit analysis assesses whether the benefits gained from having a sea defence (e.g. the costs of flooding, loss of life, etc.) outweigh the costs of construction.

Planning options

Many experts consider planning controls, managed retreat and beach nourishment as the most sustainable options. Planning options are shown in the table below:

Do nothing	Prevent and discourage	Managed retreat	Build defences
Allow natural processes of erosion to continue, until a new balance has been achieved. Unlikely option where urban areas need defending.	Planning controls prevent further development at vulnerable sites. Mortgages refused and cost of insurance increased.	Defend the coast further inland and allow the present coast to be eroded. Provide compensation and resettlement schemes for farmers and house owners, etc. Maybe viable only in areas of low population.	'Hard' defences such as sea walls, rip-rap, groynes, gabions, revetments and earth embankments. 'Soft' defences such as beach nourishment (see Figure 3.12)

Figure 3.12 Types of coastal defence (approximate costs)

Description	Effects	Advantages	Disadvantages
Type: Seawall ('hard' defence) see Figure 3.14 ref. 3 and 6			
• Concrete wall of different designs; can include flat 'decks' for walking or car parking. • Cost: £4000–5000/m	• Deflects wave energy back into the next wave.	• Capable of withstanding high energy waves. • Efficient and effective. • Strength and height reassures public fear of flooding.	• High cost of building and repair. • Reflection can cause turbulence and scouring of the beach. • Not very attractive. • Access to beach difficult.
Type: Rip-rap (rock armour) ('hard' defence) see Figure 3.14 ref. 5			
• Jumble barrier of large, irregularly shaped rocks or concrete, dumped on the beach parallel to the coast. • Cost: £4000/m	• Absorbs wave energy in gaps and voids between the boulders.	• Very efficient. • Relatively cheap.	• Costs rise if rock imported (e.g. from Norway). Rocks must be large enough to remain stable (3 tonnes). • Difficult access to beach; attractive but dangerous for young children.
Type: Groynes ('hard' defence) see Figure 3.14 ref. 2 and 3			
• Low walls of timber or concrete built at right angles across the beach. • Cost: £10 000 each	• Traps sand moving along the beach by longshore drift. • Beach built up between the groynes is able to absorb more wave energy.	• Cheaper than sea walls. • Maintains beach for tourists. • No problems of access	• Beaches further along the coast may be starved of a supply of sand and become more vulnerable.
Type: Beach nourishment ('soft' defence) see Figure 3.13			
• Beach made higher and wider by feeding sand and shingle brought in by lorries or dredgers. • Often used to extend life span of hard defences by burying them. • Cost: £50/cu.m	• Beach more able to absorb wave energy, particularly in storm conditions.	• Very effective. • Relatively cheap. • Maintains natural appearance of coast. • Preserves a beach for leisure purposes.	• Beaches probably need to be re-nourished if storms cause erosion, increasing the cost. • Offshore dredging may increase erosion in another location.

> It would be useful to know one case study of a coastline where the effectiveness, cost and impact of different types of defence strategy can be assessed.

PROGRESS CHECK

1. Is beach nourishment a 'hard' or 'soft' type of sea defence?
2. What is the meaning of the policy of 'managed retreat'?

2. Abandon the present coastline to the erosion of the sea. Build defences further inland. People who lose their land and property to the sea may get compensation.

1. Soft

Case study: Holderness and Lincolnshire coasts

Figure 3.13 Flood risk and beach nourishment sites along the east coast

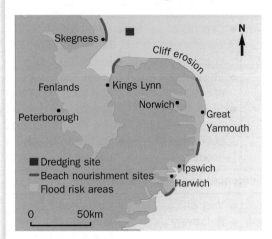

The east coasts of the UK south of Flamborough Head (Yorkshire) are vulnerable to erosion and flooding due to several factors:

- Much of the area is low lying with many parts less than 5m above average sea-level.
- Cliffs are formed of soft, easily eroded rocks such as glacial till (boulder clay).
- East Anglia is slowly sinking relative to sea-level.
- Global warming is likely to cause...
  – a rise in sea-level, particularly threatening low-lying coasts
  – increased storminess in the North Sea, and storm surges are more likely.

Figure 3.14 Management problems and solutions along the Holderness and Lincolnshire coasts

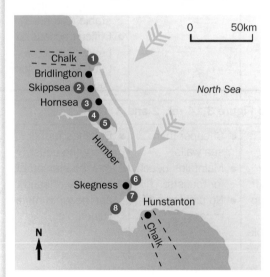

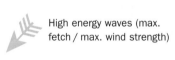
High energy waves (max. fetch / max. wind strength)

Direction of longshore drift

1 **Flamborough Head – no defences required**
High chalk cliffs being slowly eroded into small headlands and bays. Arches and stacks left on the wide wave-cut platform.

2 **Skippsea – groynes**
Low-lying coast: town and caravan sites defended by a wide beach, which is maintained by many wooden groynes trapping the sand moved south by longshore drift.

3 **Hornsea – high seawall and groynes**
After they were constructed in 1924, beaches to the south were starved of sand (e.g. Mappleton). The cliffs in soft glacial till (boulder clay) were eroded much more quickly. Erosion increased from 1.9m to 4.5m per year, with the loss of farmland, houses and roads.

4 **Mappleton – long rock groyne**
Village threatened by rapid cliff erosion (see Hornsea). Rock groyne has trapped sand and shingle moving south to create a high, wide beach, protecting the cliffs from further erosion. Beaches to the south **now** starved of sand – too narrow to prevent rapid cliff erosion. Significant loss of farmland and buildings. Long-term threat to Easington Gas Terminal.

5 **Spurn Head – rip-rap**
Erosion has almost broken through the spit at its northern end; rip-rap has been used to absorb the wave energy. The road that leads to the lifeboat station and Humber pilots' base at the end of the spit is in danger of being cut off.

6 **Mablethorpe to Skegness – heavily defended by seawalls and beach nourishment**
Low-lying land, much of it is below high tide. The towns are growing with new estates of bungalows mostly for retired people, and there are large investments in the tourist industry. Defences are expensive to maintain.

7 **Gibraltar Point (NNR) – natural defences**
Wide beach and extensive sand dunes absorb the wave energy.

8 **The Wash, Freiston Shore – earth embankment, managed retreat**
Low-lying rich agricultural land reclaimed from the Wash in the past, defended by high embankment and wide saltmarshes. At Freiston Shore recent erosion of the embankment has led to managed retreat; agricultural land has been returned to saltmarsh.

PROGRESS CHECK

1 Which part of the UK has a very large area at risk from coastal flooding?

1. The Fenlands / East Anglian coast.

Managing coasts for heritage and conservation

Case study: Dorset Heritage Coast

Figure 3.15 Conflicting demands on a coastline

Economic Issues					
Continual demand for more caravan and camping sites: • Pressure on footpaths, access to beach • Seasonal increase in demands for waste and sewage disposal	Important fishing grounds sustaining 400 boats. International venue for watersports.	17 million tourist visitors per year: • Season extending (ageing population) • Major source of employment • 200 000 educational visitors per year • Pressure on car parks, amenities and footpaths	UK's largest onshore oilfield: • Infrastructure concealed by trees, etc. • Expensive underground pipeline	Port and ferry services (Poole Harbour), and fishing: • Danger of marine pollution • Provides employment	Offshore sand and gravel reserves: • Removal can change wave patterns and rates of erosion • Conflict with fishing and marine archaeology

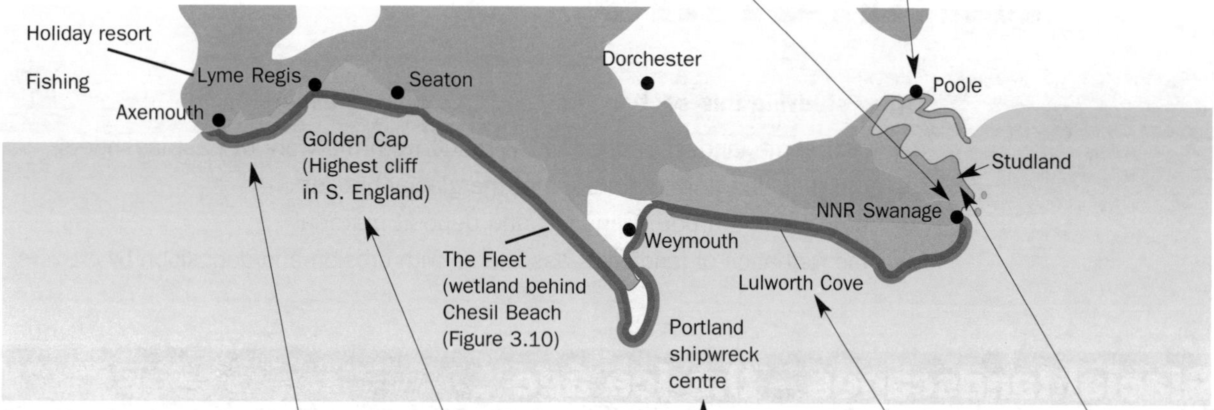

Holiday resort

Fishing

Lyme Regis

Seaton

Dorchester

Poole

Axemouth

Golden Cap (Highest cliff in S. England)

Studland

NNR Swanage

The Fleet (wetland behind Chesil Beach (Figure 3.10)

Weymouth

Lulworth Cove

Portland shipwreck centre

Key:
- AONB (Area of Outstanding Natural Beauty)
- Heritage Coast
- Protected geological and wildlife sites
- World Heritage Sites

Lyme Bay marine conservation areas (Lyme Bay reefs). Possible conflicts with: • Fishing • Water sports • Marine archaeology	Coastline of great beauty and rich cultural heritage. There is a need for interpretation centres, e.g. fossil collecting sites.	Important for marine archaeology based on 600 known shipwrecks.	Outstanding scientific and educational value (geology and landforms).		Exceptional range of wildlife habitats in National Nature Reserve and Poole Harbour (heathland, sand dunes and salt marshes – important bird reserve).
Conservation Issues					

Integrated Coastal Zone Management (ICZM)

The EC-backed ICZM initiative (2000) establishes a framework to...

- involve all groups of people (stakeholders) who interact (through work / leisure) with the coastline
- give all stakeholders the opportunity to express their views on the management of their local 'zone'
- resolve issues and conflicts in the zone, allowing it to **function** in a **sustainable** (long-term) way for the benefit of all users.

> Investigate the progress made for the coastal zone covering a coastline you have studied.

In the UK, initiatives have mostly been led by Council planning offices (Coastal Forums):

- Most councils have undertaken reviews, though some have gone further in bringing groups together to discuss how the local coast should be managed in the future.
- There have been difficulties in consulting with the many varied groups, i.e. Kent identified over 100 stakeholders in their coastal zone.
- There have been problems with funding.

4 Glacial landscapes

The following topics are covered in this chapter:

- Glacial processes and landforms
- Human activities in an upland glaciated area

4.1 Glacial processes and landforms

After studying this section you should be able to understand:

- that some landscapes in the UK result from the work of past icesheets
- the meaning and importance of the glacial budget
- how glaciers erode, transport and deposit material
- the formation of landforms associated with erosion and deposition by glaciers

Glacial landscapes – the ice age

AQA A	✓
AQA B	✗
EDEXCEL A	✗
EDEXCEL B	✓
OCR A	✓
OCR B	✗
WJEC A	✗
WJEC B	✗
CCEA	✗

The spectacular landscapes found in upland areas of the UK such as North Wales, the Cairngorms and the Lake District, are mainly the result of the work of ice in the past.

The 'ice age' consisted of many cold periods (glacials) separated by periods of warmer temperatures (interglacials). This was a time called the **Pleistocene** epoch (see Figure 4.1):

- In a long cold period 450 000 years ago, **icesheets** extended over much of the UK, as far south as a line drawn from Bristol to London. This was the **Anglian ice age**.
- During the last long glacial period (**Devensian ice age**) ice sheets advanced across the country again (see Figure 4.2). By 10 000 years ago, however, only valleys in the high mountain (e.g. The Lake District) were occupied by **glaciers**, which gradually melted as the climate warmed up (**Post glacial**).

> **KEY POINT**
>
> **Icesheets** flow out of polar and upland areas to cover the whole landscape.
> **Glaciers** occupy valleys in upland areas, leaving the highest mountains exposed.

Causes of the ice age

Scientists still debate why major ice ages occur. Explanations include:

- Variations in the Earth's orbit.
- Changes in the Earth's atmosphere (e.g. more or less CO_2, see chapter 6).
- Variations in solar energy.
- Movements of the tectonic plates.

Figure 4.1 Climate change during the Pleistocene epoch in the UK

Approx. age (years before present) *Not to scale*	Period	Epoch	Stage	Climate	Flora	Mean sea level (OD)	Archaeology	Impacts
10 000	Quarternary	Holocene	Post-glacial				Mesolithic	
17 000		upper	Devensian ice age	Cold Max. ice advance (see Figure 4.2) Cold	Tundra Polar desert Forest declining	Increasing -80m	Palaeolithic	Ice retreating (depositional landforms) Ice advancing (severe erosion in upland areas)
110 000		Pleistocene	Ipswichian interglacial	Temperate (warmer than today)	Pine, mixed oak forest	+8m		Raised beaches, e.g. Brighton and Islay (W. Scotland)
130 000		middle	Wolstonian cold phase	Cold				
			Hoxnian interglacial	Temperate				
150 000 450 000			Anglian ice age	Max. ice advance (see Figure 4.2)	Polar desert			Ice retreating (depositional landforms) Ice advancing (severe erosion in upland areas)

Figure 4.2 Maximum extent of the Anglian and Devensian icesheets (see Figure 4.1)

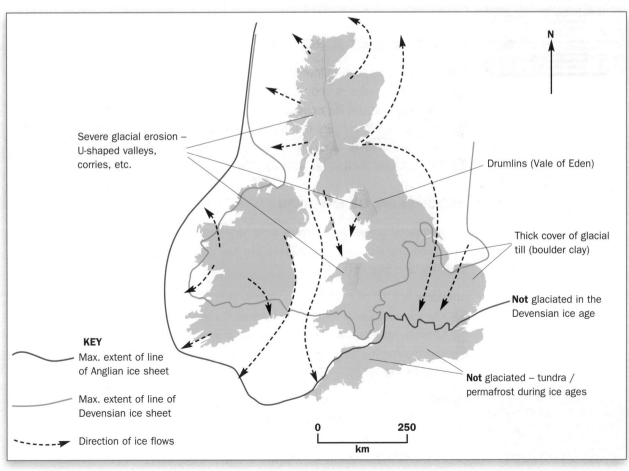

Severe glacial erosion – U-shaped valleys, corries, etc.

Drumlins (Vale of Eden)

Thick cover of glacial till (boulder clay)

Not glaciated in the Devensian ice age

Not glaciated – tundra / permafrost during ice ages

N

KEY

Max. extent of line of Anglian ice sheet

Max. extent of line of Devensian ice sheet

Direction of ice flows

0   250
km

The glacial budget

AQA A	✓
AQA B	✓
EDEXCEL A	✓
EDEXCEL B	✗
OCR A	✓
OCR B	✗
WJEC A	✗
WJEC B	✗
CCEA	✗

> **KEY POINT**
>
> The **glacial budget** is the balance between the inputs and outputs of a glacier.

The main **inputs** are snowfall and snow avalanches, which mostly occur on the higher parts of the glacier, called the **zone of accumulation**. The main **outputs** are evaporation, meltwater and icebergs (coastal sites), which mostly occur from the lower parts of a glacier, called the **zone of ablation**.

A glacier responds to changes in the local weather and climate, which might be seasonal or more long-term. Alpine glaciers receive higher snowfalls in the winter when evaporation and ice melt decreases. So, accumulation is more than ablation and the ice thickens and the glacier moves forward.

Since 1850 the Earth's atmosphere has been warming, so accumulation is less than ablation. Most glaciers and icesheets throughout the world are retreating and becoming thinner. For example, the largest glacier in France, the Mer de Glace, has retreated over 1km and is 150m thinner than it was in 1880.

Rates of retreat are increasing, which many scientists think is the result of global warming.

In Switzerland some Swiss scientists think that only the largest glaciers, e.g. Great Aletsch, will survive into the 22nd century. Consider the possible global and local impacts on sea levels, water supplies and tourism of icesheets and glaciers retreating worldwide.

Glacial erosion

AQA A	✓
AQA B	✓
EDEXCEL A	✓
EDEXCEL B	✗
OCR A	✓
OCR B	✗
WJEC A	✗
WJEC B	✗
CCEA	✗

Glacier ice is formed from the accumulation of snow in hollows. The weight of snow compacts the lower layers into **névé** (ice with many air bubbles). Further compaction and freezing over many years squeezes out the air and forms dense glacier ice.

Movement of glaciers

A glacier moves in the following way:
1. As ice accumulates and thickens it becomes heavier.
2. The weight of the ice causes it to slide downhill under gravity.
3. The movement creates friction with the rocks beneath the ice. This friction melts a thin layer of ice at the base of the glacier.
4. The released **meltwater** acts as a lubricant, helping the glacier move faster.

Processes of erosion

In cold glacial areas, freeze-thaw weathering is very active in breaking up rocks into loose angular fragments. There are two dominant processes of erosion: **abrasion** and **plucking**.

Abrasion:
1. The ice scoops up loosened rocks as it moves forward.
2. Loose fragments fall onto the glacier from rocky slopes above.
3. The moving ice uses this material to erode and scratch away the side and floor of the valley.

Use these terms when explaining the landforms produced by erosion.

Plucking:
1. Ice freezes to the rocks beneath it.
2. When the ice moves it pulls the rock apart along points of weakness (e.g. joints and bedding planes).

Landforms produced by glacial erosion

AQA A	✓
AQA B	✗
EDEXCEL A	✓
EDEXCEL B	✗
OCR A	✓
OCR B	✗
WJEC A	✗
WJEC B	✗
CCEA	✗

Corries (cirques or cwms) are linked with arêtes and pyramidal peaks. **Glacial troughs** (U-shaped valleys) are linked with hanging valleys, truncated spurs and ribbon lakes.

Corries

Corries are deep, semi-circular hollows with very steep, precipitous sides or headwalls:
- They are eroded from small hollows high up on the mountain side. The hollows allow snow to accumulate, forming névé and eventually dense glacier ice.
- They are found in many upland areas such as North Wales, e.g. Cadair Idris.

Figure 4.3 Formation of a corrie

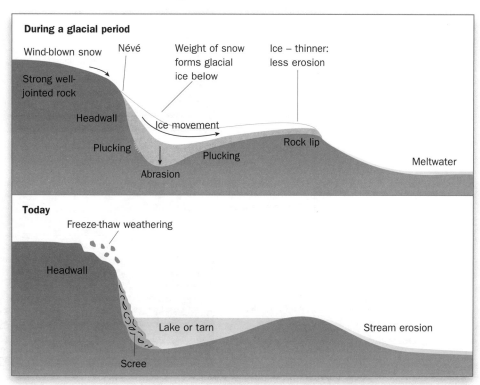

> Practise your map reading. You should be able to recognise these landforms on an OS map (e.g. OS 1:50 000 map no. 124)

> Examiners will give credit for clear, labelled drawings used to answer a question.

Arêtes are sharp, high ridges of rock where the headwalls of two corries are back-to-back. **Pyramidal peaks** are sharp, angular mountain summits, formed by the erosion of several corries, e.g. Cadair Idris.

Glacial troughs or U-shaped valleys

> Spend some time studying Figure 4.5 to recognise how a glaciated landscape is composed of many different landforms.

The following steps happen during the formation of a **U-shaped valley**:
- A valley glacier deepens, widens and straightens former river valleys.
- The V-shaped valley is eroded into a U-shape.
- The interlocking spurs are eroded and left as **truncated spurs** forming the steep valley sides.
- Tributary valleys, which would not have deepened as much as the main valley, are left as **hanging valleys** high up on the valley sides (they are marked today by **waterfalls** or steep gorges).
- Softer, less resistant rocks along the main valley floor, which would have been excavated more deeply, are now filled with water and are called **ribbon lakes**.

> Find an aerial photograph of N. Wales or the Lake District and try to identify some features of glacial erosion.

A glacial trough is the common valley shape in N. Wales, the Lake District, N. Scotland and Alpine areas.

Figure 4.4 Formation of a glacial trough

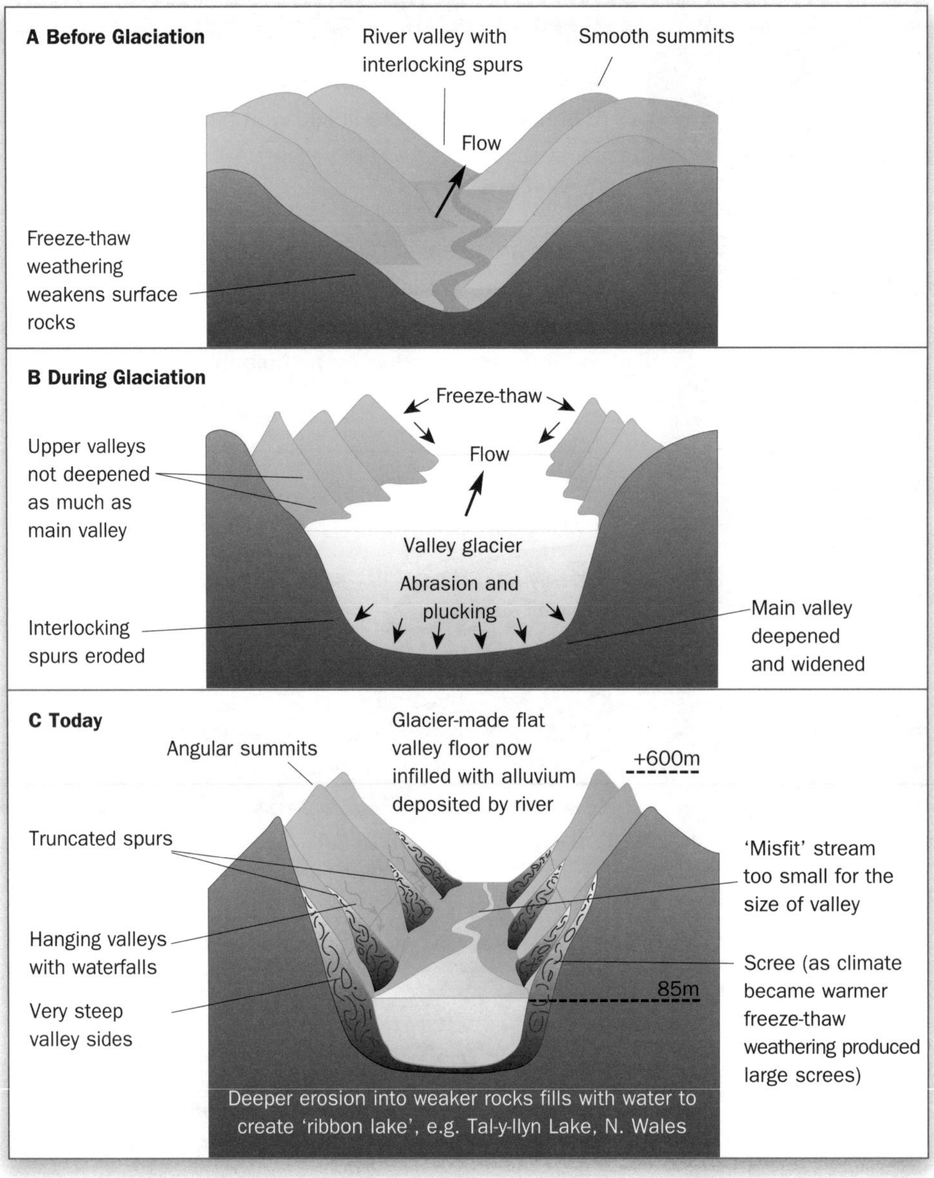

A Before Glaciation

River valley with interlocking spurs

Smooth summits

Flow

Freeze-thaw weathering weakens surface rocks

B During Glaciation

Freeze-thaw

Flow

Upper valleys not deepened as much as main valley

Valley glacier

Abrasion and plucking

Interlocking spurs eroded

Main valley deepened and widened

C Today

Angular summits

Glacier-made flat valley floor now infilled with alluvium deposited by river

+600m

Truncated spurs

'Misfit' stream too small for the size of valley

Hanging valleys with waterfalls

Scree (as climate became warmer freeze-thaw weathering produced large screes)

Very steep valley sides

85m

Deeper erosion into weaker rocks fills with water to create 'ribbon lake', e.g. Tal-y-llyn Lake, N. Wales

Case study of Cadair Idris, Wales – an upland glaciated area

Figure 4.5A Block diagram of Cadair Idris

Fig 4.5B Outline map of the Cadair Idris area (OS 1:50 000 map no. 124)

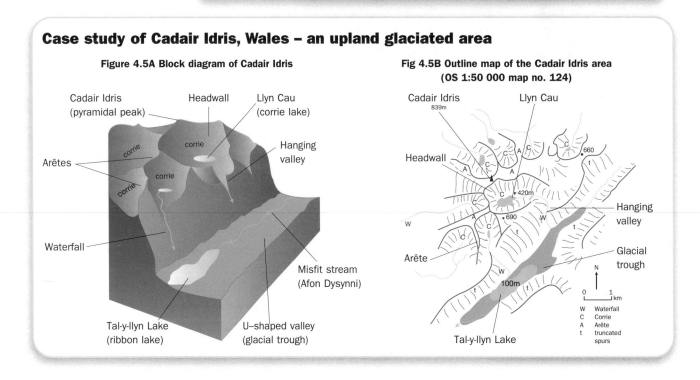

Cadair Idris (pyramidal peak)

Headwall

Llyn Cau (corrie lake)

corrie

corrie

Arêtes

corrie

corrie

Hanging valley

Waterfall

Misfit stream (Afon Dysynni)

Tal-y-llyn Lake (ribbon lake)

U–shaped valley (glacial trough)

Cadair Idris 839m

Llyn Cau

Headwall

420m

660

Hanging valley

690

Arête

Glacial trough

100m

Tal-y-llyn Lake

N

0   1 km

W Waterfall
C Corrie
A Arête
t   truncated spurs

Landforms of transportation and deposition

AQA A	✓
AQA B	✓
EDEXCEL A	✓
EDEXCEL B	✗
OCR A	✓
OCR B	✗
WJEC A	✗
WJEC B	✗
CCEA	✗

Transportation by ice

The large amount of rock carried by a glacier is known as its **load**. The load consists of...

- angular fragments of rock
- large boulders to fine clay (unsorted).

Figure 4.6 Formation of lateral and medial moraines

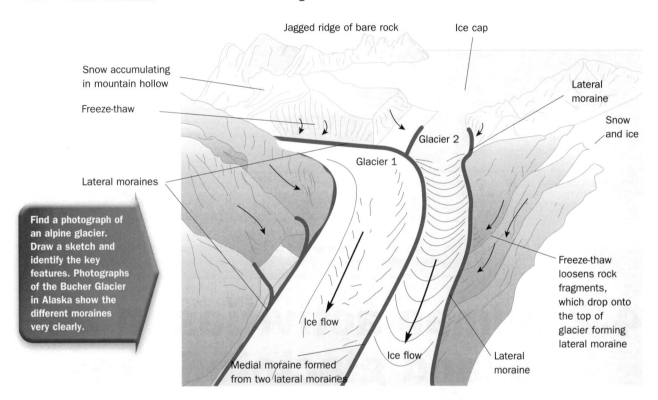

> Find a photograph of an alpine glacier. Draw a sketch and identify the key features. Photographs of the Bucher Glacier in Alaska show the different moraines very clearly.

Landforms produced by glacial deposition

The end of the last ice age was marked by the following characteristics:
- A gradual increase of global temperatures and lower snowfall.
- The glaciers melted faster than the rate at which they moved forwards.
- The glaciers became smaller, retreated and slowly disappeared from the UK.

> Glacial till is the more accurate and scientific name.

The material carried by the ice was left behind as **moraine**, deposited on the rocks and landscape below the ice. These deposits are known as **glacial till** or **boulder clay**. Glacial till is spread like a blanket over much of lowland UK, particularly in eastern areas such as Holderness, Lincolnshire and East Anglia.

Landforms formed of glacial till include the following:
- **Terminal moraines** – low ridges of till, marking the furthest position reached by the ice front.
- **Lateral moraines** – ridges of till, along the side of the valley floor, formed from rocks falling from the mountain sides above the glacier.
- **Drumlins** – streamlined shapes of till, formed under the ice, face up-valley. Their origin is still unclear, but they are often found in groups such as in the Eden Valley, Cumbria (OS 1:50 000 map no. 91).
- **Erratics** – larger rocks transported by the ice and left in an area of very different rocks, e.g. rocks from Norway are found in East Anglia.

Figure 4.7 Landforms of glacial deposition

Glacier snout

Lateral moraine: ridge of glacial till at the side of the valley

Terminal moraine: ridge of glacial till marking the furthest position reached by the glacier

Glacier retreating, i.e. forward movement of ice less than the rate of melting

Valley side

Meltwater stream

Drumlins: streamline shapes of glacial till

Glacial till spread over the old landscape

Solid rocks

Erratic: larger rocks carried from another area and deposited

No glacial till beyond the terminal moraine

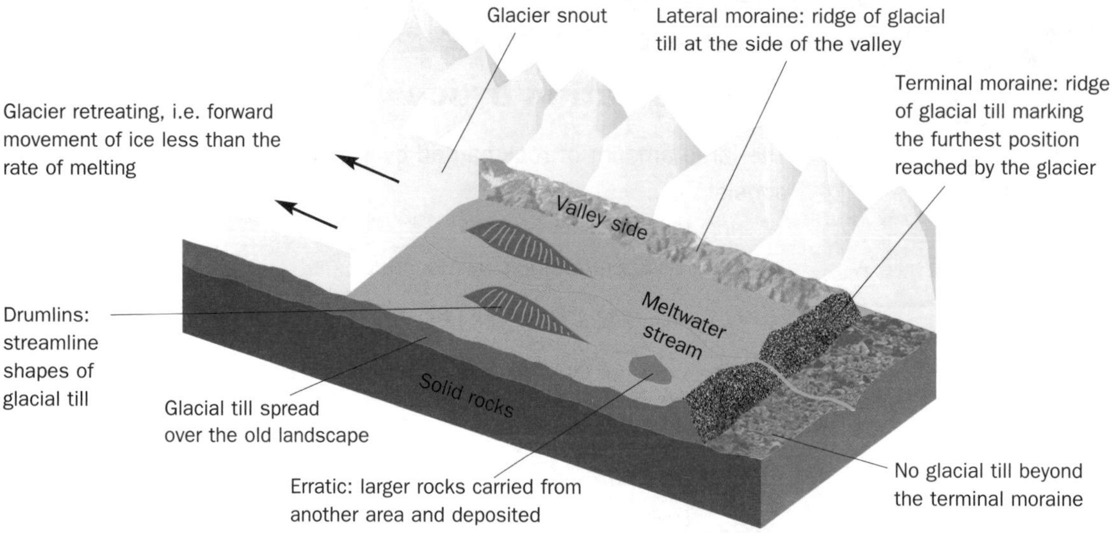

PROGRESS CHECK

1. Which weathering process is very active in glaciated areas?
2. What is the name given to sharp, high ridges of rock where the headwalls of two corries are back-to-back?
3. Use a diagram to describe and explain two features of glacial deposition.

1. Freeze–thaw 2. Arêtes 3. **Accept any two of the following:** Terminal moraines; lateral moraines; drumlins; erratics. **Make sure your diagrams and labels are clear** (see Figures 4.5 A & B and page 49).

4.2 Human activities in an upland glaciated area

LEARNING SUMMARY	**After studying this section you should be able to understand:**
	• how upland glaciated areas are used for human activities (see also chapter 8)

The Lake District National Park

AQA A	✓
AQA B	✗
EDEXCEL A	✓
EDEXCEL B	✗
OCR A	✓
OCR B	✗
WJEC A	✗
WJEC B	✓
CCEA	✗

Human activities in the Lake District National Park

The most important land-use in the Lake District is pastoral farming, raising sheep and cattle. To increase income many farmers are diversifying into tourist activities, e.g. farmhouse B&Bs, pony trekking, caravan sites and campsites.

Extensive upland areas and steep valley sides are planted with forests for commercial use; 75 000 tonnes of timber are cut and sold each year.

Communications are difficult because main roads mostly follow valleys.

> Investigate some of the more extreme sports associated with areas such as the Lake District.

Tourism is very important and increasing; in 1998 there were 12 million visitors. The Park authorities monitor and develop sustainable solutions for the impact of tourist activities on the local community and environment such as car parking, footpath erosion and mountain biking.

Case study: The Lake District National Park

The following are **physical characteristics** of the Lake District National Park:

- Much of the scenery and landforms are the result of the work of ice and glaciers in the past.
- High mountain areas, such as Coniston Fell (800m), are separated from each other by deep, steep-sided, U-shaped valleys.
- Many valleys are partly filled by long, deep ribbon lakes such as Coniston Water, Windermere and Ullswater.
- Very high rainfall (Coniston has 2200mm/year compared with London 600mm/year) and impermeable rocks give rise to many tarns, mountain streams, waterfalls and lakes.
- Cool summers (July average 15°C, compared with London, 22°C) and mild winters (January average 5°C, compared with London, 7°C).
- Much steeply sloping land with poor, thin soil cover.

> Locate the Lake District in your atlas and identify some of these places.

Figure 4.8 A sketched cross-section of the Coniston Valley (based on OS 1:50 000 map no. 97)

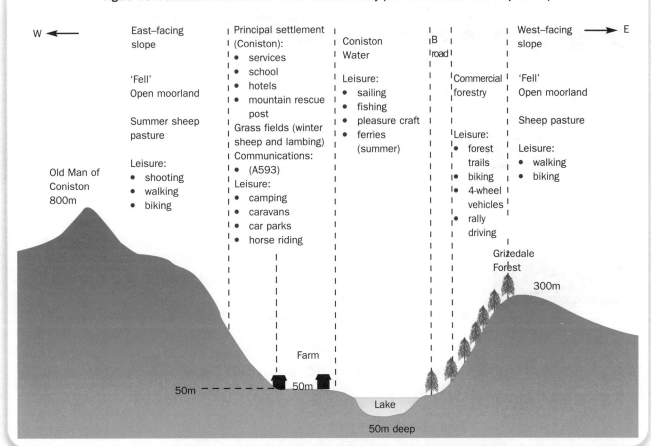

PROGRESS CHECK

1. Describe two ways in which sheep farmers in the Lake District have diversified to increase their income.

1. **Accept any suitable answers, e.g.** providing campsites, mountain bike hire, pony trekking.

Desert landscapes

The following topics are covered in this chapter:

● Hot deserts

5.1 Hot deserts

LEARNING SUMMARY

After studying this section you should be able to understand:

● that hot deserts are an example of an extreme environment
● that both physical and chemical weathering are important in creating landforms
● how the wind plays an important role in creating the landscape
● that although arid, running water makes an important contribution to desert landscapes

The desert environment

AQA A	✗
AQA B	✗
EDEXCEL A	✗
EDEXCEL B	✗
OCR A	✓
OCR B	✗
WJEC A	✗
WJEC B	✗
CCEA	✗

> **KEY POINT**
>
> **Deserts** are very dry (arid) areas receiving less than 250mm of rainfall each year. Water loss from evaporation is greater than annual rainfall. There is a permanent water deficit.

Location

Most deserts are found in one of four locations:

● Around **30° north and south**. These are zones of tropical high pressure (see Figure 6.4) where hot descending air prohibits cloud development, e.g. Saharan, Australian and Thar (India) deserts.
● In the **rainshadow of high mountains**, e.g. Mojave (USA) and Patagonian deserts.
● In the **centre of large land masses** far from sources of moist air, e.g. Australian deserts.
● Around **23.5° north and south**, on the west coast of continents where the prevailing winds are offshore (easterly), e.g. Namibian (West Africa) and Atacama (Chile) deserts.

Use an atlas to locate an example of each location.

Types of desert

Deserts can be described by the nature of the desert surface:

● **Hammada** – desert areas consisting only of bare rock and boulders.
● **Reg** – stony deserts, where the sand has been blown away.
● **Erg** – sandy deserts.

Most desert areas are either hammada or erg.

Climatic characteristics

Deserts have several climatic characteristics (see climate graph Figure 7.10A):

- Very hot summers and cooler winters. The annual range can be more than 25°C.
- An extreme daily temperature range (greater than 40°C), particularly in summer. The absence of cloud cover permits strong solar heating during the day (greater than 50°C) and rapid cooling at night.
- Very low rainfall, less than 250mm per year. There are extremes, e.g. the Atacama desert receives only 15mm (compare with UK Figure 6.17B).
- Rainfall is unpredictable, often falling in brief sudden downpours, causing flash floods.
- Evaporation rates often exceed rainfall.

Weathering in deserts

Most weathering is a combination of both **physical** (mechanical) and **chemical** processes.

Physical weathering:

- **Exfoliation** – outer layers of rock peel away like the layers of an onion (sandstone rock will disintegrate).
  - Caused by excessive daytime temperatures heating the surfaces of the bare rock whilst lower layers remain cooler. Process is increased if moisture from dew or rain is present.
- **Salt weathering** – rock disintegrates as crystals of salt grow in pores and cracks in the rock. (This is similar to freeze-thaw in colder climates.)
  - Caused by high temperatures evaporating moisture from the rocks, leaving behind salts in the surface layers.

Chemical weathering:

- Water is intermittently available from rainfall, but low night-time temperatures cause dew to form more regularly.
- Moisture is absorbed by different minerals in the rock. The minerals expand, weakening the rock and causing disintegration.
- Chemical processes are boosted by high daytime temperatures.

Landforms resulting from weathering

The following landforms result from weathering:

- **Mushroom rocks** – weaker rocks near to the ground, e.g. sandstone, disintegrate faster than those above, producing a mushroom shape.
- **Duricrusts** – the accumulation of salts near the surface cement the sand and stones together, creating a very hard layer that can be more than a metre thick.
- **Rock fans** – weathered rock from cliff faces falls under gravity to form fans. (This is similar to scree from freeze-thaw, see Figure 1.5.)

Wind (Aeolian) processes

AQA A	X
AQA B	X
EDEXCEL A	X
EDEXCEL B	X
OCR A	✓
OCR B	X
WJEC A	X
WJEC B	X
CCEA	X

Wind plays a major role in the formation of desert landscapes.

Transportation

The ability of the wind to transport material depends on several factors:
- Wind speed and turbulence (very effective when it exceeds 20km / hour).
- Persistent winds from one direction (prevailing winds).
- The size of the material covering the ground (dust is most easily moved).
- The amount of vegetation (there is most movement in places where there is no vegetation).

Sand is moved in two ways:
- By **surface creep** – rolling grains along the ground.
- By **saltation** – lifting finer sand briefly into the air and moving it along in a bouncing movement. Each impact disturbs further grains and a powerful stream of moving sand is found close to the surface (can be up to 1m thick).

Dust is carried in **suspension**. It is lifted high into the air, often as dust storms, and carried long distances. (Saharan dust can be carried across the Atlantic.) For example, every spring, Beijing is choked by huge dust storms blowing out from the Mongolian deserts. In 2006, a storm deposited 330000 tonnes of dust on Beijing in one night!

Figure 5.1 Transport of sand and dust by wind

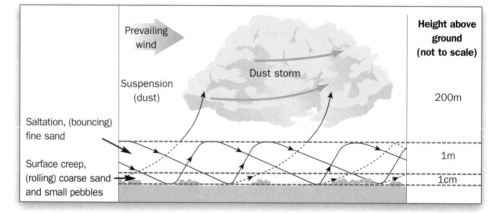

Erosional landforms

The following landforms result from erosion:
- **Deflation hollows** – moisture collects in small hollows and then chemical weathering breaks up the rock until the pieces are small enough to be removed by the wind. The removal of the rock fragments enlarges and deepens the hollow. For example, the vast Qattara Depression in north Egypt measures 160km by 320km and has been deepened to about 130m below sea level.
- Boulder strewn **hammada** desert areas may result from the wind removing all the sand and dust.
- **Abrasion** is the sand blasting action of large quantities of sand being moved close to the ground by saltation. This action creates...
  - **ventifacts** – rocks and pebbles that become highly polished on surfaces facing the prevailing wind
  - **yardangs** – rock surfaces cut into deep grooves separating sharp-crested ridges. The grooves can be up to 10m deep and extend more than 100m downwind.

Depositional landforms

Depositional landforms are associated with the **erg** or sand deserts. They are found mostly in the Sahara (Algeria) and Arabian deserts (E. Egypt).

Most sand deserts are covered by **sand ripples** (up to $\frac{1}{2}$m high), **dunes** (up to 30m high) or **draa or mega dunes** (up to 400m high).

Where the wind is impeded by vegetation, large rocks or cliffs, simple dunes can be deposited to the windward side (**fore dunes**) or downwind side (**lee dunes**).

In areas where sand is deep, extensive dunes can be found in different shapes. The dune's shape will depend on the direction of the prevailing winds and the relative strength of winds from other directions:

- **Seif dunes** (**linear**) are long ridges of sand **parallel** to a strong prevailing wind. They are mostly stationary features, often extending over many kilometres.
- **Transverse dunes** form at **right-angles** to the prevailing wind. They can be very mobile, particularly barchan type dunes (see Figure 5.2).
- **Star dunes** result from three or more seasonal changes in wind direction.

> Seif dunes are the most common dune found in sandy deserts.

Figure 5.2 Movement of a barchan dune (transverse)

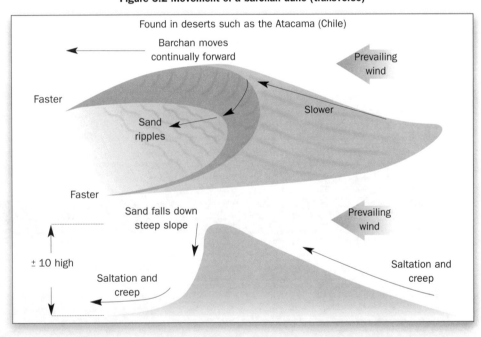

Water processes

AQA A	✗
AQA B	✗
EDEXCEL A	✗
EDEXCEL B	✗
OCR A	✓
OCR B	✗
WJEC A	✗
WJEC B	✗
CCEA	✗

Although rainfall is very low, running water plays an important role in many desert landscapes. There is evidence to show that many deserts have experienced wetter climates in the past. Some present landforms may have been shaped when more water was present.

Running water

Running water makes a substantial impact due to several factors:

- There is little vegetation, therefore, there is no interception or roots to bind the surface together.
- There is extensive duricrust (hard and impermeable) so little infiltration, which encourages surface run-off (overland flow).
- Most rainfall occurs during intense storms, so surface run-off is more likely.

> Make use of the correct terms, i.e. 'interception', 'infiltration', etc. (see chapter 2).

Run-off will either pour across the surface as **sheet floods**, or surge through gullies as **flash floods**:

- Both types of flood cause rapid erosion and will transport away vast 'loads' of loose sand, pebbles and rocks.
- Events are sudden and sporadic. Streams are **intermittent** and will dry up quickly after a storm.

Landforms associated with water

The following landforms result from the effects of water:

- **Wadis** are deep, steep-sided rocky gullies eroded by flash floods.
- **Alluvial fans** are fan-shaped deposits of rocks and pebbles that are found where flood waters emerge from a wadi, spread out and lose their energy to transport.
- A **pediment** is a gently sloping area of bare rock that remains as the mountain edge is eroded back.
- **Mesas** are flat-topped, steep-sided remnants of the mountains that are left isolated on a pediment.

> Note the similarity to a wave-cut platform and stacks (see chapter 3).

Figure 5.3 A hot desert landscape

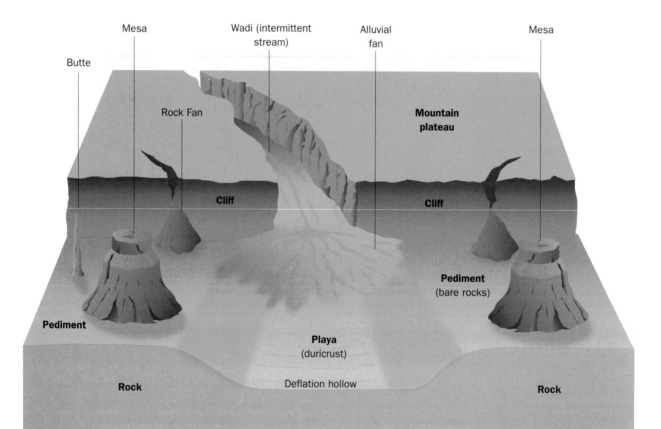

A landscape of mesas, buttes and wadis which was made famous in early film and adverts is Monument Valley (South West USA).

6 Weather and climate

The following topics are covered in this chapter:

- **Weather and climate**
- **Weather hazards**
- **Climate change**

6.1 Weather and climate

LEARNING SUMMARY

After studying this section you should be able to understand:
- the differences and relationships between weather and climate
- that solar radiation is the main source of energy in the atmosphere and that variations in solar energy over time (seasons) and space (latitude) are important in explaining weather and climatic patterns
- how atmospheric conditions can be measured and the processes explained
- how depressions and anti-cyclones affect the UK weather
- the factors affecting climate
- how to describe and compare climates in different parts of the world

Weather

AQA A	✓
AQA B	✗
EDEXCEL A	✗
EDEXCEL B	✗
OCR A	✗
OCR B	✗
WJEC A	✓
WJEC B	✓
CCEA	✓

> **KEY POINT**
>
> *Weather describes the atmospheric conditions at a particular place and time together with the changes taking place over the short term (hour-by-hour or day-by-day).

*It is important to distinguish weather from 'climate'.

At a weather station all the instruments have precise locations, so that the data gathered is reliable and comparable.

Recording the weather

Meteorologists are responsible for recording and analysing the weather. Data on the weather is obtained from...

- daily readings of instruments at a weather station
- automatic instruments in remote locations, e.g. ocean buoys
- ships and aeroplanes
- satellites (polar and geostationary) and radar images.

Data is recorded at least once every 24 hours. The information is plotted on maps or synoptic charts and then analysed to obtain a weather forecast.

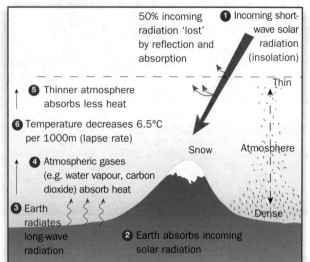

Figure 6.1 Heat received by insolation

① Incoming short-wave solar radiation (insolation)

50% incoming radiation 'lost' by reflection and absorption

⑤ Thinner atmosphere absorbs less heat

⑥ Temperature decreases 6.5°C per 1000m (lapse rate)

④ Atmospheric gases (e.g. water vapour, carbon dioxide) absorb heat

③ Earth radiates long-wave radiation

② Earth absorbs incoming solar radiation

Thin · Atmosphere · Snow · Dense

Recording data

Temperature:

- Air temperature is recorded in the shade (in a Stevenson's Screen).
- It is recorded using a **maximum / minimum thermometer** (highest and lowest temperatures in the last 24 hours).
- It is recorded in degrees **centigrade** (**Celsius**) or **Fahrenheit**.
- Solar radiation or **insolation** is the main source of heat energy to the atmosphere.
- The atmosphere is warmed mainly from **long wave radiation** emitted by the Earth.
- Temperature decreases with height at an average rate of 6.5°C per 1000m (**lapse rate**).

Air pressure is the weight of the atmosphere at the Earth's surface:

- It is recorded using an **aneroid barometer**.
- It is measured in **millibars (mb)**, reduced to sea level (average pressure at sea level is 1013mb).
- On maps the differences in pressure are shown by **isobars**, which are lines joining points of equal pressure.
- Air pressure varies with...
    - temperature: warmer, lighter air is forced to rise creating areas of low pressure; heavier, colder air descends creating areas of high pressure
    - height – as the atmosphere becomes thinner, pressure decreases.

Figure 6.2 Pressure systems

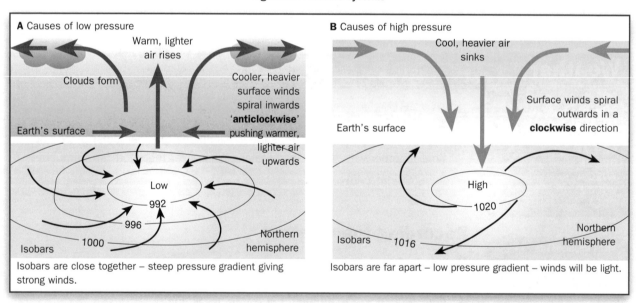

A Causes of low pressure

Warm, lighter air rises · Clouds form · Cooler, heavier surface winds spiral inwards 'anticlockwise' pushing warmer, lighter air upwards · Earth's surface · Low 992 · 996 · 1000 · Isobars · Northern hemisphere

Isobars are close together – steep pressure gradient giving strong winds.

B Causes of high pressure

Cool, heavier air sinks · Surface winds spiral outwards in a **clockwise** direction · Earth's surface · High 1020 · 1016 · Isobars · Northern hemisphere

Isobars are far apart – low pressure gradient – winds will be light.

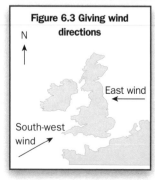

Figure 6.3 Giving wind directions

N · East wind · South-west wind

Wind is the horizontal movement of air across the Earth's surface:

- Wind is recorded as...
    - **direction**, using a **wind vane** (recorded as the direction from which the wind is blowing)
    - **speed**, using an **anemometer**, measured in **knots, kilometres per hour** or on the **Beaufort Scale**.
- Wind is caused by differences in air pressure. The wind flows from high pressure (sinking) to low pressure (rising). The greater the pressure difference, the stronger the wind blows (see Figures 6.2A and 6.2B)

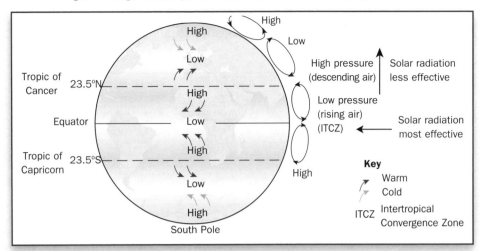

Figure 6.4 High and low pressure belts with associated winds (global scale)

> Recognising the global pressure and wind patterns is important when explaining the climate in different places.

Precipitation is the deposition of moisture from the atmosphere as rain, drizzle, hail, snow, fog or dew:

- It is recorded using a **rain gauge**.
- It is measured in **millimetres (mm)**. (Snow is recorded as rainfall equivalent.)
- The atmosphere contains **water vapour**, which, if the air is cooled sufficiently, will form visible water droplets.

> Precipitation mainly occurs when air is forced to rise.

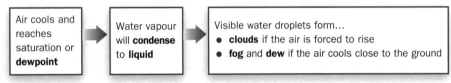

| Air cools and reaches saturation or **dewpoint** | → | Water vapour will **condense** to **liquid** | → | Visible water droplets form...
• **clouds** if the air is forced to rise
• **fog** and **dew** if the air cools close to the ground |

There are different types of rainfall:

- **Relief** rainfall (orographic) is where air is forced to rise over hills or mountains.
- **Convectional** rainfall is where air, heated by the hot ground, is forced to rise.
- **Frontal** rainfall is when two air masses of different temperatures meet. The warmer air mass is undercut and forced to rise by the heavier cold air.

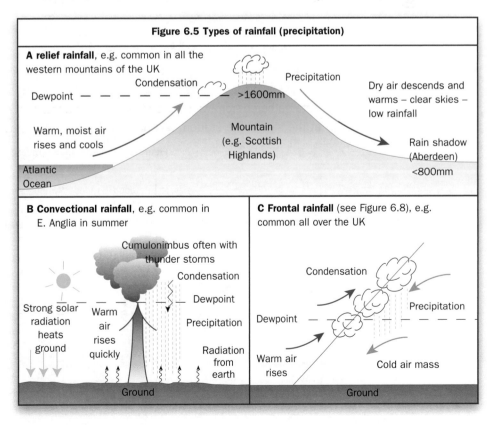

Figure 6.5 Types of rainfall (precipitation)

Clouds are visible masses of water droplets or ice crystals:
- They are recorded by observation, normally described by their shape and height.
- Cloud cover is measured in **oktas** (i.e. eighths of sky covered).

Figure 6.6 Types of clouds

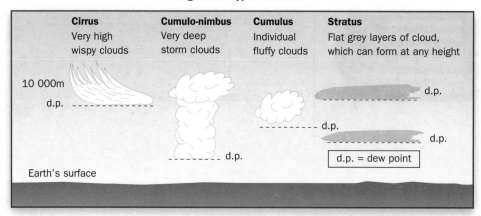

Sunshine is recorded using a **sunshine recorder** and measured in **hours per day**.

Relative humidity (**RH**) is the amount of water vapour in the air:
- It is recorded by a **hygrometer** or **wet and dry thermometer**.
- It is measured as a percentage of the maximum water vapour that can be held by air of that temperature. It can be expressed in the following equation:

$$\frac{\text{Water vapour present}}{\text{Maximum water vapour that can be held by air of that temperature}} \times 100$$

- Warm air can hold more water vapour than cold air.
- If warm air is forced to rise and cool, RH will increase until the air becomes saturated, i.e. RH = 100% = **dewpoint** and clouds form (see Figure 6.6).

Weather maps (synoptic charts)

KEY POINT

Weather maps or **synoptic charts** summarise the weather data for a particular time.

Data gathered from weather stations is represented as a group of symbols located at the site of the station. **Isobars** are drawn joining places of equal pressure.

Figure 6.7 Weather map symbols

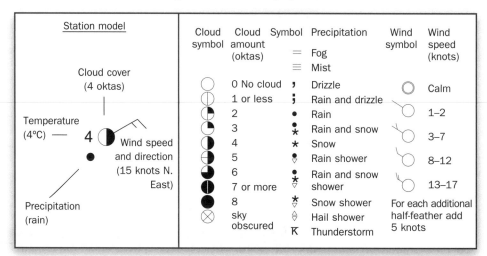

Weather systems – depressions and anticyclones

KEY POINT

Depressions are areas of low pressure, formed when a warm air mass meets a cold air mass. Fronts form at the boundaries of the two air masses.

Given a synoptic chart for the UK, be prepared to...
- describe the weather at a given place when provided with the weather symbols (Figure 6.7)
- explain why it is raining close to the fronts that are shown (Figure 6.8B)
- provide a forecast for a place ahead of the depression (Figure 6.8C).

Depressions frequently form over the North Atlantic Ocean where warm, moist tropical air moving north, meets cold polar air moving south. The depressions move east towards the UK, developing fronts (see Figure 6.8A).

1 The cold air undercuts the warm air forming a cold front and the warm air is forced upwards.

2 The warm air is pushed forward and is forced to rise over the cold air ahead, forming a warm front.

3 As warm air rises, clouds form and precipitation occurs along both fronts (see Figure 6.8B).

Winds in the Northern hemisphere spiral inwards in an **anti-clockwise** direction. Winds will be strongest in deep depressions when the isobars are closer together.

Meteorologists use their knowledge of depressions and fronts to make weather forecasts (see Figure 6.8C). Depressions are the main cause of the very changeable weather in the UK.

Figure 6.8A The formation of a depression

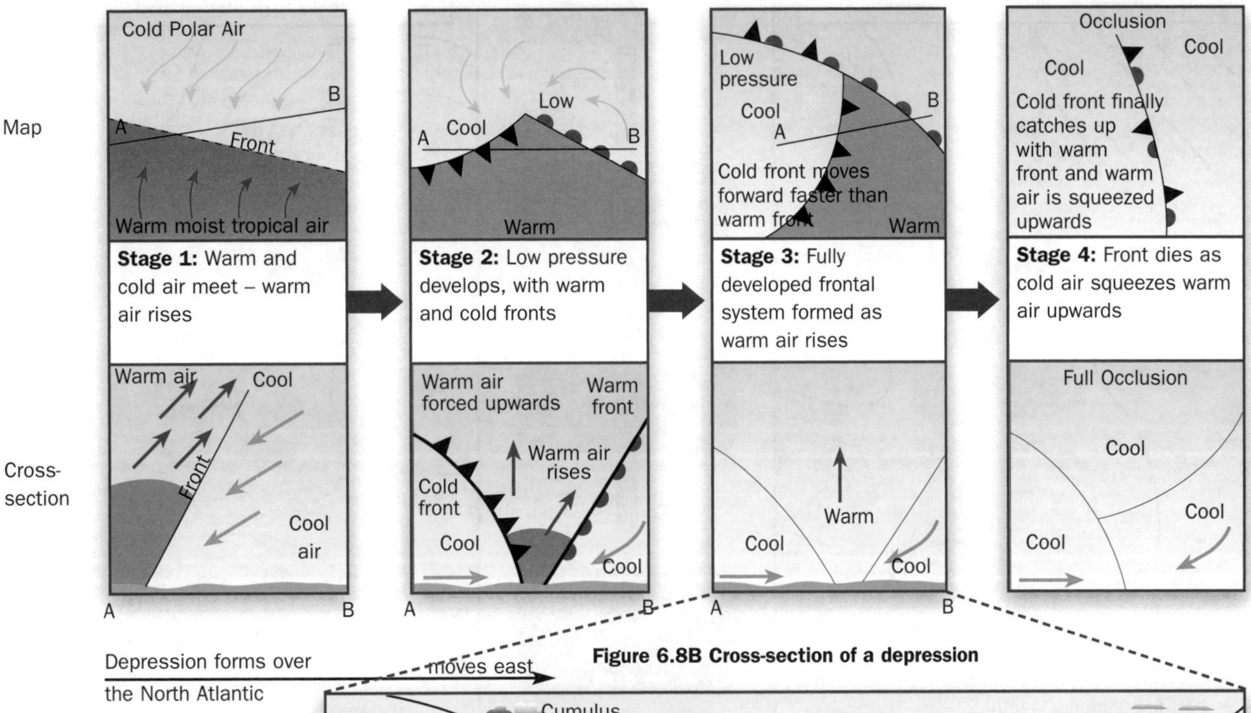

Figure 6.8B Cross-section of a depression

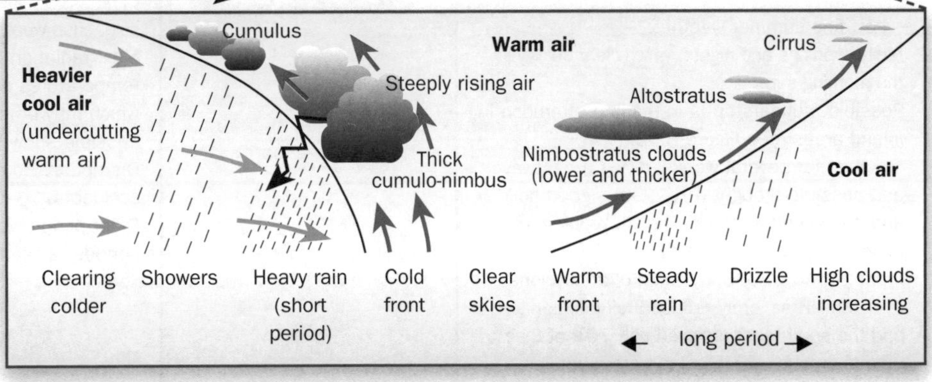

Figure 6.8C Weather forecast for Norwich

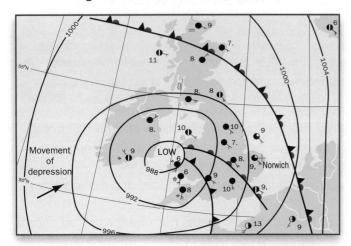

'The weather for the next 24 hours will be very changeable. Clouds will rapidly increase with drizzle and then more persistent rain. It will become slightly warmer as the winds swing more southerly. Skies may clear briefly, before more heavy cloud and rain. There is a possibility of some thunder. Skies will slowly clear to give colder conditions.'

KEY POINT

Anticyclones are areas of high pressure.

In anticyclones, the air is **sinking** and warming. Warmer air can hold more water vapour, so clouds are unlikely to form. Anticyclones can become stationary over the UK, giving settled weather for several days or weeks.

Figure 6.9 Anticyclones in summer and winter

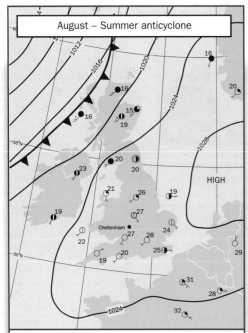

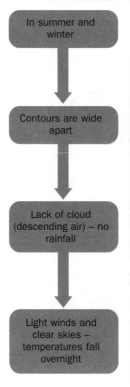

In summer and winter

↓

Contours are wide apart

↓

Lack of cloud (descending air) – no rainfall

↓

Light winds and clear skies – temperatures fall overnight

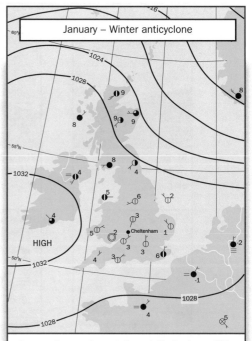

Average August temperature at Cheltenham: 27°C

Clear skies – high solar heating – max. radiation – hot, fine summer weather.

Misty evenings and nights, which clear quickly in the morning sun.

Possible thunderstorms in the late afternoon in inland areas (see Figure 6.5B).

May last for several weeks, giving a heatwave and possible drought (UK 1990) – good holiday and harvesting weather – health problems if pollen counts become high.

From 2004 to 2006, a series of anticyclones over the UK severely reduced rainfall. London and the south east received only 70% of their normal amount, threatening water supplies.

Average January temperature at Cheltenham: 3°C

Clear skies – low solar heating – max. radiation – cold, crisp weather.

Max. radiation through long winter nights – temperatures drop below 0°C – frosts and fogs, which may be slow to clear in the mornings.

Possible snow showers.

Disruptions to commuter traffic, ice may cause accidents.

Older people vulnerable to cold. Extended cold periods raise cost of heating.

Figure 6.10 Temperature inversions

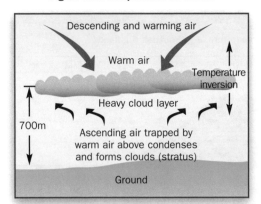

Descending and warming air

Warm air

Temperature inversion

Heavy cloud layer

700m

Ascending air trapped by warm air above condenses and forms clouds (stratus)

Ground

Winter anticyclones can cause **temperature inversions**, where a layer of warm air forms high above the ground and traps the clouds beneath it. During the winter the sun is not strong enough to 'burn off' the clouds. Car and lorry fumes are also trapped (bad air pollution can create health problems for the elderly and those with asthma). In January 2006, a temperature inversion reduced sunlight in London to 3.6 hours over nine days (25% of normal). A gloomy start to the New Year!

Climate

AQA A	✓
AQA B	✗
EDEXCEL A	✗
EDEXCEL B	✓
OCR A	✗
OCR B	✗
WJEC A	✓
WJEC B	✓
CCEA	✓

You should refer to these factors when explaining the climate of any region.

KEY POINT

Climate describes the average weather conditions of a place or area. It is the result of weather data recorded over a long period of time (normally 30 years).

Factors affecting climate

Factors affecting climate include **latitude**, **altitude**, **distance from the sea**, **prevailing winds** and **ocean current**.

Latitude:
- As distance increases from the Equator, temperatures decrease as solar energy (insolation) is less concentrated towards the Poles.
- Seasonal differences in temperature are greater due to the effects of the tilt of the Earth's axis as it orbits the sun.

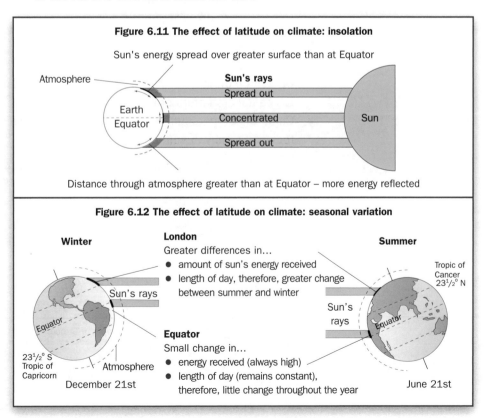

Figure 6.11 The effect of latitude on climate: insolation

Sun's energy spread over greater surface than at Equator

Atmosphere

Sun's rays

Spread out

Earth Equator

Concentrated

Sun

Spread out

Distance through atmosphere greater than at Equator – more energy reflected

Figure 6.12 The effect of latitude on climate: seasonal variation

Winter

London
Greater differences in...
- amount of sun's energy received
- length of day, therefore, greater change between summer and winter

Summer

Tropic of Cancer 23½° N

Sun's rays

Sun's rays

Equator

Equator
Small change in...
- energy received (always high)
- length of day (remains constant), therefore, little change throughout the year

23½° S Tropic of Capricorn

Atmosphere

December 21st

June 21st

Altitude affects climate because the temperature falls, on average, 6.5°C for every 1000 metres in height (see Figure 6.13).

Figure 6.13 Altitude affects temperature, e.g. Scottish Highlands

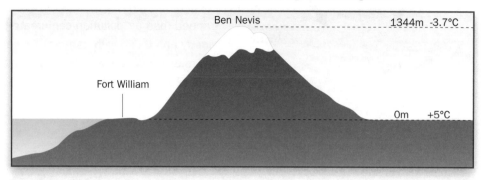

Distance from the sea:

- The seas absorb and store heat to a greater depth than the land.
- The seas, therefore, warm up slowly in summer, storing heat that is slowly released through the winter. The land heats up more quickly, but also cools more quickly.
- Coastal areas are kept cooler in summer and warmer in winter than inland areas, more distant from the sea.
- Islands and areas near the coast, such as the UK, have a **maritime** or **oceanic climate** with only a small range of temperature, e.g., London 14°C, latitude **51½°N** (see Figure 6.18).
- Inland regions, such as central Germany, experience a more extreme **continental climate** with a large annual temperature range, e.g., Berlin 21°C, latitude **52½°N** (see Figure 6.16).

Prevailing winds:

- Prevailing winds are the most frequent winds affecting an area.
- Winds blowing from the sea are generally warm and moist at all times.
- Winds blowing out from large land masses are generally hot and dry in summer and very cold and dry in winter.

Ocean currents:

- Warm and cold currents move large distances across oceans.
- Currents moving from the Equator towards polar areas bring warm conditions to coastal areas further north.
- Currents moving south from polar areas carry cold water south, causing sea fogs particularly in summer.

Figure 6.14 The Labrador Current and North Atlantic Drift

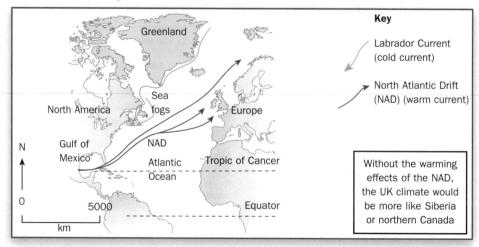

Climatic regions

Climate graphs

At the global scale, the continents can be divided into climatic regions. These are extensive areas that have similar characteristics of temperature and precipitation.

- **Climate graphs** show the **average** monthly temperatures and precipitation for a weather station and illustrate the main characteristics of each region (see Figures 6.16 and 6.18).
- Maps show the extent and pattern of climatic regions. They illustrate the influence of ocean currents, prevailing winds, altitude and latitude.

> Within a climate region there will be many local variations of climate, often called micro-climates.

Figure 6.15 A climate map

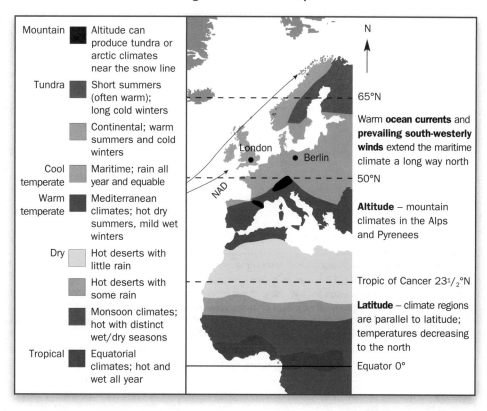

Mountain	Altitude can produce tundra or arctic climates near the snow line
Tundra	Short summers (often warm); long cold winters
	Continental; warm summers and cold winters
Cool temperate	Maritime; rain all year and equable
Warm temperate	Mediterranean climates; hot dry summers, mild wet winters
Dry	Hot deserts with little rain
	Hot deserts with some rain
	Monsoon climates; hot with distinct wet/dry seasons
Tropical	Equatorial climates; hot and wet all year

Warm **ocean currents** and **prevailing south-westerly winds** extend the maritime climate a long way north

Altitude – mountain climates in the Alps and Pyrenees

Latitude – climate regions are parallel to latitude; temperatures decreasing to the north

65°N
50°N
Tropic of Cancer 23½°N
Equator 0°

Figure 6.16 Climate graph for Berlin (52½°N – continental climate (see Figure 6.15)

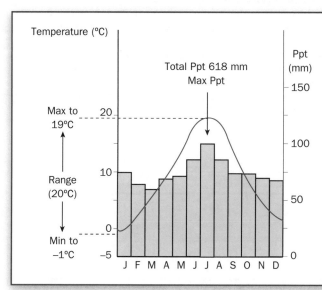

Features:
- Large temperature range (6°C greater than London, see Figure 6.18)
- Short hot summers; very cold winters (Jan. −1°C)
- Precipitation all year with summer maximum

Explanation:
- Distance from the sea; land heats up and cools down quickly
- Easterly winds in winter bring cold, dry, polar continental air (clear skies, hard frosts), and heavy winter snowfalls common
- Strong summer heating results in convectional storms and heavy rainfall

Weather and climate patterns in the UK

Make sure you can describe and explain the different patterns in summer and winter.

Figure 6.17A Seasonal temperature changes in the UK

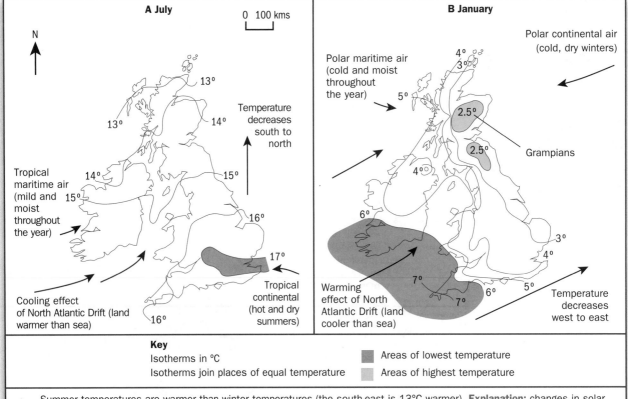

Key

Isotherms in °C
Isotherms join places of equal temperature

■ Areas of lowest temperature
■ Areas of highest temperature

- Summer temperatures are warmer than winter temperatures (the south-east is 13°C warmer). **Explanation:** changes in solar energy due to tilt of Earth's axis as it orbits the sun (see Figure 6.12).
- In summer, temperatures are highest in the south-east (17°C) and coolest in northern Scotland (13°C). **Explanation:** solar energy is less concentrated at higher latitudes (see Figure 6.11). Northern areas are more cloudy, so have less sunshine.
- In winter, temperatures in the south-west (7°C) are 4°C warmer than in north-east Scotland. **Explanation:** warming effect of the NAD (see Figure 6.14); cold polar air often reaches the north-east.

Figure 6.17B Precipitation patterns in the UK

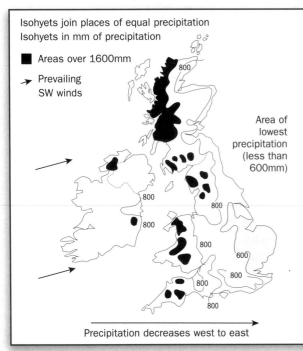

Isohyets join places of equal precipitation
Isohyets in mm of precipitation

■ Areas over 1600mm

→ Prevailing SW winds

Area of lowest precipitation (less than 600mm)

Precipitation decreases west to east

- Precipitation is highest in western areas (+1600mm) and decreases further east (less than 600mm). **Explanation:** depressions approaching from the west bring large amounts of frontal precipitation (see Figure 6.8 A, B and C). Mountains in the west, e.g. Lake District, force south-westerly prevailing winds to rise, which results in relief rainfall. Drier eastern areas are in the rain shadow (see Figure 6.5A).
- In western areas, most precipitation falls in the winter. In eastern areas more rain falls in the summer and autumn. **Explanation:** there are more Atlantic depressions in winter; summer heating in eastern areas results in convectional storms (see Figure 6.5B).

Contrasting climates

Figure 6.18 Climate graph for London (51½°N): cool, temperate maritime climate

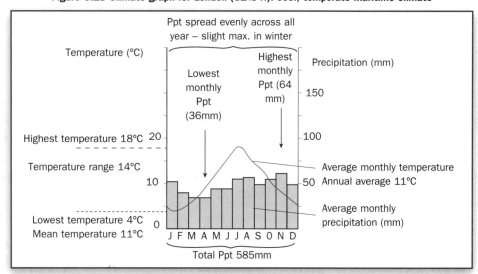

Ppt spread evenly across all year – slight max. in winter

Temperature (°C)

Lowest monthly Ppt (36mm)

Highest monthly Ppt (64 mm)

Precipitation (mm)

150

Highest temperature 18°C

100

Temperature range 14°C

Average monthly temperature Annual average 11°C

50

Lowest temperature 4°C
Mean temperature 11°C

Average monthly precipitation (mm)

J F M A M J J A S O N D

Total Ppt 585mm

Figure 6.19 Climate graph for Uaupes (1°S): tropical equatorial climate (see Figure 6.15).

> Find the location of Uaupes in your atlas.

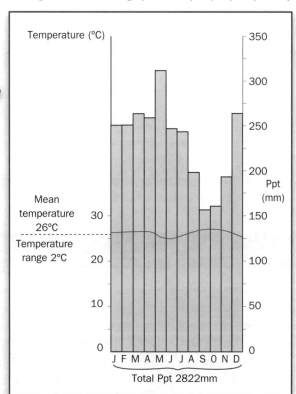

Temperature (°C)

350

300

250

200

Ppt (mm)

Mean temperature 26°C

Temperature range 2°C

30

150

20

100

10

50

0

0

J F M A M J J A S O N D

Total Ppt 2822mm

Uaupes, north west Brazil:
- This climate occurs between 5°N and 5°S of the Equator.
- There are high temperatures all year, average 26°C. **Explanation:** close to the Equator, solar radiation is very high all year (see Figure 6.11); high sunshine hours.
- There is a very small temperature range (2°C) with no summer or winter seasons. **Explanation:** minimal effect of tilt of the Earth's axis (see Figure 6.12).
- There is a large day–night variation in temperatures (diurnal) (10°C). **Explanation:** clear skies at night – Earth cools rapidly (radiation) – early morning mists.
- There is very high precipitation (2822mm), over 150mm every month. **Explanation:** high solar heating all day results in strong convection currents and clouds building up, giving heavy rain and thunderstorms every afternoon (see Figure 6.5B).

The table below shows the comparison of climate characteristics between Uaupes and London (refer to Figures 6.18 and 6.19)

	London	Uaupes	Uaupes compared with London
Mean temperature	11°C	26°C	More than double
Temperature range	14°C	2°C	Seven times smaller, no seasonal change
Highest temperature	18°C	27°C	9°C warmer all year than the summer in London
Lowest temperature	4°C	25°C	21°C warmer than January in London
Total precipitation	585mm	2822mm	Much higher, nearly five times as great; has more rain from January to March than London receives all year

6.2 Weather hazards

LEARNING SUMMARY

After studying this section you should understand:
- the causes of tropical storms, drought and desertification and wildfires
- how the effects differ between MEDCs and LEDCs
- the need to develop better strategies to predict hazards and protect people

Tropical storms

AQA A	✓
AQA B	✓
EDEXCEL A	✓
EDEXCEL B	✗
OCR A	✓
OCR B	✓
WJEC A	✗
WJEC B	✗
CCEA	✗

KEY POINT

Tropical storms are large, low pressure systems that develop over oceans in the Tropics during the summer. They move north and south away from the Equator along similar tracks. *They are known in different parts of the world as cyclones, hurricanes, typhoons and willy-willies.

*Link these different names to their origins and find out where in the world tropical storms are most common.

Tropical storms are **hazardous**, particularly if they reach land:
- Heavy rainfall (200mm per day) can cause flooding and landslides, which damage property and communications.
- Storm surges are created. Low pressure causes the sea level to rise and large waves form in shallow coastal waters (+5m high). Low-lying coasts are very vulnerable, causing severe loss of life in highly populated areas.
- High winds (often exceeding 200kph) cause severe damage to buildings, crops and electric wires.

Tropical storms form...
- over warm, tropical oceans with a water temperature of at least 27°C
- where high solar radiation causes rapid evaporation.

Stages in the development of a tropical storm

Figure 6.20 Cross-section through a tropical storm

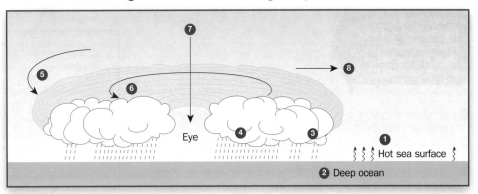

Use the sequence shown, 1–8, to develop a logical explanation.

❶ High solar heating; strong evaporation
❷ Deep ocean; hot surface water (27°C)
❸ Warm, very moist air rises quickly, cools and condenses
❹ Very deep cumulo-nimbus clouds form; heavy rainfall
❺ Low pressure develops; high winds as air is sucked into the depression
❻ Rotation of the Earth encourages violent rotating winds around the central 'eye' (anticlockwise in northern hemisphere)
❼ Central eye – descending air, clear skies, calm conditions
❽ Whole system moves forward fast in the prevailing winds and can intensify (15–25kph)

Effects of tropical storms

MEDC case study: Hurricane Katrina, August 2005

Figure 6.21 Hurricane Katrina threatens the Gulf Coast

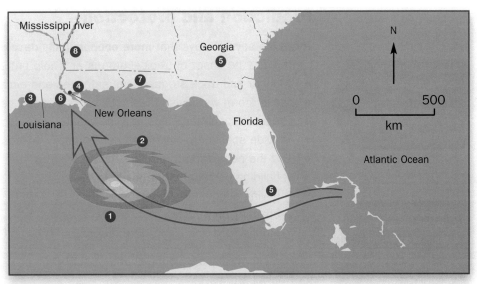

❶ Hurricane Katrina, 200km wide, moved across the Gulf of Mexico at 20kph, gaining strength and becoming a category 3 hurricane
❷ Hurricane force winds created huge 10m-high waves and pushed them north towards the coast
❸ Low-lying coast hit by an 8m-high storm surge penetrating 10–20km inland. 1500 people killed, mostly in the state of Louisiana. Early warnings allowed most people to evacuate.
❹ Surge overtopped levées and flood defences of New Orleans, flooding 80% of the city. It took over 1 month to clear all the flood water from the city
❺ Heavy rainfall and tornadoes in Florida and Georgia damaged crops, destroyed trees and brought down power lines. 3 million people without electricity, some for several weeks
❻ Thousands of homes and businesses flooded in New Orleans. High winds ripped off part of the roof of the Louisiana Superdome
❼ Coastal communities obliterated, beach resorts destroyed, oil refineries flooded and pipelines broken
❽ Interstate highways flooded and bridges destroyed, hindering evacuation and aid

Total damage was estimated at $81 billion, the costliest hurricane in USA history.

LEDC case study: Cyclone Sidr, Bangladesh, November 2007

> Locate the areas in Figures 6.21 and 6.22 in your atlas. Are there any similarities in their locations?

1 Path of the category 5 cyclonic storm funnelling into the Bay of Bengal with winds gusting to 260kph

2 In the shallow waters around the coast a storm surge reached 7m above the normal tide, flooding large areas

3 The delta of the Ganges and Brahmaputra rivers is a series of low islands covered in mangrove forest – the Sundarbans. The forest acts as a storm barrier, shore stabiliser and an important source of domestic timber and commercial shrimp hatcheries.

4 Area occupied by a dense, remote population of farmers and fishermen

5 Storm surge swamped the mangrove forest destroying inland villages. 15 000 people killed and 90 000 left without shelter

6 Fully grown crops spoiled, 100 fishing boats failed to return, shrimp hatcheries ruined – livelihoods destroyed.

7 Government investment in simple warning systems, cyclone shelters and evacuation strategies saved over 1.5m people; a similar cyclone in the area in 1991 claimed 138 000 lives

8 Recovery was slow – three months later over 1 million people were still in temporary shelters and supported by aid agencies

9 With rising sea levels and increasing frequency of storms many people in the Sundarbans needed relocating to safer areas

Figure 6.22 The cyclone path

Formed over warm waters around the Andaman Islands

Prediction and protection

> Keep up-to-date by saving newspaper reports on current hazards and disasters. Use an atlas to locate these areas.

There are several ways that **more economically developed countries** (MEDCs) can predict the onset of tropical storms and help protect people:

- Monitor and track storms using satellites and aircraft.
- Issue storm warnings at least 12 hours in advance.
- Prepare evacuation plans, e.g. designate large sports stadiums as refuges.
- Provide special training for the emergency services.
- Get the population to prepare themselves by...
    - building personal storm shelters
    - having adequate insurance cover
    - boarding-up windows
    - storing food and clean water supplies.

> Be prepared to compare an MEDC with an LEDC in terms of underlying problems due to the differences in wealth. For example, compare the GNP of Bangladesh with that of the USA.

Less economically developed countries (**LEDCs**) can do the following to prepare for tropical storms:

- Further develop sustainable warning procedures for remote areas using local villagers equipped with wind-up radios (no electricity), bicycles, klaxon horns and flags.
- Train and educate people regarding risk and evacuation procedures.
- Build more cyclone shelters (£80 000 each), which are capable of safely housing large numbers of families.
- Raise and strengthen earth banks along coasts and rivers.
- Reduce cutting and plant more mangrove trees along coasts to build up silt and absorb storm surges.
- Obtain aid from MEDCs to relocate villages to safer locations.

Drought and desertification

AQA A	✓
AQA B	✓
EDEXCEL A	✗
EDEXCEL B	✓
OCR A	✓
OCR B	✗
WJEC A	✗
WJEC B	✓
CCEA	✗

> Winter rainfall 2005–2006 in S.E. England was the lowest since the 1930s. Research the outcomes in summer 2006.

> **KEY POINT**
>
> A **drought** is a long period of time without significant rainfall.

Factors affecting the severity of droughts

Climatic factors:

- Past rainfall will affect the amounts of water in surface stores (rivers and lakes), the soil and groundwater (aquifer) stores (see Figure 2.2).
- Rock type: permeable rocks (e.g. chalk) are able to store more water than impermeable rocks (e.g. clay). Impermeable rocks lead to rapid run-off into rivers (see chapter 1).
- Temperature will affect the amount of water lost by evaporation.

Human factors:

- The size of a country's population will affect the demand for water.
- The economic wealth of a country will affect demand (e.g. swimming pools) and its ability to cope with the problems (alternative water supplies).
- Land-use: demands from agriculture (irrigation) and industry.

Causes of droughts in the UK

> **KEY POINT**
>
> An **official drought** in the UK is defined as a period of at least 15 consecutive days with 0.2mm of rain or less.

There are several factors that can contribute to causing a drought:

- Lower than average rainfall in winter and spring, with low levels of water in reservoirs.
- Summer anticyclones (high pressure systems) that become stationary over the UK for several weeks giving hot, fine summer weather (see Figure 6.9).
- Hot weather creates higher than average demand for water (e.g. showering, gardening, watering, etc).

Impact of droughts in MEDCs

There are several impacts of drought in a MEDC:

- Water rationing by using street standpipes or tanker supplies (UK 1976 and 1995).
- Reduced flows in rivers will concentrate pollutants and reduce oxygen in water, causing fish and aquatic plants to suffer or die.
- Trees and plants become stressed, particularly in urban areas.
- Reduction in yields of crops and grass may lead to increased food prices.
- Damage to housing from shrinkage and cracking of clay soils (e.g. insurance claims).
- Increased risk of wildfires (see p. 74) in forests and on heathlands, e.g. New Forest in Hampshire. Wildfires can threaten and destroy property, e.g. Sydney 2005, California 2008 and Australia (Victoria) 2009.
- Droughts are often associated with heatwaves and air pollution, particularly in urban areas, and a rise in health risks (particularly for the elderly).

Managing the effects of drought in MEDCs

Short term:

- Water conservation measures, e.g. banning hosepipes / washing cars.
- Educate people in saving water, e.g. *'Everyone in England and Wales could save four litres a day by turning off the tap while brushing their teeth, which would be enough to supply more than 600 000 homes every day'*.

Medium term:

- Compulsory water metres (Kent, UK, 2006).

Long term:

- Building new reservoirs.
- Establishing a national water supply network, transferring water from areas of high rainfall, e.g. N.W. England, to areas of high demand and low rainfall, e.g. S.E. England.

Causes of droughts and desertification in LEDCs

Case study: The Sahel

Many scientists blame climate change for disturbing the global circulation of winds and ocean currents and causing the rains to fail in the Sahel. Other scientists consider the droughts to be only short-term fluctuations of climate.

KEY POINT

The Sahel is a belt of semi-arid land that stretches across Africa from Mauritania in the west to Somalia in the east, which relies on summer rains to support the habitat and agriculture. Since 1968 the area has suffered from many severe droughts.

With **less rainfall**, the trees and grassland cannot survive and they become scrub vegetation. Less vegetation gives **less transpiration**, so less water vapour is available and there is less likelihood of rain.

Figure 6.23 Drought in the Sahel – failure of the summer rains

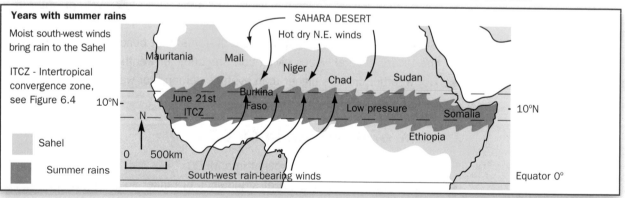

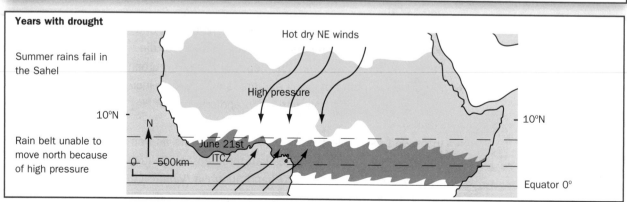

Desertification is the result of both natural and human causes.

Desertification is the process by which land becomes desert.

Drought and human activities have caused the Sahel to become more like a desert. Sahel has…

- thin, dry, sandy soils, lacking any humus to bind the sand together
- large areas of bare rock where soils have been blown away (soil erosion)
- sparse vegetation.

Desertification is also spreading north of the Sahara, in countries such as Algeria and Tunisia.

Figure 6.24 The processes causing desertification in the Sahel

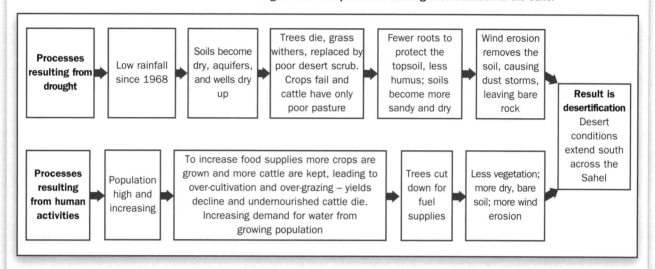

There are several impacts of drought and desertification on LEDCs:

- Food and water shortages lead to malnutrition, famine, disease and high death rates.
- Large numbers of people become dependent on food aid programmes.
- People migrate, which lowers their quality of life. They migrate…
  – from rural to urban areas, causing over-population in towns
  – to refugee camps.

Civil wars prevent aid reaching stricken areas and cause mass migrations to refugee camps, for example as in Eritrea, Ethiopia and the Sudan.

Solutions need to be sustainable.

Short term:

- Provide food aid and water supplies to prevent suffering.
- Conserve water in local, small-scale schemes, e.g. in Burkina Faso they built low stone walls across shallow slopes, capturing any rainfall and dew.

Medium term:

- Improve farming methods by encouraging schemes using sustainable, appropriate technologies, e.g. small-scale, locally made tools (i.e. not tractors).
- Provide drought-resistant seed such as millet, e.g. in northern Nigeria.
- Start tree-planting schemes to reduce soil erosion.
- Reduce population growth through education and investment in health facilities.

Long term:

- Improve water supplies by building large reservoirs and drilling deeper wells.
- International action to reduce the causes of global warming.
- Long term sustainable aid (training and education).

Wildfires

AQA A	X
AQA B	✓
EDEXCEL A	X
EDEXCEL B	X
OCR A	X
OCR B	X
WJEC A	X
WJEC B	X
CCEA	X

> **KEY POINT**
>
> **Wildfires** are uncontrolled and unpredictable fires, driven by high winds and often in wilderness areas of forest and scrubland.

Wildfires occur globally, but most frequently in areas with long, dry, hot summers, for example...

- countries with a Mediterranean climate, such as Portugal (2005–06) and Greece (2007)
- S.E. Australia (Victoria, 2009)
- Indonesia
- South Africa
- S.W. USA (Los Angeles, 2008)

> Locate these countries in an atlas.

There are several **conditions** favouring wildfires.

Climatic conditions:

- **Temperature** increases evaporation and transpiration, drying out the vegetation.
- High **winds** fan the flames and drive the fire forwards.
- **Moisture** – dry winds increase evaporation.

Fuel sources:

- Short-term sources (dry grass, pine needles) provide flashy fuels that are easily ignited and transported beyond the fire front by strong winds.
- Long-term sources are dense forests of resin-rich fir and pine trees.

Topography:

- Steep slopes – fires travel faster uphill.
- Narrow valleys (canyons) funnel winds and fires.

Case study: The Santa Ana Winds, California, USA

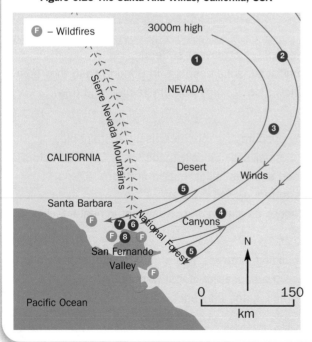

Figure 6.25 The Santa Ana Winds, California, USA

❶ **Great Basin** (Nevada/Utah)
- Desert wilderness (3000m high), cooling fast after summer heat
- Very dry, **high pressure** cell develops and winds flow outwards

❷ **Santa Ana winds** flowing **clockwise** from high to low pressure

❸ Winds start cool and dry, flowing **downslope** out of the high Great Basin. Winds become much warmer and gain in speed

❹ **N.E. winds** approaching Los Angeles are now strong, warm and dry. They suck up moisture from plants and the ground

❺ Winds funnelled into deep narrow canyons, increasing their speed up to 85mph or more

❻ Los Angeles National Forest. Trees and undergrowth, tinder dry after the summer drought, creating a very high fire hazard requiring only a spark to be fanned by the winds into a wildfire

❼ Scenic canyons and forest on edge of city attracts expensive housing developments and low-cost mobile home parks

❽ **Los Angeles Basin** (California) – compared to the Great Basin:
- Much lower pressure so inflowing winds
- Much lower altitude, 500–1000m
- Much warmer, but still dry
- Where dense urban population and development lives on the edge of the National Forest

Causes of wildfires

Causes of wildfires can be natural or from human activities, though nowadays the latter cause is more likely.

- **Natural** causes – lightning, heat of the sun, volcanic eruptions
- **Human** causes – fallen electricity lines (due to high winds), campfires, fireworks, car accidents, arson.

Impacts

> Some scrub, heathlands and forest are 'controlled burnt' by rangers. This reduces the build-up of 'flashy fuels' and encourages new growth. Some plants have adapted to natural burning and now require fire or smoke to germinate.

Case study: California, October–November 2008 (see Figure 6.25)

San Fernando Valley (35km north of downtown Los Angeles):
- Two fires extended over 70km^2.
- Over 50 multi-million dollar homes destroyed.
- Only 2 fatalities.

Montecito (outskirts of Santa Barbara):
- Three fires extended over 75km^2.
- 800 houses and 500 mobile homes destroyed.
- 30 000 people evacuated.
- 100 000 homes without power, and water supplies contaminated.
- Human carelessness thought to be the cause.

> The after-effects of a wildfire can be serious:
> - The vegetation cover lost can expose dry soils on steep slopes.
> - Torrential rain can cause land and mud slides, which block roads and rivers and cause flooding.

Prediction and protection

Prediction:
- Development of satellite technology and on-site sensor webs to monitor and provide early warnings of fire outbreaks.
- FPI (Fire Protection Index) developed by the US Forest Service to identify high-risk areas.

Protection:
- Satellite monitoring of fire fronts.
- Training of rapid deployment teams.
- Development of eco-friendly, effective fire retardants to deploy from helicopters.
- Planning controls in identified fire risk areas.

> Hi-tech responses are possible in a MEDC.

PROGRESS CHECK

1. What are tropical storms and what conditions do they require to form?
2. What is desertification?
3. Give two ways in which human activities are contributing to desertification in the Sahel.
4. Give two reasons why the Santa Ana winds in S. California often cause serious wildfires.

1. Tropical storms are large low pressure systems that form over tropical oceans with a water temperature of at least 27°C and where solar radiation causes high evaporation
2. The process caused by natural and human factors that turns land into desert.
3. **Accept two ways from:** Rapid population growth; Over cultivation; Over grazing; Trees cut down for fuel supplies (link to loss of vegetation cover and greater wind erosion) (see Figure 6.24)
4. **Accept two reasons from:** Warm dry winds suck up moisture from vegetation and soil; Winds increase in speed through the canyons; Undergrowth and trees very dry after long hot summer (link to either natural and human causes) (see Figure 6.25)

6.3 Climate change

After studying this section you should understand:

- that atmospheric conditions may be changing as a result of human activities
- that changes in atmospheric conditions will have important social, economic and political consequences
- that to meet the challenge, global, national and local strategies are required

Global warming

AQA A	✓
AQA B	✓
EDEXCEL A	✓
EDEXCEL B	✓
OCR A	✓
OCR B	✓
WJEC A	✓
WJEC B	✓
CCEA	✓

Some scientists believe that the global climates are changing, largely because of human activities.

Other scientists believe the changes being measured are just fluctuations in the atmospheric conditions, which have always occurred. For example, ice sheets have advanced across the UK several times in the last 500 000 years, and in the last 10 000 years there have been notable changes to our climate, long before human activity had significant effects.

Figure 6.26 Climate change in the Holocene

Approx. age (years before present). *Not to scale*	Period	Epoch	Zone	Climate	Historical Timescale	Impacts
150 (1850 AD)				Global warming		• Glaciers shrinking • Sea levels rising
200 (1800 AD) 600 (1400 AD)				Little ice age Violent storms Freezing winters	Georgian Medieval	• Flooding caused much loss of life, ruined farming • Famine across Europe. Thames frozen over, 'frost' fairs on the ice (e.g. as seen in Dutch paintings)
1000 2000 AD BC 3000 4000 5000	Quaternary	Holocene (post glacial)		Warmer and drier than present Cool and wet Warm and dry	Anglo-Saxons Roman occupation Iron age Bronze age Neolithic	• Vineyards common in England • Population increasing • Forest remains only in Scottish Highlands • Forest clearance for mixed farming
7500			Atlantic	Warm and dry		
			Boreal	Warm and dry	Mesolithic	
10 000				Temperate warming		• Spread of deciduous forest • Rising sea-levels creating the North Sea, English Channel and Irish Sea
		Pleistocene (ice ages)				

The greenhouse effect

Figure 6.27 The greenhouse effect

> Do not confuse the greenhouse effect with holes in the ozone layer.

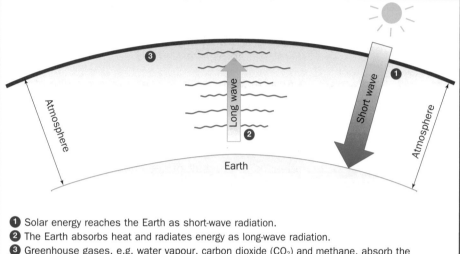

- ① Solar energy reaches the Earth as short-wave radiation.
- ② The Earth absorbs heat and radiates energy as long-wave radiation.
- ③ Greenhouse gases, e.g. water vapour, carbon dioxide (CO_2) and methane, absorb the long-wave radiation and insulate the Earth.

Global warming

Greenhouse gases occur **naturally**, but human activities have resulted in **rising concentrations** of these gases, particularly of CO_2. Greater amounts of long-wave radiation are retained in the atmosphere and so **warm it up**.

Evidence for climatic change

> Newspapers have frequent discussions on climate change, particularly when storms or flooding cause damage. Make a collection of these articles and use them in your revision.

There are several factors that indicate a climatic change is occurring:
- **Rising global temperatures** – average temperatures have increased by 0.6°C in the last 100 years and a further rise of 1.4°C to 5.8°C is predicted by 2100.
- An **increase in extreme events** – there are more intense tropical storms, and in the last few years the UK has had the driest, wettest and windiest periods of weather since records began.
- **Changing ocean currents** – currents in the S. Pacific may be changing and causing droughts and forest fires in Indonesia and the loss of important fishing grounds off Peru and Chile. The North Atlantic Drift may also be weakening.
- **Shrinking of glaciers and ice sheets** (particularly since 1985) – permanently frozen soils and rock in Siberia and on high mountains in the Alps are melting (increase in mudslides). Evidence from satellite images shows that the Antartica icesheet is losing up to 36 cubic miles of ice each year.
- **Increased rainfall** in the northern hemisphere over the past decade.

This is a popular subject for examiners to ask question about.

Causes of global warming

It is thought that some human activities are causing global warming.

The **burning of fossil fuels** (e.g. coal and oil) releases CO_2 into the atmosphere. The rate at which fossil fuels are being burned has increased rapidly in the last 100 years. Energy consumption in power stations, for domestic heating and in cars and lorries, has increased by 50% in the last ten years. A 2008 report predicts CO_2 will continue to rise by more than 3% a year unless action is taken.

Deforestation is another possible cause. Most woodlands in temperate areas, e.g. the UK, have been chopped down, and tropical rainforests are now being felled and burned. Trees convert CO_2 into oxygen through photosynthesis, so the burning of forests releases large amounts of CO_2 into the atmosphere.

Cattle farming has increased the levels of methane going into the atmosphere (cattle produce methane in their intestines). Cattle numbers have steadily increased as demand for food increases.

The use of **waste tips** means that large quantities of methane are being released as a result of decomposing materials. Commercial and domestic waste has increased enormously in recent years.

However, some scientists believe **natural processes** are the cause:
- Temperatures have changed notably during the past 500 000 years, long before human activities became notably (see Figures 4.1 and 6.26).
- CO_2 is produced in huge quantities from natural sources, e.g. volcanoes and decaying vegetation, and in far greater amounts than that produced by human sources.
- Variations in sun spot activity and cosmic radiation may be relevant.

Figure 6.28 Areas at risk from sea-level rise in the UK

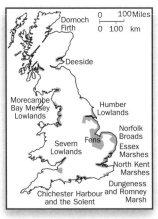

Consequences for both MEDCs and LEDCs

There are many consequences as a result of global warming.

A rise in **sea level** would create the following problems:
- The melting of ice caps and glaciers will release large amounts of water into the oceans.
- Higher water temperatures will cause ocean waters to expand, raising sea levels.
- The flooding of low-lying coastal areas, e.g. Bangladesh, Japan and the UK Fenlands, and the submersion of islands in the Caribbean and Indian Ocean will produce many millions of refugees.

Global circulation would be disturbed:
- Tropical areas are becoming drier and deserts are expanding, which will lead to widespread crop failures in central Africa, resulting in malnutrition and starvation.
- Water shortages will increase, particularly in Africa, northern China and India.
- The spread of the malarial mosquito in Africa, USA and Europe.
- Decreasing crop yields in South America, China, Africa and India.
- More temperate conditions in Canada and Siberia will improve agriculture.

It will be more difficult for LEDCs to adjust than most MEDCs.

The melting of **permafrost** in Siberia will release large amounts of methane into the atmosphere and further increase global warming. Increased evaporation will raise the amount of water vapour in the atmosphere, also increasing global warming. Greater amounts of energy in the atmosphere will increase the likelihood of **extreme events** such as tropical storms.

Global strategies to reduce global warming

One strategy to reduce global warming is to reduce emissions of greenhouse gases. This could be done in several ways:

- Develop **alternative forms of energy**, e.g. solar, tidal, wind and hydroelectricity (see page 148–149).
- Switch to nuclear power (see page 147).
- Develop **alternative energy sources** for road transport (e.g. electric cars).
- Support LEDCs in using alternative forms of energy.

International commitments could also agree to reduce emissions and limit pollution, e.g. **Earth Summits**. So far, progress has been slow as positive action requires political commitment:

- 1992 Rio de Janeiro (Agenda 21, 118 countries committed).
- 1997 Kyoto (5% cut in emissions by all MEDCs by 2012).
- 2000 The Hague (opposed by President Bush, USA, UN delegates agreed a strategy to cut world carbon emissions).
- 2005 Kyoto agreement.
- 2007 Bali agreement.

Other strategies include the following:

- Reduce **deforestation** and develop sustainable policies such as **selective cutting** (rainforest) and **replanting** (UK National Forest, e.g. Leicestershire).
- Reduce population growth and reduce energy consumption.

Local strategies to reduce global warming

- Reduce water consumption – '*put a hippo in the toilet cistern*'
- Cut at least one car journey a week – '*get a bus timetable*'
- Reduce energy use and insulate housing – '*switch off the light*'
- Recycle more and reduce landfill – '*watch out for the symbol!*'

Strategies to reduce impact of global warming

There are several strategies to reduce the impact of global warming:

- Defend and protect low-lying coastal areas from flooding.
- Improve water supplies and use them more efficiently, particularly in areas that are becoming drier.
- Encourage research into developing crops that can withstand drought and diseases.
- Develop more efficient ways of predicting and preparing for extreme weather events such as tropical storms.

Why are some MEDCs and LEDCs unwilling to reduce their emissions of CO_2?

Research further the Earth summits.

Are these ideas significant at the global scale?

LEDCs will probably be the worst affected. How will these countries afford to pay for the research and new development?

Ozone layer depletion

AQA A	X
AQA B	X
EDEXCEL A	X
EDEXCEL B	X
OCR A	✓
OCR B	X
WJEC A	X
WJEC B	X
CCEA	X

KEY POINT

Ozone (O_3) forms a protective layer of gas around the Earth that absorbs and filters ultraviolet (UV) radiation from the sun.

Ultraviolet radiation is an important component of sunlight which, in small doses, is good for people and allows the body to produce vitamin D. However, excessive exposure can be harmful.

Damage and causes of ozone depletion

Do not give this as a cause of global warming.

In 1986, scientists in Antarctica discovered a 'hole' in the ozone layer. The hole means that greater amounts of UV radiation are reaching the Earth. Measurements in 1998 showed that the hole had grown larger and amounts of **UV radiation** had increased in Australia and Argentina. A further hole was discovered over the Arctic, which is increasing in size and could affect Europe and North America.

The increased production and use of **chlorofluorocarbons** (CFCs) are responsible for slowly eroding a hole in the ozone layer. Chlorofluorocarbons...

- are light gases that rise slowly into the atmosphere
- can have a long 'life' of over 400 years
- attack and destroy ozone molecules.

> **KEY POINT**
>
> **Chlorofluorocarbons** (CFCs) are man-made chemicals used in foam packaging, aerosols and as a coolant in fridges and air-conditioning systems.

The Australian government and people treat this threat very seriously. The government has promoted the campaign: '*slap on the cream, slip on the hat*'.

Consequences

In Australia and South America...

- skin cancer has increased (it is estimated that a 1% decrease in ozone causes a 5% increase in cancer)
- incidents of eye cataracts have increased
- crops have suffered from more diseases
- marine food chains have been affected; microorganisms that are important sources of food for fish are being destroyed.

There is evidence that the 'holes' are repairing themselves, but sufficient CFCs are still present in the atmosphere to pose threats until 2020.

Solutions

An International Agreement in 1990 banned the use of CFCs by 2000:
- Most MEDCs have achieved this, though some LEDCs require more time.
- New fridges no longer use CFCs – new 'ozone friendly' aerosols and biodegradable packaging has replaced foam.

Poster campaigns and the **media** have raised public awareness about using suntan creams and reducing exposure by always wearing sunhats and long-sleeve shirts. **Weather forecasts** include information on UV intensities.

> **PROGRESS CHECK**
>
> 1. Which of the following is causing global warming?
>   a) The hole in the ozone layer
>   b) The increase in greenhouse gases
>   c) The rise in sea level
> 2. Describe three global strategies to reduce global warming.
> 3. Why is the layer of ozone, found in the upper atmosphere, beneficial to life on Earth?
>
> 1. The increase in greenhouse gases 2. **Select three from:** Develop alternative energy sources; Increase use of nuclear energy; Alternative power sources for transport; Reduce deforestation; Reduce population growth; Increased international co-operation (link to reductions in greenhouse gases, see p. 79) 3. It protects us from exposure to too much ultraviolet radiation.

7 Ecosystems

The following topics are covered in this chapter:

- The natural environment
- Global ecosystems

7.1 The natural environment

LEARNING SUMMARY

After studying this section you should be able to understand:

- the complex nature of ecosystems and their importance
- that ecosystems exist at a variety of scales
- how energy from the sun and nutrients derived from weathered rock are circulated through the system by plants and animals
- that ecosystems develop over time by the process of succession
- how most ecosystems have been destroyed or altered by human activity
- that many ecosystems need to be managed in a sustainable way

Ecosystems

AQA A	✓
AQA B	✓
EDEXCEL A	✓
EDEXCEL B	✓
OCR A	✓
OCR B	✓
WJEC A	✓
WJEC B	✓
CCEA	✓

The **natural environment** consists of the **rocks**, **soils**, **vegetation**, **animals**, **air** and **water** of the Earth. It is made up of different **ecosystems**.

> **KEY POINT**
>
> An ecosystem describes the links between the living community of animals and plants and their habitat.

The living community is the **biomass** (animals, plants, fungi and bacteria). They are linked together in a **food web**.

The **habitat** includes non-living components, e.g. rocks, soil, water and climate.

Ecosystems exist at a variety of scales, from an oak tree or rock pool on the seashore to **biomes** (large global systems) such as tropical rainforests or coral reefs. Human activity has destroyed or altered parts of many ecosystems.

Energy cycle

Understanding the basic ideas of the energy cycle, nutrient cycle and succession will help you to explain why biomes are so different.

The sun is the source of all energy in an ecosystem. Light energy from the sun is absorbed by green plants in a process called **photosynthesis**. Energy flows through the system as a food web. Plants are eaten by animals, and animals eat each other (see Figure 7.3).

The food web consists of a series of stages known as **trophic levels**. Energy is **stored** in the system as plant tissue, muscle and fat (see Figure 7.2).

Energy is **lost** from the system by **transpiration**, **respiration** (by plants and animals), **consumption** (e.g. when a worm is eaten by a bird) and **decomposition** (bacteria and fungi break down dead plants and animals).

Human activity can interfere with the food web, e.g. through farming and hunting.

Nutrient cycle

Weathered rock releases nutrients such as calcium, carbon and nitrogen into the soil. Plants and animals circulate nutrients through the system. The cycle occurs quickly in hot, wet ecosystems, e.g. a tropical rainforest, and more slowly in cold systems, e.g. tundra. Nutrients are lost into rivers (see Figure 7.4).

Human activity can affect the cycle, e.g. deforestation (increased run-off).

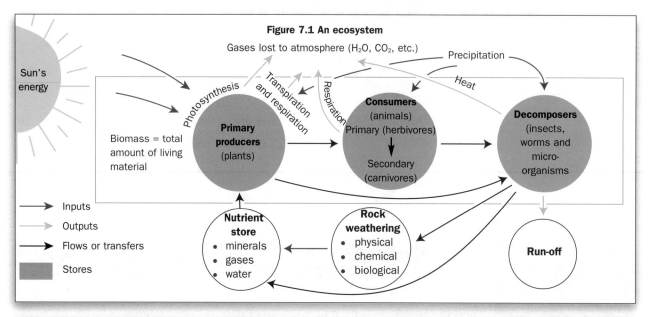

Figure 7.1 An ecosystem

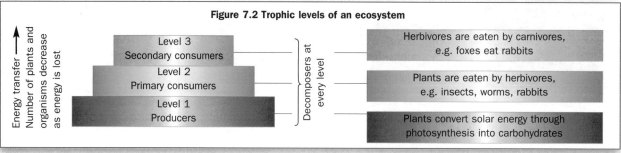

Figure 7.2 Trophic levels of an ecosystem

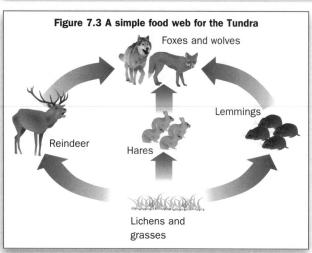

Figure 7.3 A simple food web for the Tundra

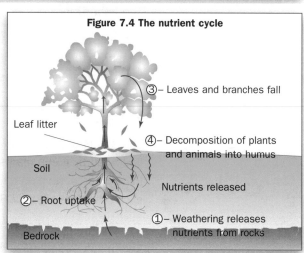

Figure 7.4 The nutrient cycle

Succession

Ecosystems develop over time by the process of succession:

1 The first plants to colonise an area are called **pioneer species**. Pioneer plants are adapted to harsh conditions. They are hardy and require only a low nutrient supply.

2 Rock weathering and the decomposition of plants increase the supply of nutrients, allowing new plants to germinate, e.g. grasses. Insect and animal life increases.

3 Soils become deeper with more nutrients, so can support larger and more varied species, e.g. shrubs.

4 Given time, a dominant species (e.g. oak or beech trees) takes over and smaller plants live beneath the dominant trees. The succession is completed.

5 Plants, insects, birds and animals exist in complex food chains and webs.

Succession can take place in four environments: on bare rock, in freshwater, on sand, and in salt water.

Figure 7.5 Typical succession to climax vegetation

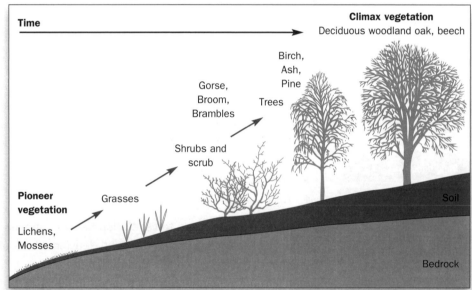

A small-scale ecosystem – sand dunes

Dunes form along coasts where there is a large supply of sand from the beach and strong prevailing winds blowing in from the sea. Dunes are common on sand spits (see Figure 3.9).

Sand is blown inland forming low embryo dunes, which are colonised by marram grass. Further sand is trapped by the grass and the dunes grow higher (see Figure 7.6).

> The plants and animals interact with the wind and sand, and the succession develops.

Marram grass helps to stabilise the dunes – the decomposition provides humus for soil development. The grass is **adapted** to the dry and windy environment:

• It grows quickly so is not smothered by fresh sand.

• It has long roots to reach the water table.

• It has strong leaves that can stand exposure to high winds and prevent excessive moisture loss.

Older dunes are more stable and have a wider variety of plants covering the ground. Shrubby plants develop, e.g. sea buckthorn, hawthorn and gorse, which are colonised by insects, birds, rabbits, birds of prey and foxes. Pine trees and eventually oak and ash (the dominant species) complete the succession.

Figure 7.6 Succession to climax vegetation on sand dunes

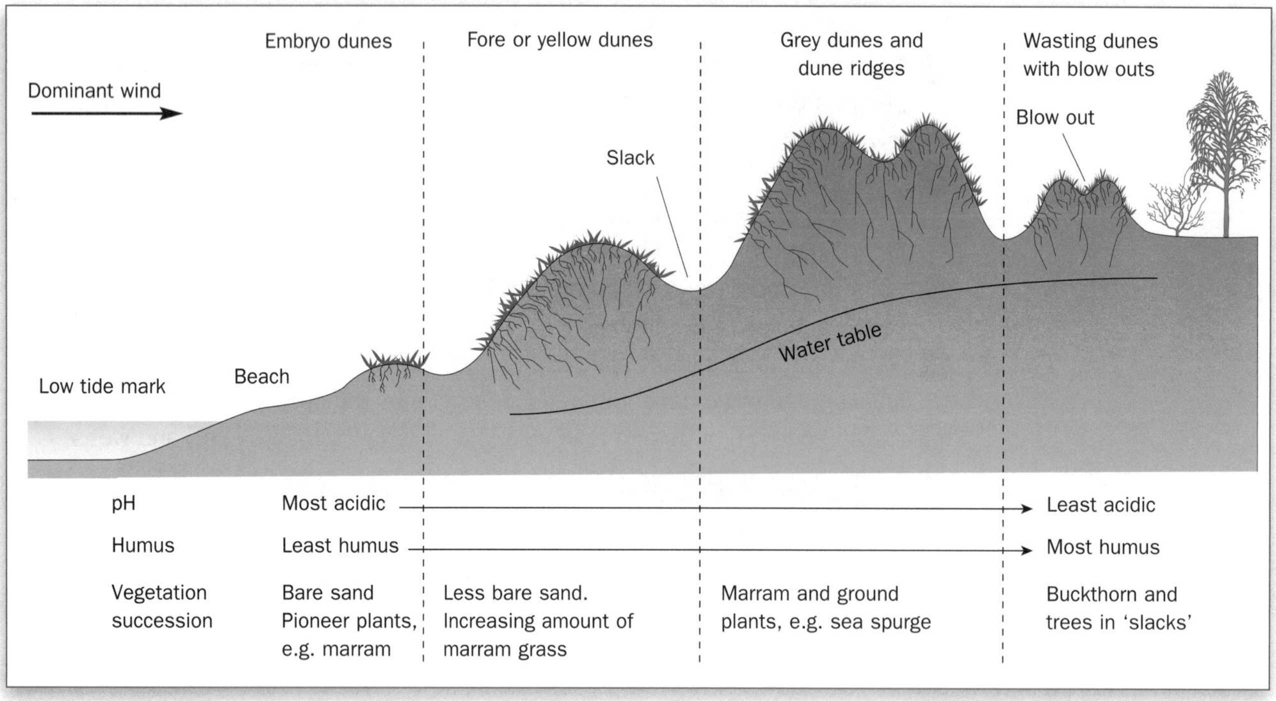

	Embryo dunes	Fore or yellow dunes	Grey dunes and dune ridges	Wasting dunes with blow outs
pH	Most acidic →			Least acidic
Humus	Least humus →			Most humus
Vegetation succession	Bare sand Pioneer plants, e.g. marram	Less bare sand. Increasing amount of marram grass	Marram and ground plants, e.g. sea spurge	Buckthorn and trees in 'slacks'

Dune management

Dunes are important coastal defences and need to be conserved. They are fragile systems and can quickly become damaged by...
- human activity, including trampling, sliding down dune faces, horse riding and fires
- over-population by rabbits
- military use.

Damage to dunes leads to vegetation being destroyed and bare sand being exposed. The wind removes the sand, leaving 'blow-outs'. Root systems then become exposed, which kills marram grass and in turn leads to a greater exposure of bare sand and more wind erosion.

Damage can be reduced by various management techniques:
- Wooden boardwalks and fencing along popular routes through dunes.
- Information / interpretative boards to raise public awareness.
- Wardens and guides.
- Car parking charges in order to reduce demand.
- Culling and controlling rabbit populations.

> Sand dunes at Gibraltar Point, Skegness (Figure 3.13) and Studland, Dorset (Figure 3.14) are carefully managed to allow public access and to sustain the dune habitat.

PROGRESS CHECK

1. What is an ecosystem?
2. By what process do green plants absorb light energy from the sun?
3. In a food web, what is the name given to herbivores such as rabbits?
4. What is the principal source of nutrients in an ecosystem?
5. What name is given to plants that first colonise an area?

1. It describes the links between the living community of animals and plants and their habitat
2. Photosynthesis
3. Primary consumers
4. Weathered rock
5. Pioneer species

7.2 Global ecosystems

LEARNING SUMMARY	After studying this section you should be able to understand:
	• the natures, scale and distribution of some major biomes
	• the important links that exist between climate, soils and the living community in different biomes
	• the need for vegetation and animals to adapt to their habitat
	• the impact of human activity
	• the need for careful management if biomes are to remain sustainable

Biomes (continental)

AQA A	✓
AQA B	✓
EDEXCEL A	✓
EDEXCEL B	✓
OCR A	✓
OCR B	✓
WJEC A	✓
WJEC B	✓
CCEA	X

> **KEY POINT**
>
> **Biomes** are large ecosystems at the global scale where the climate, vegetation and soils are broadly the same.

There are eight major biomes:

- Tundra (cold desert)
- Temperate deciduous woodland
- Mediterranean
- Savanna grassland

- Coniferous forest (taiga)
- Temperate grasslands
- Hot desert
- Tropical rainforest

Figure 7.7: Six of the major biomes

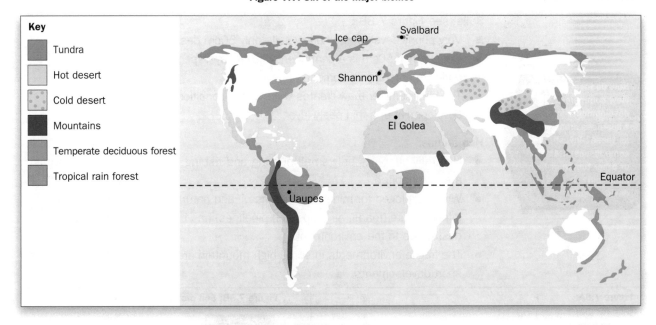

Key
- Tundra
- Hot desert
- Cold desert
- Mountains
- Temperate deciduous forest
- Tropical rain forest

> **KEY POINT**
>
> The tundra and desert biomes are examples of **extreme environments**:
> - Both experience extremes of temperature and low irregular precipitation.
> - Soils are mostly thin and poorly developed.
> - The number of species of plants and animals is low because of the need to adapt to the harsh environment.

Tundra (and High Alpine)

Tundra means 'barren land'. It is a treeless landscape due to the harsh environment.

Location (see Figure 7.7):
- Found mostly along and within the Arctic Circle: Alaska, northern Canada, northern Europe, Russia and Siberia bordering the Arctic Ocean.
- Also found in high mountains above the tree line close to the permanent snow line, e.g. Rocky Mountains, Andes and the Himalayas.

Climate (see Figure 7.8A):
- Very long, intensely cold, dark winters for about 8 months. Temperatures are below freezing with extreme temperatures (-30°C). Many months are without daylight.
- Brief summers with max. temperatures rarely exceeding 15°C. There is a very short **growing season** (less than 50 days).
- Low precipitation (less than 300mm). The cold air is unable to hold much water vapour and mainly falls as winter snow.
- Frequent winds, which are often strong and drying.

Vegetation and animals:
- Vegetation is dominated by low growing mosses, lichens, hardy grasses and dwarf shrubs.
- Very few species (compared with the tropical rainforest).
- Vegetation greatly disturbed in summer by processes such as frost-heave, solifluction and freeze-thaw (see chapters 1 and 4).
- Only small herbivores remain all year (e.g. lemmings and hares) together with hunters (e.g. arctic foxes and owls). Most animals are summer visitors only, e.g. reindeer migrate south into the coniferous forest in winter and there are summer breeding sites for arctic terns who migrate south to W. Africa in September.

> Study the food web for the Tundra (Figure 7.3). If owls were added to the web and the lemming population suddenly increased, what might the effect be?

Soils (see Figure 7.8B):
- Very poorly developed, shallow soils only 50cm deep.
- Deeper than 50cm is a permanently frozen layer (permafrost), which prevents drainage or root development.
- The brief summer thaw creates waterlogged conditions at the surface and the development of a thin peaty layer.

> How do local people view commercial developments in wilderness areas such as these? Investigate some issues in Alaska or other tundra or high mountain environments.

Human use:
- Naturally supports only small hunting and fishing communities. Large areas are uninhabited.
- Where exploited for minerals, such as oil and natural gas, the development of infrastructure (roads, air strips and pipelines) has been difficult and often destructive to the environment.
- The fragile environments in some high mountain areas have suffered from winter sport developments.

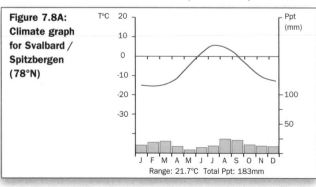

Figure 7.8A: Climate graph for Svalbard / Spitzbergen (78°N)

Range: 21.7°C Total Ppt: 183mm

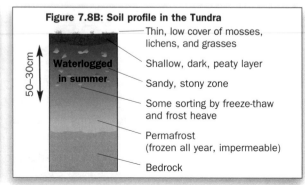

Figure 7.8B: Soil profile in the Tundra
- Thin, low cover of mosses, lichens, and grasses
- Shallow, dark, peaty layer
- Sandy, stony zone
- Some sorting by freeze-thaw and frost heave
- Permafrost (frozen all year, impermeable)
- Bedrock

Waterlogged in summer

50–30cm

Temperate deciduous woodland

Location (see Figure 7.7):

- Found mostly on the east coast of continents, between 40°N to 60°N, e.g. eastern USA, much of China and Japan. Also in New Zealand and S.E. Australia.
- Also found in N.W. Europe (including the UK and Eire).

Climate (see Figure 7.9A):

- Cool summers and mild winters. The growing season is seven months.
- Precipitation is 500–1000mm/year, falling throughout the year.

Vegetation and animals (see Figure 7.9B):

- **Deciduous** trees (oak, beech, ash) shed leaves in winter. This reduces transpiration when the colder temperatures reduce effectiveness of **photosynthesis**.
- Relatively few species compared with tropical rainforest.
- Oak represents **climax vegetation**.
- There are some layers beneath the upper canopy because sunlight is able to penetrate, particularly in spring (deciduous trees).
- Thick leaf litter, but many decomposers cause rapid recycling of nutrients.
- Deer, foxes, squirrels, badgers and many bird species.

Soils (see Figure 7.9C):

- Brown **earth**, which is deeper and more fertile than tundra soils (see Figure 7.8B).
- Leaf litter decomposes quickly and is incorporated into the soil by many earthworms.
- Fairly uniform, well-drained soil, which is deeply penetrated by root systems of trees.

Human activity:

- Severe deforestation, which is the result of clearance and use over the past 1000 years (see Figure 6.26)
- Significant uses today include game management, timber production and recreation. Multi-purpose is seen as best way of conservation.

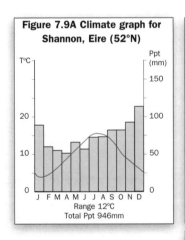

Figure 7.9A Climate graph for Shannon, Eire (52°N)

Range 12°C
Total Ppt 946mm

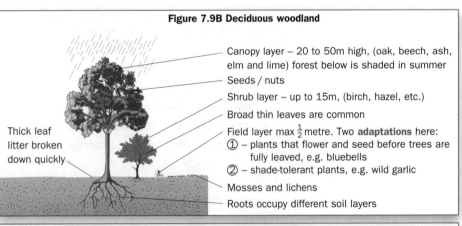

Figure 7.9B Deciduous woodland

Canopy layer – 20 to 50m high, (oak, beech, ash, elm and lime) forest below is shaded in summer

Seeds / nuts

Shrub layer – up to 15m, (birch, hazel, etc.)

Broad thin leaves are common

Field layer max $\frac{1}{2}$ metre. Two **adaptations** here:
① – plants that flower and seed before trees are fully leaved, e.g. bluebells
② – shade-tolerant plants, e.g. wild garlic

Mosses and lichens

Roots occupy different soil layers

Thick leaf litter broken down quickly

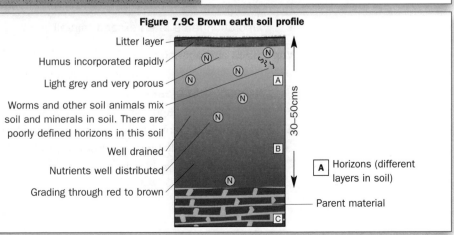

Figure 7.9C Brown earth soil profile

Litter layer

Humus incorporated rapidly

Light grey and very porous

Worms and other soil animals mix soil and minerals in soil. There are poorly defined horizons in this soil

Well drained

Nutrients well distributed

Grading through red to brown

30–50cms

A Horizons (different layers in soil)

Parent material

Carry out research to discover how these schemes are progressing.

There are several schemes that have re-established multi-purpose uses:

- The **Community Forest Organisation** (1991) has been responsible for planting 3500 hectares of native trees in twelve community forests in the UK, mostly on brownfield sites on the edges of cities, e.g. Great North forest (Newcastle), Mersey forest (Liverpool–Manchester).
- The **National Forest** aimed in 1990 to plant a third of the Midlands (Staffordshire, Derbyshire and Leicestershire) with new trees.
- The **Woodland Trust** owns and cares for over 1000 woods and all have open access.
- **Brownfield sites** have been used for different purposes, for example...
  - old mine tips have been used for commercial forestry
  - old quarries have been used for leisure pursuits, e.g. cycling, fishing, walking and wildlife reserves (see chapter 1).

Hot deserts

Most hot deserts are found in one of four **locations**: (see Figure 7.7):

- Around 30° north and south. These are zones of tropical high pressure (see Figure 6.4) where hot descending air prohibits cloud development, e.g. Saharan, Australian and Thar (India) deserts.
- In the rainshadow of high mountains, e.g. Mojave (USA) and Patagonian deserts.
- In the centre of large land masses far from sources of moist air, e.g. Australian deserts.
- Around 23.5° north and south, on the west coast of continents where the prevailing winds are offshore (easterly), e.g. Namibian (West Africa) and Atacama (Chile) deserts.

Use an atlas to locate one example from each group.

Climate:

- Very hot summers and cooler winters. The annual range can be more than 25°C.
- An extreme daily temperature range (greater than 40°C), particularly in summer. The absence of cloud cover permits strong solar heating during the day (greater than 50°C) and rapid cooling at night.
- Very low rainfall, less than 250mm per year. There are extremes, e.g. the Atacama desert receives only 15mm (compare with Shannon Figure 7.9A).
- Rainfall is unpredictable, often falling in brief sudden downpours, causing flash floods.
- Evaporation rates often exceed rainfall.

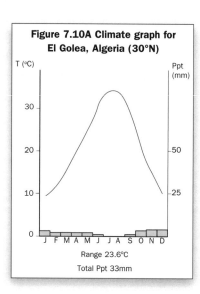

Figure 7.10A Climate graph for El Golea, Algeria (30°N)

Range 23.6°C

Total Ppt 33mm

Vegetation and animals:

- Sparse vegetation, mostly low-growing shrubs and trees surrounded by bare sand and rocky areas.
- Mobile areas of sand dunes support very little vegetation.
- Few plant and animal species (compared with the tropical rainforests).
- There are relatively large numbers of reptiles (lizards, snakes) and insects. The food chains are simple.

There are three main ways that plants have adapted to tolerate extreme aridity (see Figure 7.10B):

- **Xerophytes** develop shallow, extensive root systems that capture a lot of water when rain falls, e.g. creosote bush.
- **Phreatophytes** develop deep roots (many metres long) to reach the water table, e.g. mesquite bushes.
- **Succulents** store water in fleshy cells protected by tough outer layers (cuticle), e.g. cacti and yuccas.

Animals have **adapted** to tolerate extreme aridity by...

- being small enough to shelter under stones and rocks by day, e.g. spiders
- living in burrows during the day, foraging and hunting at night (nocturnal), e.g. kangaroo mice
- storing water and passing little urine, e.g. tortoises
- having tough waterproof skins to reduce water loss, e.g. lizards.

Soils:

- Poorly developed, with no clear layers.
- Little or no humus due to lack of vegetation and chemical breakdown.
- Soils are often highly saline. Strong evaporation draws moisture to the surface and leaves salt deposits behind (see Figure 7.10B).

Figure 7.10B Cross-section of Death Valley in the Mojave Desert, USA, showing how vegetation responds to changes in access to water

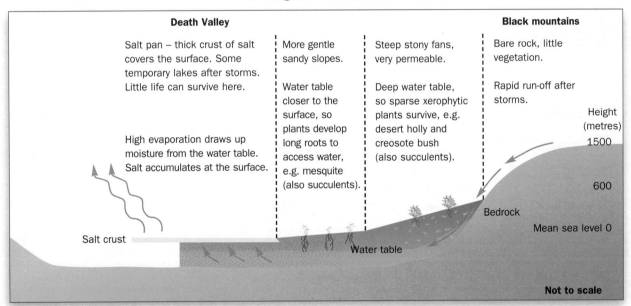

Human use:

- Traditionally supports only low populations of mostly nomadic herdsmen, e.g. Bedouin tribes in the Arabian Desert.
- Increasing populations, larger herds and restricted access to traditional grazing grounds (political pressure) has lead to over grazing, desertification and loss of livelihood. (See chapter 6, p.72 and 73).
- Irrigation farming raises the water table, increases salt content in soils and ruins farmland, e.g. Lower Nile Valley in Egypt.
- Providing water supplies for growing cities surrounding deserts, e.g. Los Angeles, lowers the water table, which reduces river flows and dries out shallow lakes. This threatens wildlife.
- Leisure activities involving 4WD vehicles can severely affect this fragile environment, causing increased erosion particularly in sandy areas.

Find photographs of desert landscapes and make simple labelled drawings describing and explaining the principal features of the vegetation.

Construct a simple food web for a hot desert, see Figure 7.3.

Tropical rainforests

Location (see Figure 7.7)**:**

- Found between 5°N and 5°S of the Equator.
- Areas include Amazon Basin (Brazil), West Africa (southern Nigeria, Congo), S.E. Asia (Indonesia) and N.E. Australia (state of Queensland).

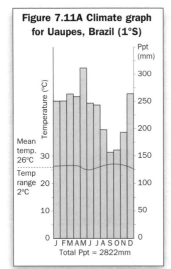

Figure 7.11A Climate graph for Uaupes, Brazil (1°S)

Ppt (mm)
300
250
200
150
100
50
0
Temperature (°C)
Mean temp. 26°C
30
Temp range 2°C
20
10
0
J F M A M J J A S O N D
Total Ppt = 2822mm

Climate (see chapter 6)**:**

- High temperatures all year round (average 26°C). There is a small annual temperature range (2°C) and 12-month continuous growing season.
- Annual rainfall is very high (over 2000mm). It falls throughout the year (some areas slightly away from Equator have a short 'drier' season).
- High humidity and rising air gives daily afternoon convectional storms.

KEY POINT

Tropical rainforests are the biomes that have the most diverse vegetation and animal life. For example, the Amazon rainforest has up to 300 species of tree per square km, mostly hardwoods, e.g. ebony, teak and mahogany.

Vegetation and animals:

- **Deciduous trees**, which grow and shed leaves throughout year, give an evergreen appearance. Flowers, fruits and seeds are available all year from different species of tree. There is a huge continuous supply of leaves to the forest floor.
- Distinct layers of vegetation with the tallest trees up to 50m tall (**emergents**).
- Trees have shallow roots, but develop **buttress roots** above ground to support their great height.
- Leaves are thick and waxy to reduce transpiration if exposed to the sun. They have **'drip tips'** in order to shed the heavy rainfall efficiently.
- **Epiphytes** grow on trunks and branches, but do not feed on the trees' nutrients.
- At ground level the forest is dark as little sunlight can penetrate the dense canopy. Undergrowth is, therefore, limited, but there is dense growth if trees are cut down.
- Huge variety of animals occupy different levels of the forest, (rich, all-year food supply). The rivers contain many species of fish and reptiles.

Figure 7.11B Cross-section through a tropical rainforest

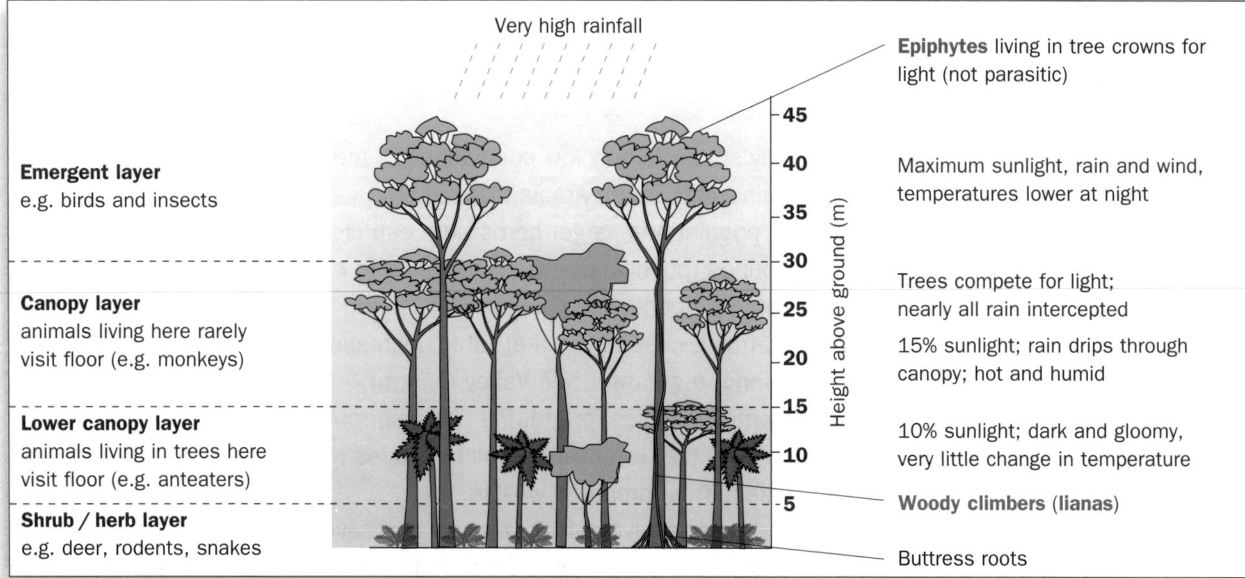

Very high rainfall
Emergent layer
e.g. birds and insects
Canopy layer
animals living here rarely visit floor (e.g. monkeys)
Lower canopy layer
animals living in trees here visit floor (e.g. anteaters)
Shrub / herb layer
e.g. deer, rodents, snakes
45
40
35
30
25
20
15
10
5
Height above ground (m)
Epiphytes living in tree crowns for light (not parasitic)
Maximum sunlight, rain and wind, temperatures lower at night
Trees compete for light; nearly all rain intercepted
15% sunlight; rain drips through canopy; hot and humid
10% sunlight; dark and gloomy, very little change in temperature
Woody climbers (lianas)
Buttress roots

Soils:

- Red clay soils rich in iron and aluminium oxides.
- Large numbers of decomposers.
- High temperatures and humidity cause rapid chemical weathering:
  - There is a rapid breakdown of leaf litter and fast recycling of nutrients through dense root systems. Soils keep few nutrients and are infertile. Nutrients are stored in the biomass.
  - Rapid weathering of parent rock gives very deep soils – up to **20 metres**.
- Soils have a weak structure and erode easily if exposed to heavy rain, e.g. after deforestation.

Figure 7.11C Tropical soil profile

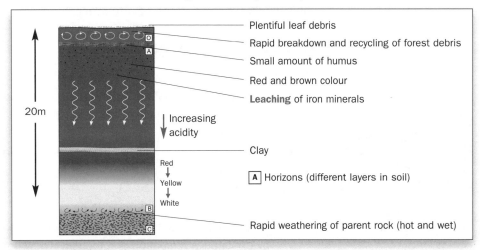

Human activity:

- **Shifting cultivation** (slash and burn). The traditional form of agriculture is followed by local (**indigenous**) farmers (see chapter 13).
- Farming is supplemented by hunting, fishing and gathering (different fruits available all year round).
- Extensive areas of forest are required to support a small number of families.
- In many areas the system is under pressure from...
  - population growth: cleared areas are not given sufficient time to recover before being used again (**fallow period** is reduced) – soil erosion more likely and yields decline
  - large areas of forest are cut down for logging and other new developments, which reduces the forest available for traditional farmers.

Figure 7.12 Flow diagram of shifting cultivation in the rainforest

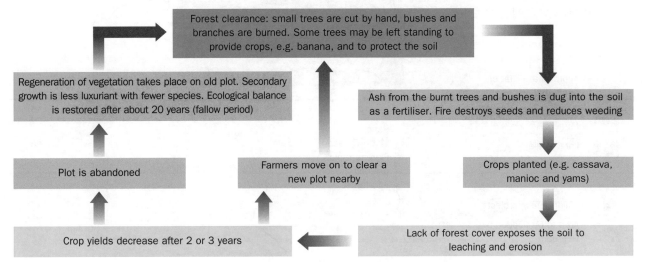

Deforestation of tropical rainforests

AQA A	✓
AQA B	✓
EDEXCEL A	✓
EDEXCEL B	✓
OCR A	✗
OCR B	✓
WJEC A	✓
WJEC B	✓
CCEA	✗

> **KEY POINT**
>
> **Deforestation** is the cutting down and removal of areas of forest, in any part of the world.

50% of tropical rainforest has been destroyed in the last 100 years. The rate of destruction has been increasing rapidly in the last twenty years and some scientists estimate that if the current rate of clearance continues, most forests will have disappeared in the next ten years.

Causes of deforestation

There are many reasons why forests have been felled:

- Extension of commercial agriculture, e.g. forest is cleared for cattle ranches.
- Timber extraction – producing hardwood for MEDCs such as Japan and the UK.
- Mining operations.
- Developing electricity supplies – HEP projects (reliable high rainfall).
- Road building – new roads allow easier access in and out the forest.
- Population growth...
  - within forest communities (shifting cultivators)
  - by government resettlement schemes of urban poor, alongside the new roads
  - by exploitative recreation and tourism – new hotels and leisure complexes.

> Link these causes to examples in the Brazilian rainforest or another rainforest you have studied.
> *N.B. It is important to remember place names.*

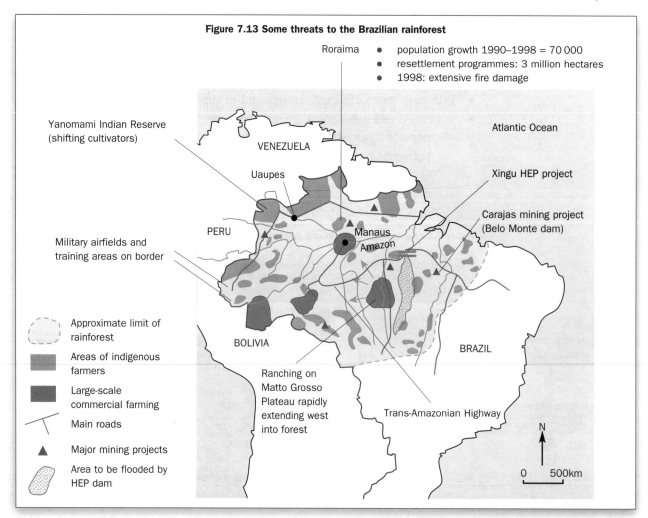

Figure 7.13 Some threats to the Brazilian rainforest

Roraima
- population growth 1990–1998 = 70 000
- resettlement programmes: 3 million hectares
- 1998: extensive fire damage

Yanomami Indian Reserve (shifting cultivators)

Atlantic Ocean

VENEZUELA

Uaupes

Xingu HEP project

PERU

Manaus
Amazon

Carajas mining project (Belo Monte dam)

Military airfields and training areas on border

BOLIVIA

BRAZIL

Ranching on Matto Grosso Plateau rapidly extending west into forest

Trans-Amazonian Highway

N

Approximate limit of rainforest

Areas of indigenous farmers

Large-scale commercial farming

Main roads

▲ Major mining projects

Area to be flooded by HEP dam

0   500km

Benefits from deforestation

Most rainforest is located in LEDCs, e.g. Brazil and Indonesia. Money earned from the export of timber and ores will increase the country's GDP and lead to economic and social development and improve quality of life (schools and hospitals). The LEDCs need the income to pay off loans from MEDCs.

Many jobs are provided by mining, logging and tourism. Resettlement provides a better quality of life for people living in urban 'shanty towns'.

Problems from deforestation

Nutrients are stored in the biomass. Cutting a tree down will leave behind an infertile soil. New farmers will only obtain satisfactory yields for three or four years. After that they will need to cut down more forest or abandon the farm.

The exposed soils are quickly eroded by heavy rainfall. Clay soil is washed into rivers, which causes deposition and flooding. Navigation becomes difficult, fishing is ruined and water supplies polluted.

The rapid run-off of heavy rainfall on exposed areas causes flash floods and bank erosion.

N.B. There is a conflict between the need for LEDCs to develop and improve the quality of life of their people and global environmental considerations.

Indigenous people are losing their livelihoods, homes and culture. They can catch diseases introduced by settlers, raising death rates.

Vaccines for diseases such as malaria have been developed from rainforest plants. Deforestation may prevent the discovery of new plants that might have possible medical value.

Deforestation may also be affecting climate change:
- Trees absorb CO_2 (a greenhouse gas), so if there are fewer trees, the concentrations of CO_2 in the atmosphere will increase. This is a possible cause of global warming.
- Burning trees releases more CO_2 into the atmosphere.

> **KEY POINT**
>
> MEDCs suggest that LEDCs stop deforestation because they say it is increasing global warming. However, MEDCs have a huge need for timber and are the largest importers of this commodity. MEDCs also burn 80% of the world's fossil fuels, which is the principal cause of global warming.

Solutions for the Amazon rainforest

Proposals to protect the rainforests include sustainable conservation schemes such as **agroforestry** and **biosphere reserve**.

Agroforestry is a technique that imitates the protection 'layers' of the natural forest, which protects the soils from erosion (see Figure 7.14).
- It maintains the humus layer in the soil and improves fertility.
- It retains the surrounding forest for hunting and gathering.
- It provides annual crop-for-cash sales and longer term tree resources.
- It supports a large population that can be self-sufficient.
- It discourages non-indigenous 'new settlers'.

Figure 7.14 Agroforestry

How are these plans sustainable? What are the advantages and disadvantages for different groups such as indigenous farmers, loggers and the government?

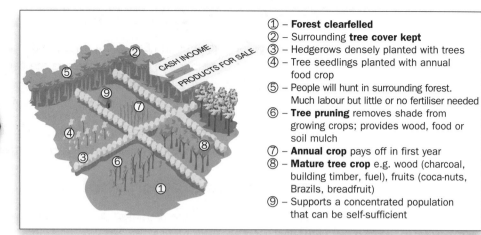

① – **Forest clearfelled**
② – Surrounding **tree cover kept**
③ – Hedgerows densely planted with trees
④ – Tree seedlings planted with annual food crop
⑤ – People will hunt in surrounding forest. Much labour but little or no fertiliser needed
⑥ – **Tree pruning** removes shade from growing crops; provides wood, food or soil mulch
⑦ – **Annual crop** pays off in first year
⑧ – **Mature tree crop** e.g. wood (charcoal, building timber, fuel), fruits (coca-nuts, Brazils, breadfruit)
⑨ – Supports a concentrated population that can be self-sufficient

A biosphere reserve establishes three 'zones', which have designated non-intrusive uses.

- It retains a large area of 'natural' forest for research.
- It maintains a secure zone for indigenous shifting cultivators.
- It provides an income from harvesting tree crops.
- It creates minimum disturbance of the forest.

Figure 7.15 Biosphere reserve

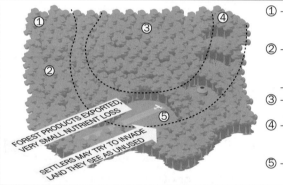

① – **Extraction Reserve Zone** owned by collectors of products from wild trees, e.g. rubber, brazil nuts
② – Forest canopy preserved. Only selected products harvested in small amounts
  – Few people employed
③ – **Core Zone** Large area used only for research and genetic materials
④ – **Buffer Zone** More activities allowed at low population density (shifting cultivators)
⑤ – **Eco-tourism** in accessible areas (see chapter 16)

Environmental groups such as the **WWF (World Wide Fund)** and **Friends of the Earth** campaign to make the public aware and to persuade industry and governments to respond to the issues.

The **Forest Stewardship Council** links timber producers to customers and gives assurances that timber and timber products are only from areas of sustainable logging. MEDCs contribute to share the 'cost' of conserving the rainforest, and ensure that the living standards of all people in LEDCs improve. Strategies such as 'reduce, recycle, reuse' reduce the demand for timber resources.

Marine biomes – coral reefs

AQA A	X
AQA B	X
EDEXCEL A	X
EDEXCEL B	✓
OCR A	X
OCR B	X
WJEC A	X
WJEC B	X
CCEA	X

A **marine biome** describes a large scale ecosystem in which the habitat and the living community of animals and plants are broadly the same.

> **KEY POINT**
>
> **Corals** come from the same family as jelly fish, but they secrete hard skeletons of limestone that surround and protect their soft bodies. **Reefs** are formed by large colonies of corals that slowly build hard structures upwards on the remains of previous colonies. This forms a habitat for themselves and for a huge variety of other animals and plants.

Reefs are found around the UK, e.g. Lyme Bay in Dorset (see chapter 3).

Location

Corals are found in many marine environments, but **colonial corals**, which are responsible for reefs, are found only in tropical waters between 30°N and 30°S along Pacific, Atlantic and Indian coastlines.

To grow, corals require warm water and sunlight, but only a low nutrient supply. Most coral reefs are found in clear shallow water (up to about 30m deep).

Reefs are rich in coral species (400 on a single reef is not uncommon), which have a huge variety of growth forms reflected closely in their common names, e.g. staghorn coral, plate coral and brain coral.

This is known as a symbiotic relationship, meaning they depend on each other.

Microscopic plants (algae) live in the coral's skin and produce sugars by photosynthesis (so they need sunlight). The sugars form the principal food supply for the coral whilst the algae benefits from a protected home.

Types of Reef

There are three main types of reef:
- **Fringing reefs** grow in shallow waters separated from the coast by a narrow channel, e.g. the Tanzanian coastline in E. Africa and the Coral Triangle off the coasts of Malaysia and Papua New Guinea.
- **Barrier reefs** are larger and more continuous. They grow parallel to the coast, but are further seaward on the continental shelf, e.g. the Great Barrier Reef in Queensland, Australia, is the largest in the world at 2000km long.
- **Coral atolls**, often low circular reefs enclosing a lagoon, are formed around a volcanic island that has subsided. They are common in the S. Pacific, e.g. the Hawaiian group.

Use an atlas to locate these examples.

Importance of coral reefs

Coral reefs are considered by scientists to be possibly the most diverse, productive communities on earth. They are the marine equivalent to the tropical rainforest and are in need of priority protection and conservation.

Reefs provide protection from coastal erosion by absorbing much of the energy of storm surges created by cyclones or tsunamis, e.g. on the low lying islands in the Caribbean.

Being so productive, reefs are rich fishing grounds, for example, the resources of the Coral Triangle are estimated to support the livelihoods of over 100 million people. They are also attractive tourist venues for snorkelling and scuba diving in warm, clear waters. Servicing tourism is an important economic activity, e.g. at Cairns and Port Douglas for the Great Barrier Reef.

The complex diversity and productivity of reefs offer opportunities to source products for new medicines and drugs (similar to the tropical rainforest).

Threats to coral reefs

Reefs are fragile features and even a slight change to their environment, such as muddy water, can be threatening.

Natural threats include:
- Predators, e.g. 'crown-of-thorns' starfish in the Pacific atolls.
- Hazards – storm waves can break up the upper active parts of a reef.
- Diseases, e.g. 'white band' is a growth that smothers the coral and threatens the sustainability of the reef.

Threats from **human activity** include:

- Overfishing – this destroys the delicate balance and allows the spread of algae (food for many fish).
- Decreased catches encourage fishermen to catch juvenile fish or use destructive methods such as explosives. These methods destroy the reef, e.g. the Coral Triangle.
- Higher sewage outflow, due to rising coastal populations, increases nutrient levels in the sea, e.g. Hawaiian islands.
- Poor farming practices in parts of Queensland are said to be increasing the amount of sediment in rivers reaching the sea close to the Great Barrier Reef.
- Increased tourism can cause accidental damage.
- Climate change – oceans naturally absorb CO_2 from the atmosphere, so increasing CO_2 emissions means oceans absorb more acidity. This raises their average pH and reduces the ability of corals to produce limestone (see chapter 1).

Sustainable coral reef management

There is worldwide recognition of the importance of coral reefs, the threats that currently exist and the need to establish sustainable management plans for their survival.

Initiatives to protect coral reefs include:

- Great Barrier Reef Protection Plan (GBRPP).
- Coral Reef Targeted Research (CRTR (Tanzanian coast)).
- Coral Triangle Initiative (2007) (CTI).

Initiatives often include:

- Substantial investment from the Global Environment Fund (and the World Bank).
- Declaration of Marine Park status (with associated protection laws and zoning).
- Support from global wildlife charities, e.g. World Wildlife Fund (WWF).
- Support from centres of marine science research (local and international).
- Provision of awareness and educational programmes with local populations.
- Sustainable programmes to support local economies.

These are called mutilateral initiatives.

Research one of these initiatives and develop a case study of sustainable management.

PROGRESS CHECK

1. Between which latitudes are tropical rainforests found?
2. In which biome are xerophytic plants important?
3. Name the soil type commonly found in temperate deciduous woodland.
4. Which biome has a low rainfall and only brief summers?
5. Give two reasons why coral reefs need to be conserved.

1. 5°N and 5°S of the Equator
2. Hot desert
3. Brown earths
4. Tundra
5. **Select two from the following and develop both with reference to examples:** rich biodiversity; coastal protection; employment (fishing / tourism)

8 Tectonic Activity

The following topics are covered in this chapter:

- The Earth's structure
- Volcanoes and earthquakes

8.1 The Earth's structure

LEARNING SUMMARY

After studying this section you should be able to understand:

- that the earth is made up of a core, mantle and crust
- that the crust of the Earth is divided into two different types of plates: continental and oceanic
- that most tectonic activity is associated with the plate boundaries or margins
- that plate margins can be divided into three main types depending on how the plates are moving in relation to each other
- that each type of plate margin is linked to different combinations of tectonic activity
- the formation of fold mountains and their associated human activity.

Plate tectonics

AQA A	✓
AQA B	✓
EDEXCEL A	✓
EDEXCEL B	✓
OCR A	✓
OCR B	✓
WJEC A	✓
WJEC B	✗
CCEA	✓

To understand the **location**, **distribution** and **causes** of volcanoes and earthquakes, it is necessary to study **plate tectonics**.

> **KEY POINT**
>
> **Plate tectonics** is the theory that explains the movement, formation and destruction of the plates that make up the Earth's crust.

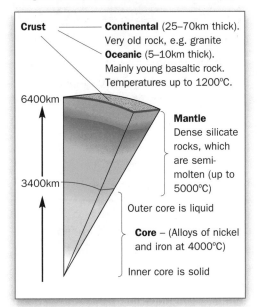

Figure 8.1 The internal structure of the Earth

Crust — **Continental** (25–70km thick). Very old rock, e.g. granite
Oceanic (5–10km thick). Mainly young basaltic rock. Temperatures up to 1200°C.

6400km

Mantle Dense silicate rocks, which are semi-molten (up to 5000°C)

3400km

Outer core is liquid

Core – (Alloys of nickel and iron at 4000°C)

Inner core is solid

The crust

The **crust** forms the **outer surface** of the Earth. The crust...

- is cool enough to behave as a more or less rigid shell
- is up to 90km thick (compared with a total radius of the Earth of 6400km)
- floats on hotter, semi-molten rock (called the **mantle**).

The crust is sub-divided into **plates**. There are...

- seven large plates, e.g. Pacific plate and Eurasian plate
- twelve smaller plates, e.g. Philippine plate and Juan de Fuca plate (see Figure 8.2).

Plates

There are two types of plate:

- **Oceanic plates**
- **Continental plates**

200 million years ago all the land masses of the Earth formed one continent known as Pangaea. Note how South America closely fits the shape of the west coast of Africa.

Oceanic plates are composed of basaltic rock and are 5–10km thick. They are denser and younger than continental plates and are often destroyed beneath the continental plates.

Continental plates are mainly composed of granite and are 25–90km thick. They are less dense than oceanic plates so can 'float' on top of the oceanic plates.

Figure 8.2 Principal crustal plates and plate margins

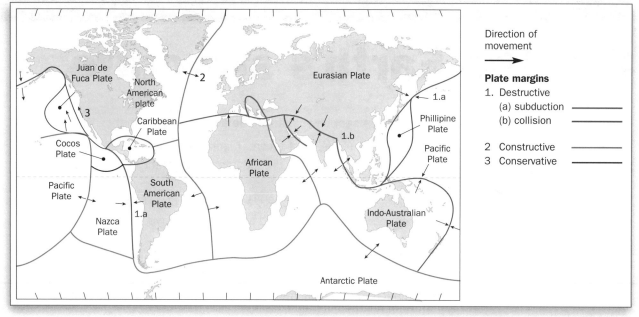

Figure 8.3 How crustal plates move

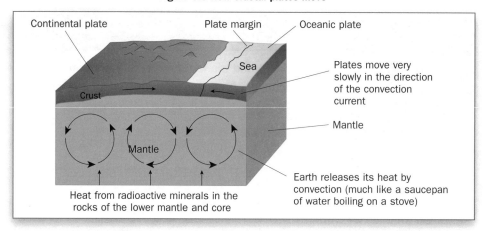

Plate Margins

The place where two plates meet is called a **plate margin**. The plates are slowly moved by convection currents in the mantle (see Figure 8.3). Plates move in different directions and at different speeds, which causes stress and friction along the plate margins.

It is important to understand the difference between these margins. You need to know examples of where they occur, and relate them to your case studies of volcanoes and earthquakes.

Stress and friction are mostly responsible for...
- earthquakes and volcanic activity
- the creation of **fold mountains**, e.g. the Himalayas and the Alps.

Plate margins can be divided into three types:
- **Destructive** margins (or compressional or convergent margins). These can be split into subduction zones and collision zones (see Figures 8.4 and 8.5).
- **Constructive** margins (or extensional or divergent margins) (see Figure 8.6).
- **Conservative** margins (or tensional or transform margins) (see Figure 8.7).

Figure 8.4 Destructive margin – subduction zone

A subduction zone is the location of many violent and destructive earthquakes (e.g. Kobe in Japan, 1995) and volcanoes (e.g. Mt St Helens in the USA, 1980)

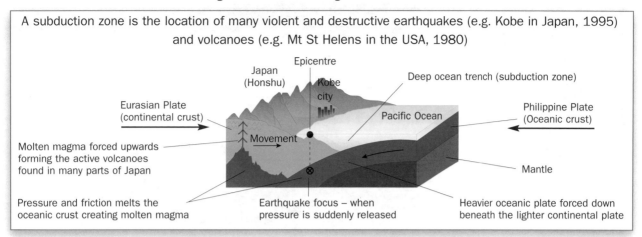

- Epicentre
- Japan (Honshu)
- Kobe city
- Deep ocean trench (subduction zone)
- Eurasian Plate (continental crust)
- Pacific Ocean
- Philippine Plate (Oceanic crust)
- Movement
- Molten magma forced upwards forming the active volcanoes found in many parts of Japan
- Mantle
- Pressure and friction melts the oceanic crust creating molten magma
- Earthquake focus – when pressure is suddenly released
- Heavier oceanic plate forced down beneath the lighter continental plate

Figure 8.5 Destructive margin – collision zone (Himalayas and Alps)

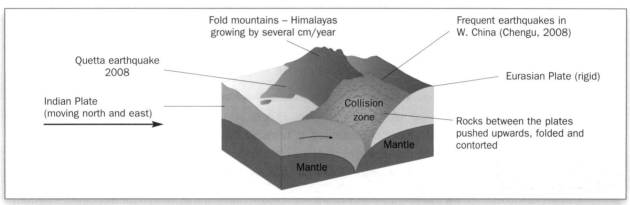

- Fold mountains – Himalayas growing by several cm/year
- Frequent earthquakes in W. China (Chengu, 2008)
- Quetta earthquake 2008
- Eurasian Plate (rigid)
- Indian Plate (moving north and east)
- Collision zone
- Rocks between the plates pushed upwards, folded and contorted
- Mantle
- Mantle

Figure 8.6 Constructive plate margin (Mid-Atlantic Ridge)

The Mid-Atlantic ridge is a zone of gentle volcanoes and earthquakes, mostly on the ocean floor.

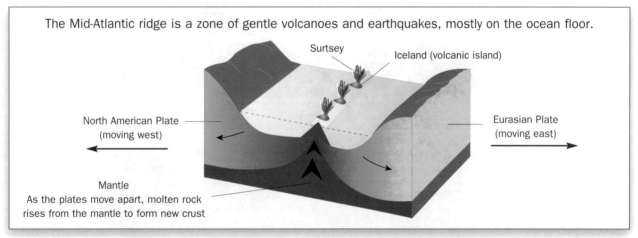

- Surtsey
- Iceland (volcanic island)
- North American Plate (moving west)
- Eurasian Plate (moving east)
- Mantle
- As the plates move apart, molten rock rises from the mantle to form new crust

Figure 8.7 Conservative plate margin (San Andreas fault, California)

Use labelled diagrams like these in your revision and do not be afraid of using them in an exam. They are quick to draw, and show your knowledge and understanding clearly.

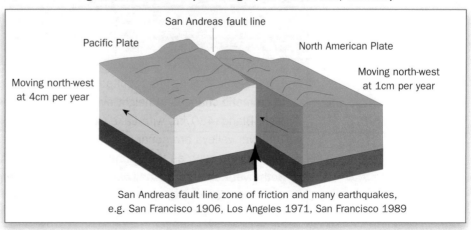

- San Andreas fault line
- Pacific Plate
- North American Plate
- Moving north-west at 4cm per year
- Moving north-west at 1cm per year
- San Andreas fault line zone of friction and many earthquakes, e.g. San Francisco 1906, Los Angeles 1971, San Francisco 1989

Formation of fold mountains

AQA A	✓
AQA B	✗
EDEXCEL A	✓
EDEXCEL B	✗
OCR A	✓
OCR B	✗
WJEC A	✗
WJEC B	✗
CCEA	✗

Case study – The Alps

Figure 8.8 Diagrammatic sketch showing formation of the Alps

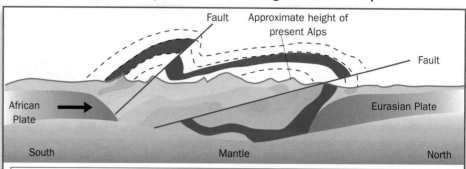

> How are rocks containing marine fossils found high up in the mountains?

> To help your understanding, try adding labels to Figure 8.8 using these bullet points.

- The African plate moved towards the **rigid** European plate (destructive margin – collision zone, see Figure 8.5)
- Between the two plates were thick beds of weak sedimentary rocks that had been laid down in a deepening sea.

- As the plates converged, the sedimentary rocks were squeezed upwards into huge folds (in the Neogene Period, 20 million years ago, see Figure 1.3).
- More compression led to complex folding and faulting.
- The movements created great pressure and heat, which changed some of the sedimentary rocks into much harder metamorphic slates and marbles.

- Weathering and erosion by rivers and ice has produced the landscape of high mountain ranges and deep river valleys that we see today.

Figure 8.9 Alpine ranges and rivers

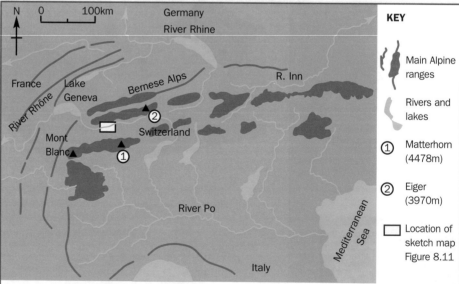

- The tectonic activity has resulted in a complex geology, which can give rise to dramatic changes in height over short distances. Compare the height of Mont Blanc (4807m) with Lake Geneva (321m), only 70km apart.
- The river valleys are separated by high mountain ranges, e.g. Bernese Alps.
- Major rivers such as the Rhône and Rhine have their sources in the Alps. Both rivers emerge as meltwater from beneath large glaciers.
- Both rivers follow deep steep-sided, flat-floored 'glacial troughs' (see chapter 4).

Human activity in an Alpine region

Case study – The Swiss Alps in the Upper Rhône Valley

Figure 8.10 Sketch cross-section of Upper Rhône Valley near Sion

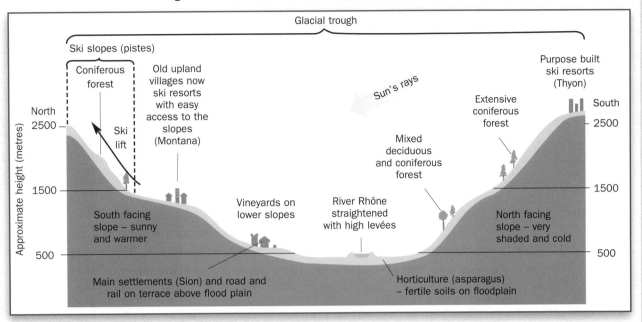

Glacial trough

Ski slopes (pistes)

Coniferous forest

Old upland villages now ski resorts with easy access to the slopes (Montana)

North
2500

Ski lift

Approximate height (metres)

1500

South facing slope – sunny and warmer

500

Main settlements (Sion) and road and rail on terrace above flood plain

Vineyards on lower slopes

River Rhône straightened with high levées

Sun's rays

Mixed deciduous and coniferous forest

Horticulture (asparagus) – fertile soils on floodplain

Extensive coniferous forest

Purpose built ski resorts (Thyon)

South
2500

1500

North facing slope – very shaded and cold

500

Physical features:

Check out these landforms in chapter 4.

- High snow-capped mountain ranges (Figure 8.9 Bernese Alps, Mont Blanc Massif).
- Deep glacial troughs (Rhône valley) with hanging valleys (waterfalls and alluvial fans) and truncated spurs.
- Cirques and arêtes (Wildhorn–Arpelistock Ridge, Figure 8.11).
- Many rapidly flowing rivers, with steep rocky courses.
- Large rivers flow across floodplains in the wide flat-floored glacial troughs (Rhone).
- Deep Alpine valleys have contrasting local micro-climates on the north and south facing slopes, which can affect human activities (Figure 8.10).

Figure 8.11 Sketch map of Upper Rhône Valley

Give named places to support your answers.

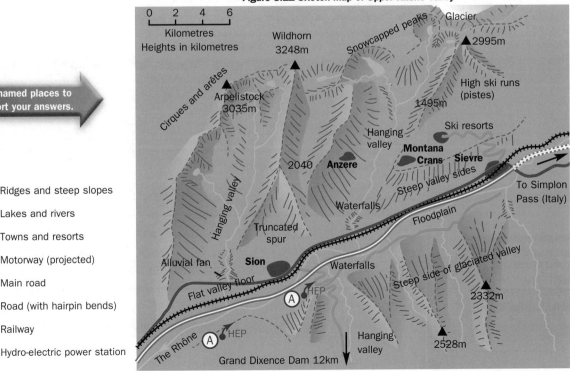

0   2   4   6
Kilometres
Heights in kilometres

Wildhorn 3248m

Snowcapped peaks

Glacier

▲2995m

Cirques and arêtes

Arpelistock 3035m

1495m

High ski runs (pistes)

Ski resorts

Hanging valley

Montana Crans **Sievre**

2040 **Anzere**

Steep valley sides

To Simplon Pass (Italy)

Hanging valley

Waterfalls

Floodplain

Truncated spur

Alluvial fan

Sion

Flat valley floor

Waterfalls

Steep side of glaciated valley

2332m

(A) HEP

The Rhône (A) HEP

Grand Dixence Dam 12km

Hanging valley

2528m

Ridges and steep slopes

Lakes and rivers

Towns and resorts

Motorway (projected)

Main road

Road (with hairpin bends)

Railway

Hydro-electric power station

Case study – The Swiss Alps in the Upper Rhône Valley (cont.)

Human activities
- Winter sports, e.g. skiing.
- Summer tourism (touring and walking based in towns such as Sion).
- Agriculture and forestry (horticulture and vineyards).
- Communication routes – main roads and railways follow main valleys – tunnels and high passes, e.g. the Simplon Pass and Gotthard tunnel provide important links with Italy.
- Rivers such as the Rhône have been straightened and embanked to prevent flash floods.
- Dams and hydro-electric power stations provide electricity.

Hydro-electric power (HEP) accounts for 60% of Switzerland's electricity production. One third of this power is generated at the power stations marked A and A on Figure 8.11. These power stations produce nearly 2000MW (cf. Heysham 2 (UK) 1250MW). The turbines are driven by water falling through pipes from a reservoir in a mountain valley 1500m above. The deep, narrow hanging valleys provide good dam sites, e.g. The Grand Dixence Dam (see Figure 8.11).

Electricity is used in Switzerland to power the railways and urban public transport as well as serving industrial and domestic demands.

Hazards in Alpine areas:
- Flash flooding from heavy rain or rapid snow melt.
- Convectional storms with thunder and lightning.
- Avalanches, mudslides and rock falls.

Avalanches

Avalanches occur in all mountainous areas of the world. They have become a more recognised hazard due to the growth of winter sports in countries such as Austria, Switzerland, Italy and western USA.

Over 100 people die from avalanches each year and many more become trapped and need to be rescued.

Avalanches are hazardous because they...
- are very unpredictable
- often involve large masses of snow or slabs of ice, which are capable of destroying and burying villages
- descend very rapidly, reaching speeds up to 100km per hour.

Avalanches often occur...
- where large amounts of snow and ice have accumulated on upper slopes
- on steep upper slopes (30° angle) with steeper valley slopes below (insufficient snow accumulates on very steep slopes)
- when the weight of the snow is sufficient to overcome friction and descend due to the force of gravity
- if triggered by rapid changes in temperature, vibrations or loud noise (often echoed)
- where slopes have been deforested.

Avalanches are most common in late winter / spring. Research current case studies using the Internet.

The **hazard threat** can be reduced in several ways:

- Satellites, webcams and remote sensors can be used to predict avalanches and slopes can be evacuated if there is a threat.
- Controlled avalanches can be started using explosives and other means.
- Snow fences and avalanche sheds over roads and railways can be built on known avalanche paths.
- Planting trees in high risk areas (afforestation).
- Using effective warning systems and issuing advice to those venturing off-piste or into wilderness areas.

PROGRESS CHECK

1. What are the two types of plate that form the Earth's crust?
2. What type of plate margin is found close to Japan, at the boundary of the Eurasian and Pacific Plates?
3. What type of plate margin is found along the Mid-Atlantic Ridge?
4. Describe two ways in which tourism has affected the Upper Rhône valley.
5. Give two reasons why avalanches are so dangerous.

1. Oceanic and continental
2. Destructive / subduction zone
3. Constructive
4. **Accept two from:** Winter sports; Summer walkers and campers; Coach tours; Employment; Traffic congestion (linked to landscape, places, routeways)
5. **Accept two from:** Unpredictable; Large mass movements; Rapid descent (link to dangers to skiers, valley settlements, difficult to predict and control)

8.2 Volcanoes and earthquakes

LEARNING SUMMARY

After studying this section you should be able to understand:

- that tectonic activity often results in earthquakes and volcanoes
- the main characteristics of earthquakes and volcanoes
- the hazards and benefits of volcanic activity
- the impact of earthquakes and volcanic activity in an LEDC and an MEDC
- the management issues (such as prediction and preparedness) associated with reducing the impact of earthquake and volcanic activity

Where are earthquakes and volcanoes located?

AQA A	✓
AQA B	✓
EDEXCEL A	✓
EDEXCEL B	✓
OCR A	✓
OCR B	✓
WJEC A	✓
WJEC B	✗
CCEA	✓

There is a clear pattern for the distribution of both **earthquakes** and **volcanoes**. The patterns are closely linked to the distribution of plate margins (see Figure 8.2).

Global distribution of volcanoes

Volcanoes occur...
- in narrow bands; a pattern similar but not identical to the distribution of earthquakes, e.g. volcanoes are not found along collision margins (Himalayas)
- most often at destructive plate margins, e.g. around the Pacific Ocean – the 'Ring of Fire'
- along constructive plate margins, e.g. the Mid-Atlantic Ridge
- at 'hot spots' in the centre of plates where the crust is thin, e.g. Mauna Loa in Hawaii.

Figure 8.12 Global distribution of volcanoes

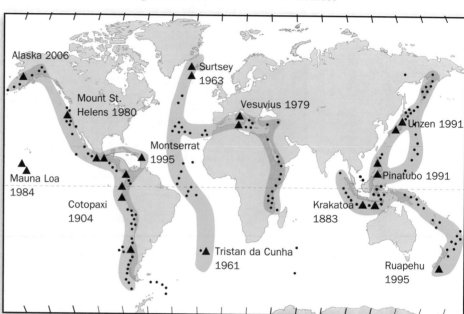

Questions often ask you to describe 'patterns' that are shown on a map. Figures 8.12 and 8.13, are good for practising your technique.

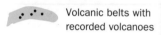 Volcanic belts with recorded volcanoes

▲ Major volcanoes

Global distribution of earthquakes

Earthquakes occur...
- in long narrow bands
- along all types of plate margin
- close to volcanoes
- on land or under water
- in a dense ring around the Pacific Ocean.

Figure 8.13 Global distribution of earthquakes

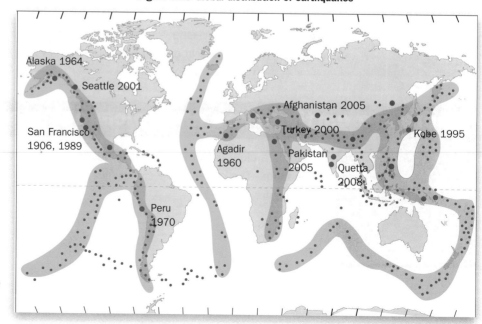

 Earthquake belts and recorded earthquakes

● Some recent major earthquakes

Volcanoes

AQA A	✓
AQA B	✓
EDEXCEL A	✓
EDEXCEL B	✓
OCR A	✓
OCR B	✓
WJEC A	✓
WJEC B	✗
CCEA	✓

KEY POINT

Volcanoes occur where weaknesses in the Earth's crust allow magma, ash, gas and water to erupt onto the land and seabed.

Figure 8.14 Characteristics of a composite volcano (e.g. Soufriere Hills volcano, Montserrat in the Caribbean)

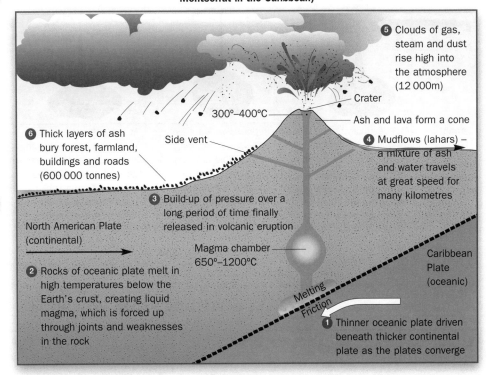

Be prepared to use a labelled diagram similar to this in an exam to explain the processes involved in a volcanic eruption.

Types of volcano

Volcanoes can be classified by how active they are:

- **Active** volcanoes are ones that have erupted recently, e.g. Soufriere Hills in Montserrat; Mt St Helens in N.W. USA and the Augustine volcano in Alaska (2006).
- **Dormant** volcanoes are ones that have not erupted for a long time, e.g. Mt Rainier, N.W. USA. The Soufriere Hills volcano in Montserrat had been dormant for 400 years before its violent eruption in 1996.
- **Extinct** volcanoes are ones that are no longer areas of tectonic activity, i.e. there has been no record of volcanic activity since records began, e.g. Castle Rock in Edinburgh.

Dormant volcanoes always pose a risk for the people living nearby.

KEY POINT

Supervolcanoes are catastrophic, violent eruptions at a global scale. They result from massive upwellings of magma into the crust, which causes high temperatures and pressure close to the Earth's surface.

Supervolcanoes are dormant for long periods, e.g. the last one erupted 75 000 years ago in Indonesia. It was many thousand times greater than the eruption of Mt St Helens in 1980. Ash blacked out the sunlight and global temperatures plummeted. The Yellowstone National Park (Rocky Mountains, USA) that is famous for its geysers and hot springs, is possibly the largest known supervolcano. Another eruption (the last was 640 000 years ago) would devastate North America and cause a global catastrophe.

Figure 8.15 The classification of volcanoes by how they erupt

Margin type	Destructive (subduction)	Hot spot	Constructive	Destructive (subduction)
Volcano type	Composite (ash and lava)	Shield	Usually shield	Composite (ash and lava)
Eruption	Explosive	Gentle oozing	Usually gentle	Explosive
Products	Nuées, ash, lava	Lava	Lava, ash	Nuées, ash, lava
Margin/plate	Caribbean / South American	Pacific	North American / Eurasian	Juan de Fuca / North American
Volcano	Soufriere, Montserrat	Mauna Loa, Hawaii	Surtsey, Iceland	Mount St Helens, USA

| Formation | At a destructive margin, one plate dives beneath the other. Friction causes it to melt and become molten magma. The magma forces its way up to the side of the actual plate margin (the ocean trench). A number of volcanoes may reach the surface to form a string of islands called an island arc, e.g. Japan. | In places where a plate is particularly thin, magma may be able to escape to the surface. Such a place is called a 'hot spot'. A shield volcano, like those on Hawaii, will be formed. | At a constructive margin where two plates are moving apart, new magma can reach the surface through the gap. Volcanoes forming along this crack create a submarine mountain range called an ocean ridge, e.g. the Mid-Atlantic Ridge. | Sometimes destructive margins involve continents. Instead of forming islands, volcanoes occur within a range of mountains, e.g. the Rocky Mountains and the Andes. |

Hazards resulting from volcanoes

Hazard	Description	Examples
Lava flows	Molten rock (magma) flowing down the volcano sides. Very hot basaltic lava flows very fast.	Frequent rapid lava flows on Mt Etna, Sicily, threaten local settlements.
Lahars	Mudflows, a mixture of ash and water, travel at great speed down the mountain sides.	Ruiz volcano, Columbia, erupted in 1985. The eruption melted snow around the summit and a mixture of water, ash and rock turned to mud and buried the town of Armero. 22 000 people drowned in the mud.
Dust and ash clouds	Ash thrown high into the atmosphere shuts out the sun and causes gloomy days. On settling, ash can completely bury buildings and crops.	When the Soufriere Hills volcano in Montserrat erupted in 1996, ash clouds deposited 600 000 tonnes of ash burying the landscape and farms (see Figure 8.17).
Nuée ardente (glowing cloud)	Flows of superheated ash and gases, flowing at very fast speeds.	In 1980, nuée ardente from the eruption of Mt St Helens in north-west USA destroyed every tree over a very large area (see Figure 8.18).

Benefits from volcanoes

These benefits help to explain why large numbers of people live in the danger areas surrounding volcanoes.

Volcanic ash will weather to produce very fertile soils that are excellent for intensive farming, e.g. the lower slopes of Mt Etna in Sicily. Volcanoes produce geothermal energy. Iceland uses energy from volcanic water and steam to supply heat and electricity. Volcanic rock also makes good building stone.

Check out the Iceland Tourist Board for the attractions they offer.

Volcanoes attract adventurous tourists to visit sites in Iceland, New Zealand and southern Italy (Vesuvius and Stromboli), providing employment.

Predicting volcanoes

Careful monitoring has allowed scientists to become more successful at predicting volcanic eruptions. Early evacuation can be advised and lives saved. The main monitoring methods include the following:

- Checking earthquake activity – the activity will increase prior to eruption due to the magma rise in the crust.
- Measuring gas emissions – these will change with increasing sulphur.
- Using lasers and tiltmeters to measure changes in the shape of the volcano. Bulges and domes suggest a build-up of magma.
- Measuring ground temperature changes using satellites.
- Using ultrasound to detect movements of magma.
- Studying past activity of a volcano as it may provide evidence.

Responding to a volcanic hazard

Although little can be done to control volcanoes, some measures can be taken to respond to the threats:

- Diverting lava flow from vulnerable areas.
- Halting lava flow using water sprays.
- Designing buildings that shed ash.
- Preparing communities for a disaster by...
  - preventing settlements in vulnerable areas
  - organising and practising evacuation procedures
  - improving public awareness.

LEDC case study: Montserrat, Caribbean, (British Territory) 1995–97 (see Figure 8.12)

Figure 8.17 Montserrat eruptions 1995–1997

------ Roads
• Settlements
Flows of mud, ash and lava (lahars):
May–July 1996 ⟶
June 1997 ⟶
Aug–Sept 1997 ⟶

Montserrat factfile:

- Population: 11 000 (1995).
- An island in the island arc on the destructive plate margin between the North American and Caribbean plates (see Figure 8.12).

Effects of the eruption:

- Forests and rich farmland were destroyed by lahars and covered with deep layers of ash.
- Many villages were buried in ash; 23 people killed.
- Many people were evacuated to the north of the island, to neighbouring islands and to the UK.
- The capital city, Plymouth (port, industrial and administrative centre) was almost totally destroyed and abandoned.
- The island's only hospital was destroyed.
- Many roads destroyed; the only airport was engulfed in ash.
- Dust covered the whole island, making it difficult to breathe.

Short-term responses:

- The authorities and people were totally unprepared because the volcano had been dormant for 400 years.
- People were evacuated to the north of the island. They were housed in tents and makeshift homes with little food, poor sanitation and no power.
- The UK government gave £55 million in compensation and redevelopment (e.g. they funded the building of 250 prefabricated houses).

LEDC case study: Montserrat (cont.)

> The effects of volcanoes and earthquakes are more severe and long-lasting in LEDCs than in MEDCs. Be prepared to explain why.

- The hospital re-opened in a former school.
- Communications were difficult and expensive to repair.
- Many people were unemployed because the tourist industry collapsed.
- Little farmland was available to reclaim in the south because of the thick cover of ash.
- The capital city, Plymouth, was abandoned.

Long-term responses:

- The volcano is still active with a new lava dome still growing. A volcanic observatory has been established to monitor activity and advise residents and tourists of the dangers.
- An exclusion zone exists over much of the southern part of the island and for 2km offshore.
- The population is about 5000, less that half of what it was in 1995. Everyone lives in the north of the island (where very few people lived before the eruption).
- There is no capital city. The ash-covered remains of Plymouth remain in the exclusion zone.
- Services have been expanded in the north – there are reliable electricity and water supplies and education is available for all children over 5 years old.
- New roads have been built in the south and are being extended.
- Agriculture and fishing once employed nearly 500 people, now it is only 200. The government is concentrating on poultry production and other ways to reduce the island's dependency on imports.
- Construction of an industrial park is in progress.
- Tourism is seen as the major enterprise in the future; outside investment is encouraged but growth is slow. The tourist department advertises 'volcano experiences', 'diving and snorkelling', and 'weddings and honeymoons' as attractions. International access is only via a one-hour ferry trip from Antigua.

MEDC case study: Mt St Helens, N.W. USA, 1980 (see Figure 8.12)

> Volcanic activity still continues and is carefully monitored at both case study locations. Research the latest information.

Figure 8.18 Effect of Mt St Helens' eruption

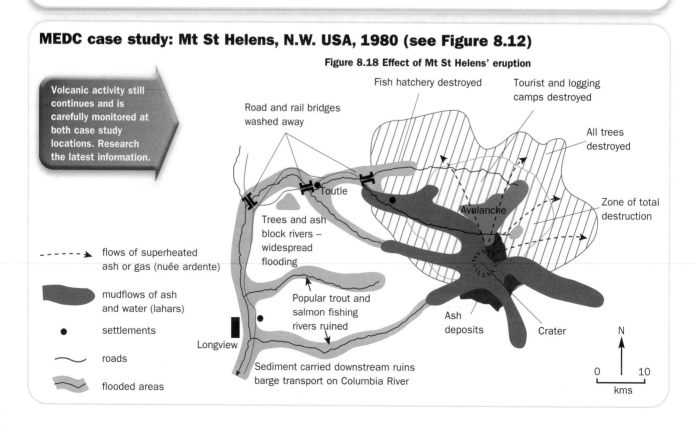

Mt St Helens factfile:

- Mt St Helens lies on the destructive margin where the Juan de Fuca Plate (oceanic) is disappearing below the North American Plate (see Figure 8.12).

Effects of the eruption:

- Early warnings were given as volcanologists monitored the volcano, so most people were evacuated to safety.
- Extensive forests and logging camps destroyed by nuée ardente (see Figure 8.18)
- Ash and flooding destroyed crops and livestock.
- Lava flows and ash clogged prime salmon and trout rivers.
- 63 people were killed, most from poisonous gases.
- Flooding washed away road and railway bridges.

Response to the eruption:

- Ten million trees were replanted.
- Agriculture benefited from fertile ash.
- Rivers were dredged and restocked with fish.
- People were re-housed.
- Bridges were rapidly rebuilt.
- Tourism has increased, attracted by the event. A new tourist centre has been built, attracting 1 million visitors a year. New tourist lodges have also been built.
- The volcano is still active and carefully monitored by volcanologists.

Earthquakes

AQA A	✓
AQA B	✓
EDEXCEL A	✓
EDEXCEL B	✓
OCR A	✓
OCR B	✓
WJEC A	✓
WJEC B	✗
CCEA	✓

KEY POINT

An **earthquake** is the vibration of the Earth's crust, caused by shock waves travelling outwards from a sudden movement deep within the crust.

The source of the shock waves is known as the **focus**, and the point on the Earth's surface immediately above is the **epicentre**. Most earthquakes are associated with movements along plate margins, but some occur at other weaknesses in the crust, such as fault lines.

Figure 8.19 Characteristics of an earthquake

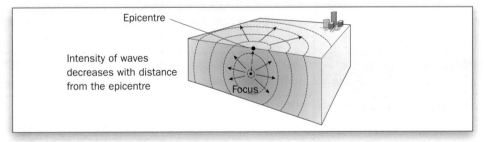

Measuring earthquakes

The shock waves of an earthquake are recorded and measured on a **seismograph**. The seismograph measures the strength or **magnitude** on the **Richter Scale**. The **modified Mercalli Scale** measures the **intensity** of an earthquake. It quantifies the effects as witnessed by people.

Figure 8.20 Measuring earthquakes by the Richter and Mercalli Scales

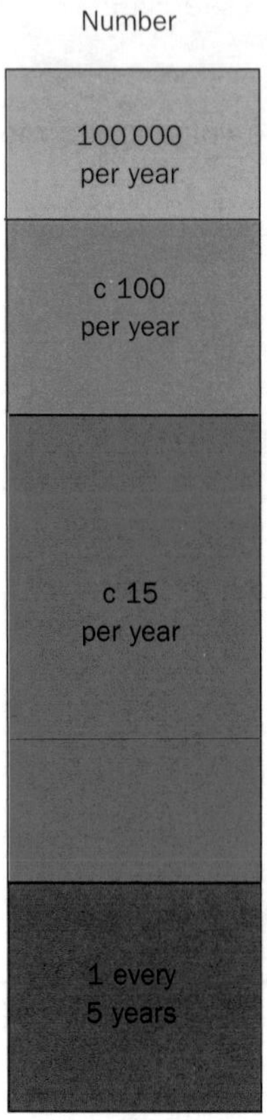

Number	Examples	Scale Richter Mercalli		Observable effects
100 000 per year		1		None, only detected by instruments
			I	
		2		
c 100 per year			II	Felt by a few people, especially on upper floors
		3		
		4	IV	Faint tremor, like the vibrations of a lorry
		5		
c 15 per year	Market Rasen, 2008 5.2 North Wales, 1984 5.4 (largest UK quake)		VI	Difficult to stand. Structural damage to chimney pots. Trees shake
		6	VII	Distinct shaking, poorly built houses collapse
	Kobe, 1995 7.2 W. China, 2008 7.8	7	IX	Major earthquake, large buildings destroyed, ground badly cracked, landslides
		8	XI	
1 every 5 years	Banda Aceh 9.0+ (Sumatra), 2004	9	XII	Total damage, few buildings / bridges left standing. Waves seen on ground, wide cracks appear

The impact of an earthquake

Primary impacts include deaths, collapse of buildings and damage to roads, water and gas mains. **Secondary impacts** include fire and flooding, people made homeless, injuries, disease and loss of business.

> 'The greater the strength of an earthquake, the higher the death toll'. Is this statement correct? Look at Figure 8.21.

> Add other examples of more recent earthquakes to Figure 8.21.

Table 8.21 The impact of individual earthquakes

Year	Place	Richter Scale	LEDC / MEDC	Impact
1960	Agadir, Morocco	5.7	LEDC	12 000 deaths, many homeless
1976	Tangshan, China	7.8	LEDC	250 000 deaths, 650 000 homeless
1989	San Francisco, USA	7.1	MEDC	62 deaths
1999	Turkey	7.3	LEDC	18 000 deaths, many remote villages destroyed
2001	Seattle, USA	7.0	MEDC	1 death, 250 injuries, billions of dollars worth of damage
2005	Pakistan	7.6+	LEDC	100–150 dead, countless homeless
2008	Market Rasen, UK	5.2	MEDC	Minor structural damage over a limited area

Factors affecting the impact of an earthquake

The **strength** of an earthquake is measured on the Richter Scale. The impact of an earthquake will be affected by several factors:

- The depth of the **focus** (see Figure 8.19).
- The distance from the epicentre.
- The nature of the surface rocks, e.g. soft rocks can absorb water and become very mobile, e.g. Mexico City, 1985.
- Population density, because densely populated urban areas are very vulnerable, e.g. Kobe, 1995.
- The remoteness of an area will affect the time that emergency services and aid take to reach the area, e.g. Afghanistan, 1998 and Pakistan, 2005.
- Resources available and preparedness of an area; MEDCs can afford better services.
- Time of day – at night time more people will be indoors and in danger from building collapse.
- The time of year / climate can affect survival and the spread of disease.

Tsunamis

> **KEY POINT**
>
> **Tsunamis** (Japanese for 'harbour wave') are powerful ocean waves caused by earthquakes. Tsunamis are not tidal waves. They can travel long distances across oceans very quickly.

Locate this area on an atlas map.

In December 2004 a severe **submarine earthquake** (Richter Scale 9.0) occurred along the destructive plate margin off the west coast of Sumatra (Indian Ocean). An upward thrust of 20m of the seafloor sent a series of fast moving powerful waves in all directions.

Within 15 minutes the waves had reached the shallow coastal waters of the island of Sumatra. They quickly built up to 20m high waves that submerged coastal areas, flooded busy tourist resorts and ripped vegetation from mountainsides some 800m inland. The city of Banda Aceh was destroyed and tens of thousands of people were killed.

Within two hours, similar waves hit Sri Lanka, still without warning. Some 4000 people died in the region around the city of Galle alone. The total death toll of this tsunami has been estimated at 230 000 in 11 countries.

Responding to earthquakes

Control:
Research in the USA has experimented with injecting fluids along the San Andreas fault to lubricate zones of friction (see Figure 8.7). However, there is little evidence that this works.

Despite much research, it is still not possible to precisely predict earthquakes.

Prediction:
It is possible to predict where earthquakes are likely to happen but not exactly when. On-going research is investigating...

- evidence from past earthquakes (distribution, patterns)
- patterns of small tremors
- unusual animal behaviour
- gas emissions from the ground.

One of the reasons for the low death toll and injuries in Seattle (2001) was that large sums of money had been spent over the previous 20 years to ensure that buildings could withstand major shocks. The Space Needle, built to withstand a 9.1 magnitude earthquake, shuddered violently but no damage occurred. Compare this with the high death toll in Pakistan (2005) where flats and schools collapsed immediately.

Preparation:

There are several things that can be done to prepare for earthquakes and their aftermath:

- Looking at land planning to prevent building on weak rock, e.g. reclaimed land from the sea.
- Using more flexible gas, water and power lines.
- Planning and practising emergency and evacuation procedures. In November 2008, S. California held its largest earthquake drill involving 5 million people – 'drop – cover – hold on'!.
- Having greater public awareness, e.g. education in schools (Japan and California).
- Improving building designs.

Building designs might be improved using the following:

- Reinforced foundations deep in bedrock.
- Rubber shock absorbers between the foundations and superstructure.
- 'Bird cage' interlocking steel frames.
- Rolling weights on roof to counteract the shock waves.
- Automatic shutters that come down over windows to prevent pedestrians being showered with glass.
- Panels of marble and glass flexibly anchored into the steel superstructure.
- Open areas surrounding buildings where pedestrians can safely assemble if evacuated.

MEDC case studies: Kobe, Japan, 1995

Kobe factfile:

- **Location:** Kobe, Japan (see Figure 8.13); a heavily populated urban area.
- **Time and date:** 5.46am on 17th January 1995.
- **Magnitude on Richter Scale**: 7.2.
- **Plate margin**: destructive, subduction zone (see Figure 8.4).

Short-term effects:

- 5477 deaths and 35 000 injured.
- 316 000 people left homeless.
- Many houses collapsed despite earthquake-proof designs.
- Large number of buildings destroyed by fire when gas mains fractured.
- Many people evacuated to schools, parks and community centres. Tents and emergency rations provided.
- Rescue teams arrived quickly on scene with equipment.
- National government set up emergency headquarters in two days.
- Injured people transferred to hospitals in nearby cities.
- Electricity restored in six days.
- Search for survivors concluded in ten days.
- Earthquake refugees started moving into temporary housing within two weeks.
- Much industry, communications and shopping restored within three months.
- All temporary shelters for the homeless closed in seven months.

Long-term effects

- Many businesses closed.
- Extra jobs created in rebuilding.
- Many people moved away from area permanently.
- Overall cost was 10 billion yen (about £6 million).

LEDC case study: Quetta, S.W. Pakistan, 2008

Quetta factfile:
- Location: Quetta, Baluchistan, Pakistan (see Figure 8.13), a well-populated, remote, mountainous area (2000–3000m high) bordering Afghanistan.
- Time and date: 5.00am 28th/29th October 2008.
- Magnitude on Richter Scale: 6.4.
- Plate margin: Destructive, collision zone (see Figure 8.5).

Short-term effects:
- 300 deaths and large numbers injured.
- 20 000 people left homeless, many around the hill town of Ziarat 50km north of Quetta.
- Nearly all the mud houses collapsed during the initial quake, burying families asleep.
- The severe tremors triggered many landslides along the steep sided valleys, burying villages and destroying roads and communications.
- Large numbers of people camped in makeshift shelters made from wood and polythene, but these were inadequate for the harsh mountain climate at the onset of winter.
- Army rescue teams were sent immediately and army hospitals put on standby.
- The rescue and retrieval of bodies continued for many weeks.

> Be prepared to explain why the effects are more severe in LEDCs than in MEDCs.

Longer-term effects
- International aid agencies were mainly responsible for rehabilitation. By December 2008 international aid of $1M had been committed for emergency relief, tents and blankets.
- Some villages and roads may well remain unrepaired for a long time.
- Families left destitute as farmland has been ruined and livestock killed by landslides.

> Further research into the longer term effects might be useful. Keep a look out for any future earthquake activity in this region.

- Geologically this is an unstable area. A destructive plate margin extends for nearly 1800km across the country along which there have been many destructive earthquakes. For example, May 1935 near Quetta – 7.6 magnitude – 30 000 deaths, October 2005 near Rawalpindi – 7.7 magnitude – 80 000 deaths.
- The Pakistan government is still coping with the recovery from the 2005 earthquake. Italy has committed $2M in bilateral aid to assist rebuilding.
- The latest disaster (unlikely to be the last) places further financial demands on a limited budget. (The Pakistan GNP per head = US$689 compared to UK = US$19 950).

PROGRESS CHECK

1. What is the name given to the molten rock that flows down the sides of some volcanoes?
2. How is tectonic activity of benefit to Iceland?
3. What is the name given to the point on the Earth's surface immediately above the focus of an earthquake?
4. What scale is used to measure the strength or magnitude of an earthquake?
5. Describe three ways in which the impact of earthquakes might be reduced.

1. Lava 2. Tourism and geothermal energy 3. Epicentre 4. Richter Scale 5. **Accept three from:** Improved prediction; Planning controls; Better building design; Flexible pipes for services; Developing emergency and evacuation plans; Improving public awareness (link to examples where possible)

9.1 Population density and change

LEARNING SUMMARY	After studying this section you should be able to understand:
	• the main features of the world pattern of population density
	• the main reasons for population change and the effect on population structure

The world pattern of population density

AQA A	✗
AQA B	✗
EDEXCEL A	✓
EDEXCEL B	✓
OCR A	✓
OCR B	✓
WJEC A	✓
WJEC B	✓
CCEA	✓

KEY POINT

Population density is measured as the number of people living in an area. It is usually measured in people per square kilometre (km²).

Make sure that you know some examples of places with different population densities.

Figure 9.1 World population density

Scale	Densely populated	Sparsely populated
International	S.E. Asia; Western Europe	Sahara Desert; Antarctica
National	Singapore; Netherlands	Australia; Mongolia
Regional	S.E. England; S.E. Brazil	Western Australia; Amazonia
Local	Hong Kong; Rio de Janeiro	Snowdonia; Alaska

Figure 9.2 World population distribution

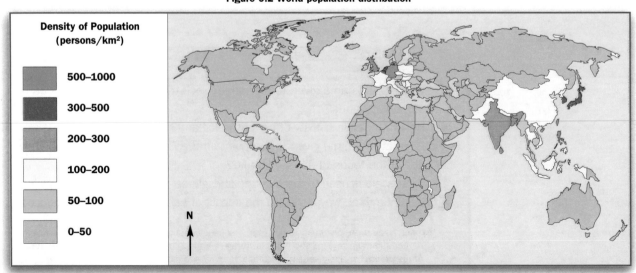

Density of Population (persons/km²)

- 500–1000
- 300–500
- 200–300
- 100–200
- 50–100
- 0–50

N

Reasons for the differences in population distribution and density

The factors affecting the distribution and density of population include…

- **physical factors**, e.g. relief, climate, soils, vegetation and minerals
- **social factors**, e.g. the proportion of urban to rural population and history
- **economic factors**, e.g. resources, the amount of industrialisation, employment, trade and transport networks
- **political factors**, e.g. government policy on birth control.

> It is useful to have an example of one MEDC and one LEDC.

> **KEY POINT**
>
> **Population distribution** describes the pattern of people in an area (how the population is spaced or spread out). The three main patterns of distribution are…
> - uniform or even
> - nucleated or clustered
> - a random pattern.

MEDC case study: population density in the United Kingdom

Figure 9.3 Population density in the United Kingdom

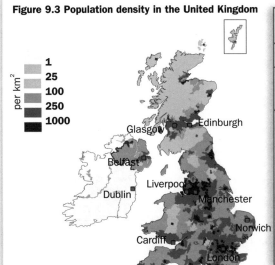

per km²
- 1
- 25
- 100
- 250
- 1000

United Kingdom factfile	
Area	241 590 km²
Population density	250 people per km²
Description	The United Kingdom has a belt of high population density running from London and the South East, in a north westerly direction, through Birmingham and the West Midlands to Liverpool and Manchester in the North West. Scotland, Wales and Northern Ireland tend to have lower population densities, although they do contain denser areas around their cities.

LEDC case study: population density in Ghana

Figure 9.4 Population density in Ghana

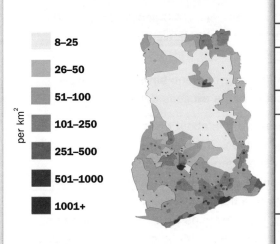

per km²
- 8–25
- 26–50
- 51–100
- 101–250
- 251–500
- 501–1000
- 1001+

Ghana factfile	
Area	230 940 km²
Population density	101 people per km²
Climate	Warm tropical
Population	23 382 848, but there is a high mortality rate due to AIDS. Life expectancy is 59 years and 38% of the population is under 14 years. Most of the population is located in a series of coastal cities
Description	Capital city is Accra. The country has many natural resources, but is heavily dependent on international finance and technical assistance.

World population growth

AQA A	✓
AQA B	✓
EDEXCEL A	✓
EDEXCEL B	✓
OCR A	✓
OCR B	✓
WJEC A	✓
WJEC B	✓
CCEA	✓

The best estimate of the world's population total is 6.7 billion (6 700 000 000) people. This number has doubled since 1960, with most of the growth in LEDCs. The growth rate was highest in 1963.

In 1900 Europe contained 24.7% of the world's population, but this share had fallen to 12% by 2008.

Some experts think the total world population will reach 9 billion by 2040. Others believe that the social and economic changes taking place in LEDCs will slow down their population growths. Many countries take a census (questionnaire survey) every ten years, which counts their population.

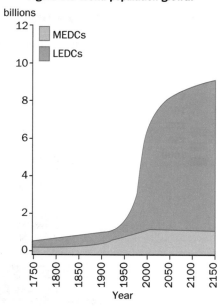

Figure 9.5 World population growth

Population change: the balance of birth and death rates

AQA A	✓
AQA B	✓
EDEXCEL A	✓
EDEXCEL B	✓
OCR A	✓
OCR B	✓
WJEC A	✓
WJEC B	✓
CCEA	✓

KEY POINT

The birth rate is the number of live births per 1000 people per year. The death rate is the number of deaths per 1000 people per year.

Natural population increase is the difference between **birth** and **death** rates. Natural increase occurs if the number of births exceeds deaths.

Birth rates are high in LEDCs, for example it is about 48 in the Democratic Republic of the Congo and 46 in Afghanistan. There are several reasons for this:

- Children provide labour on family-subsistence farms.
- There are no old age pensions, so children provide security for old age.
- Large families are seen as a sign of a husband's virility.
- Girls are expected to marry early, which extends their child-bearing years.
- Women stay at home and raise a family and with little education they do not know about birth control.

> You should know one case study of population change for both a LEDC and a MEDC.

- Some religions do not approve of contraception.
- High infant mortality encourages large families to ensure that some children survive.

Birth rates are low in MEDCs, e.g. UK, Sweden and Germany. There are several reasons for this:

- People marry later.
- Women are educated and delay having a family so that they can have a career.
- High costs of living make having children expensive.
- Some couples prefer material possessions such as a car, house and holidays.
- Birth control (the contraceptive pill in particular) is freely available.
- Governments discourage large families in order to save the costs of building more schools.

Death rates are low in MEDCs and are falling in LEDCs. This is due to several factors:

- Better healthcare and medical care.
- People are able to retire earlier after less physically demanding jobs.
- Cures are being found for diseases such as cancer, malaria and cholera.
- People are better educated about hygiene.
- There are cleaner water supplies and sanitary facilities.

The Demographic Transition Model

AQA A	✓
AQA B	✗
EDEXCEL A	✓
EDEXCEL B	✗
OCR A	✗
OCR B	✓
WJEC A	✗
WJEC B	✗
CCEA	✗

Geographers studying the changes taking place in the populations of many countries have noticed that they follow a similar pattern. This is called the **Demographic Transition Model**. The model shows how the total population of a country changes through time as birth and death rates change.

The demographic transition model is useful for...

- studying the way population is changing
- understanding trends in births, deaths and natural increases
- predicting the changing structure of population and planning to meet its changing needs.

Figure 9.6A The Demographic Transition Model

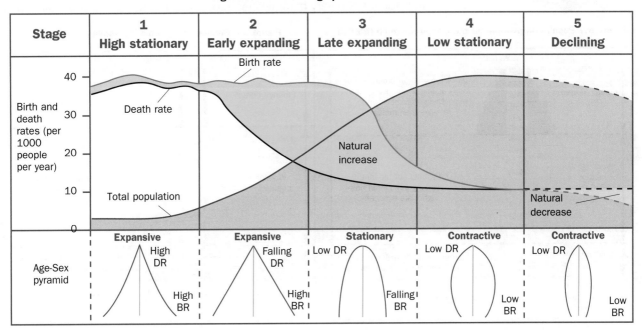

Figure 9.6B: The demographic transition model

Stage	One	Two	Three	Four	Five
Birth Rate	High	High	Falling	Low	Very low
Death Rate	High and varies	Falls rapidly	Falls more slowly	Low	Low
Population changes	Small increases or stable	Rapid increase	Growth slows	Stable or slow increase	Slow decrease
Places	Parts of the rainforest or Ethiopia	Peru, Malawi	China, Australia	Canada, USA	Hungary, Germany, Singapore
People's lives	• Subsistence agriculture • High infant mortality • Disease • Famine • Poor hygiene • Few doctors	• Better food supply • Health care improves • Lack of birth control • Improved water supply	• Living conditions and health care improve • Jobs in industry • Family planning, education	• High living standards • Affluence • Small families • Long life expectancy • Education for all	• High livings standards • Health care for all • Ageing population • Women educated and working

Geographers are uncertain about stage 5, although some European countries and possibly Singapore have entered this stage where birth rates are low. In this stage governments encourage couples to have more babies. A shortage of people of working age means that some governments encourage migrants from other countries.

There are several **limitations** of the Demographic Transition Model:
- LEDCs may not follow the patterns of change that was found in the MEDCs 30 to 50 years ago.
- Birth rates have not fallen as rapidly as suggested by the model in some LEDCs because of social customs and beliefs.
- Government planning for population change may interrupt the model, e.g. the 'One-Child Policy' in China.
- The impact of AIDS may mean some African countries are not progressing through the model because of high infant mortality and low life expectancy.
- Some industrialising LEDCs are moving more rapidly through the stages than the MEDCs did.

> This is a diagram that is often tested by examiners. Note how total population is changing at each stage.

> Note how the pyramids divide into three age groups and the two sexes.

Population pyramids

Population pyramids are very helpful when studying the structure of a population.

Figure 9.7 Population pyramid for the United Kingdom (MEDC)

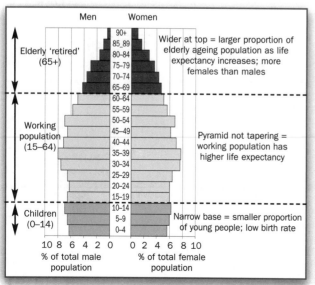

Figure 9.8 Population Pyramid for Kenya (LEDC)

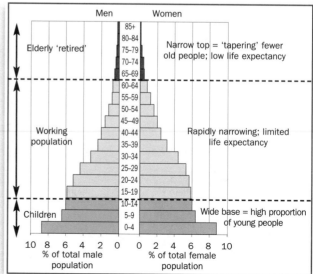

9.2 The movement of population

LEARNING SUMMARY	After studying this section you should be able to understand:
	• a range of population issues and their planned solutions

Population change

AQA A	✓
AQA B	✓
EDEXCEL A	✓
EDEXCEL B	✓
OCR A	✓
OCR B	✓
WJEC A	✓
WJEC B	✓
CCEA	✓

Population migration

Population totals change with variations in birth and death rates. Populations also change because of **migration**.

> **KEY POINT**
>
> A **migrant** is a person who moves to live in another place, either permanently or temporarily. **In-migrants** move into an area and **emigrants** move out.

> Migration is not part of natural population increase.

Types of migration

There are four types of migration:
- **Rural to rural**, e.g. a farmer retiring to a cottage near the sea.
- **Rural to urban**, e.g. people moving from the countryside to cities for jobs and amenities.
- **Urban to rural**, e.g. families moving to a village with a house with a garden from where working members commute back to the urban area.
- **Urban to urban**, e.g. people moving from one urban area to another for a job change or moving from a big city to a smaller urban area for better housing.

> Remember examples of some of these types of migration.

Forced and **voluntary** migrants is another division of migration:
- **Forced** migrants have had to move, e.g. Jews from the Nazi regime in Germany in 1939.
- **Voluntary** migrants move because they believe they will benefit by moving.

Migrants may move locally, nationally or internationally.

Understanding migration

Figure 9.9 Push–pull factors influencing migration

Push factors	Journey factors	Pull factors
• Lack of jobs • Poor housing • Poor environment, e.g. pollution, crime, traffic, dust, eyesores • War, genocide, persecution • Poor schools • Lack of health care • Retirement • Family breakdown • Racial tension • Restlessness • Decline of a community	• Cost of the journey • Other attractions on the way • Running out of money for travel • Poor transport • Natural disasters, e.g. floods • Long distances • Language difficulties • Homesickness • Political barriers • National boundaries	• Job opportunities • Better housing • Green areas, safety, privacy • Increased wealth • Good schools • Affordable health care for all • Using wealth to improve life • Slower pace of life • Friends • New experiences • New community emerging

Note the way the push–pull model helps you to understand this migration.

Rural to urban migration is taking place in many countries including Brazil, Chile, Bolivia, Uganda, Lesotho and China. For example, in Brazil rural people migrate to the cities in the south-east of the country for several reasons:

- High population increase in the rural areas causes land and food shortages.
- People believe the urban area is a place of bright lights and opportunity.
- Crop failures, insecurity, lack of capital, absentee landlords, soil exhaustion and poor education mean a life of rural poverty.
- Farm machines do the work of many labourers and so create unemployment.
- Poor health care and lack of clean water.
- Political instability with conflicts between local leaders.

Case study of regional migration in an MEDC (United Kingdom)

In many MEDCs, including the UK, people are on the move. There are several main movement patterns:

- Towards the large cities (especially the capital city) and industrial areas in search of jobs or promotions, e.g. into London.
- To the suburbs, the edge of the urban area or into the countryside for better housing and a cleaner environment, e.g. out of London and other big cities.
- For retirement to country towns and warmer areas such as Devon, Cornwall and the south coast.
- Older people moving closer to their grown up children for mutual support.
- Families moving short distances to gain access to better schools.
- Workers leaving areas of unemployment and moving to growing areas, e.g. moving from South Wales into Milton Keynes.
- Skilled workers (in areas such as information technology or finance) moving to areas with science and business parks near universities, e.g. recent graduates to Camborne in Cambridgeshire.

Case study of economic migration into California

Mexicans started to move into California in the 1950s. These Spanish-speaking people, called Hispanics, migrated to improve their standard of living, find better jobs, education and health care.

The working men move first and then bring their families once they are established. Recently more single women have moved because there are jobs for them. Many of the Mexican migrants move illegally, but they are willing to take the harder, dirtier, seasonal and low paid jobs in agriculture, the building industry, hotels and restaurants. Many find themselves living in poor housing, but they are better off financially than if they stayed in Mexico. These illegal migrants cause problems for the authorities because they present a higher health risk.

Population problems and issues

The social, environmental and political problems of population growth and movement in LEDCs

KEY POINT

Overpopulation occurs when there are too many people for the available resources. **Underpopulation** occurs when there are too few people to fully exploit the available resources.

Many LEDCs have high rates of population growth because of high birth rates and declining death rates. The problems caused by this growth include the following:

- Unemployment
- Strain on services
- Shanty towns
- Poor medical care
- Prostitution
- Lack of food
- Poor sanitation
- Housing shortages
- Overcrowded buses
- Crime

However, this growth provides a labour force and an increased domestic market.

Figure 9.10 Advantages and disadvantages of population change

	Areas losing population	Areas gaining population
Advantages	• Lowers population pressure • Reduces unemployment • Fewer mouths to feed • Birth rates fall • Money sent back by migrants • Farms become bigger	• Increases working population • Migrants willing to do unpleasant jobs • Migrants work for lower wages • Brings new culture to an area • Some may be skilled or very skilled • Ready to develop informal economy
Disadvantages	• Young workers leave • Farm production falls • Young educated people leave • Elderly population left behind • Services deteriorate • May attract even poorer migrants • Criminals may move in and take control	• Dangers of racial tension • May put local people out of work • Services become overcrowded • Arrivals may be poorly educated • Arrivals too poor to afford local housing • May build shanty towns • May bring disease

The problems of ageing populations in the EU

This is a new and growing problem and one that will often be tested in your exam.

KEY POINT

Life expectancy is the number of years that a person is expected to live at birth.

Life expectancy is increasing in many countries due to better diets, housing and health care as well as less physically demanding jobs. This has meant an increase in the number of older people, e.g. the 'greying' population in Sweden and the UK. Birth rates have also fallen in these countries.

The problems caused by ageing populations include the following:
- Increased funds needed to meet the demand for health services.
- The need for specially designed houses and serviced blocks of flats, e.g. hand rails, nonslip floors and emergency buttons.
- Provision of leisure activities for the elderly.
- Increased dependency and burden on the working population.
- Shortages of labour, recruiting overseas workers, e.g. nurses and doctors.

However, older people do undertake many worthwhile tasks, many of them voluntary. They also often support their grown-up children as they raise their young families.

The problems of rural to urban migration in LEDCs

You need to know at least one example of the source and destination of these migrants.

Migrants arrive in cities with little money and few skills for urban jobs. They cannot afford housing and are forced to settle in temporary dwellings made from scrap materials such as corrugated iron, wood, cardboard and cloth.

These residential areas have...
- little or no sanitation and poor water supplies
- unsafe electricity, taken illegally from the National Grid
- few health facilities and widespread disease
- overcrowding, unemployment and crime.

The effect of this movement is that rural areas do not have enough labour. Women, with the help of the very young and the elderly, often run small farms. As a result, farming output falls.

The problems of urban to rural migration in MEDCs

You should know at least one example of source and destination and know the effects on source and destination areas.

With improvements in public transport and increased car ownership, people are moving away from large urban areas to live in the smaller market towns and villages nearby.

The effects on the urban area are not always positive, because the people left behind are often those with fewer skills and some social problems.

This migration also causes problems for the country areas:
- Population increase places a strain on housing and health services.
- Increase in traffic creates congestion, noise and pollution.
- Schools may have to be expanded.
- Housing prices rise and local young people cannot afford to buy in the area.
- There is a loss of open space as developers build houses to meet the demand.
- Public transport becomes crowded as commuting increases.

However, the arrival of affluent people in a village can revitalise the area, allowing shops to remain open, village schools to prosper and clubs and societies to flourish.

The problems and issues raised by refugees

Some people are forced to leave their home area or country. They are called refugees and estimates suggest there are 30 million refugees in the world. There are several reasons why people become refugees:
- **Persecution** due to race, religion, nationality, social group or political beliefs. For example, people in the Democratic Republic of the Congo (DRC) moved to nearby Rwanda as civil war raged between government troops and rebels.
- **Struggles** between rival groups for control of a country, e.g. Afghans moving to Pakistan.
- **Natural disasters** such as earthquakes, volcanic eruptions, floods and droughts. For example, Ethiopians leave the Sahel region due to drought at a time of high population growth and poor harvests.

Problems and issues are raised by the influx of refugees. They arrive in neighbouring countries that do not have the resources to cope with them, e.g. Ethiopian refugees filled camps in nearby Somalia, which is itself a very poor country. Refugees usually arrive in large numbers in a very short space of time and have to be housed in tented camps, which have poor sanitary and water facilities, and disease often breaks out. They also need to be provided with food, water, medicine and shelter.

After the emergency, some refugees return home, but others stay in their new country. The ones that stay may bring valuable skills and expertise and find good employment. Others fill menial jobs that local people do not want to do. However, there are some refugees that do not settle because they find the language, currency and customs of their new country difficult. For a sense of security they tend to live together in the same neighbourhoods and create a small piece of their own country there. Racial conflict can occur.

Figure 9.11 Examples of international migration

From	To	Reason
Poland	UK	Skill shortages in host, e.g. dentists and plumbers
Central Europe	UK	Labour shortages in host, e.g. hospitality, hotels and restaurants
South Africa	UK	Doctors and nurses needed by host
India	UK	Doctors and IT specialists needed
UK	New Zealand	Shortage of doctors and nurses locally
Mexico	Canada	Jobs and education
UK	Spain	Retirement to warmer climate
Philippines	USA	Domestic workers and care assistants to undertake low paid tasks
Malaysia	Singapore	To fill labour shortages in growing economy
Caribbean	Argentina	Employment, housing and health care
Indonesia	Australia	To fill labour shortages in low paid jobs
Australia	USA	Skilled people moving for promotion or better paid jobs

Figure 9.12 The reasons for international migration

	For	Against
Spiritual reasons	• Search for greater enlightenment • To gain understanding of life • Persecution by the authorities	• Compromise spiritual values in order to survive • Challenges to personal views by people in the new place
Moral reasons	• To get a job so that the family can be supported • Responsibility to ease problems of 'home area'	• Dangers of unemployment, forced into crime and prostitution • Worries that the 'new' area may not be what it seems
Ethical reasons	• Duty to earn and send money back to 'home' area • Attitudes of local authorities to problems in the 'home' area	• Fear of failure • Concerns over the way migrants are treated in the 'new' area
Social reasons	• Better education for the individual or family • Wider variety of entertainment and social experiences	• Break up of the wider family, split with parents • Loss of friends • Decline in the community left behind
Cultural reasons	• To experience a richer cultural scene • Opportunity to express themselves more openly	• Neglect of personal heritage and culture • Dangers of entering an oppressive regime
Economic reasons	• To gain employment or promotion • To use skills from education not needed at home • Higher wages allowing money to be sent home	• Unemployment may force individuals into the informal economy • Costs may be higher in 'new' area • Expense of the move, e.g. selling home and travel

Strategies for coping with population change

AQA A	✓
AQA B	✓
EDEXCEL A	✓
EDEXCEL B	✓
OCR A	✓
OCR B	✓
WJEC A	✓
WJEC B	✓
CCEA	✓

Strategies for reducing population growth in LEDCs

Many LEDCs face increasing population totals and have more mouths to feed. This takes resources away from plans to improve the **quality of life** of people.

The strategies adopted by LEDCs to reduce population include the following:

- **Birth control** using contraceptives, abortion and sterilisation (tried in India with limited success).
- Raising the level of education, especially for girls.
- Encouraging delayed marriages or raising the age at which people may marry.
- Making polygamy (multiple spouses) illegal.
- Raising the status of women so they have more of a say over the number of children they have.
- Having better health care (less need for large families if more children survive).
- Providing financial benefits to small families.
- Providing employment and careers for women.
- Limiting the number of children parents can have, e.g. China's **one-child policy**.

> Many candidates remember the 'one-child policy' but say it applies to Japan. Remember where it was introduced.

China's **one-child policy** encourages one-child families. This policy includes the following:

- Birth control and fines if more than one child is born.
- Increased taxes for couples with more than one child.
- Public education and advertisements explaining the policy.
- Salary bonuses for those with one child.
- Priority in education, housing and health for one-child families.

The policy has been a partial success with signs of the slower growth of China's population. But, the policy is harsh and unpopular and is being relaxed in some rural areas. It created 'spoiled, only child' families and some girl babies were abandoned or murdered because their parents wanted a son to keep the family name alive.

> **KEY POINT**
>
> **Population strategies** are government plans intended to ease the problems of population growth or decline.

Strategies for increasing population in MEDCs

> This is important topic so expect examination questions on it.

Some MEDCs have low birth rates, more elderly people and a falling population total. The population is below its **replacement level**. These countries face **labour shortages** and are not able to meet economic plans for improvements in the quality of life. Different countries have adopted different strategies.

In **Japan** the government has...

- raised the retirement age to increase the workforce
- reviewed working conditions for men and women to make having a family easier
- set up local committees to help couples have families
- increased social welfare payments
- allowed males to claim paid paternity leave
- offered tax incentives to companies allowing workers time off work to support their children
- built a large number of day-care centres.

However, these policies are not being very successful.

In **Singapore** the government has...
- encouraged single people to marry
- encouraged married graduates to have more babies
- provided a Social Development Unit to help single people to meet each other
- established child-care centres for working women
- introduced flexible working hours and part-time employment for mothers
- extended the period of paid maternity leave
- given tax rebates to married couples who have more than two children
- subsidised child-care centres
- given housing priority to couples who have more than two children
- introduced the Baby Bonus scheme for having a second and a third child
- provided a Work–Life unit to promote family-friendly policies by employers, e.g. flexible hours, working from home and help with deposits for the purchase of family houses
- advertised the benefits and joys of marriage on television programmes
- shown stories of happy family life in newspapers.

Strategies for coping with ageing populations in MEDCs

> There will be purpose-built housing for the elderly in a town near you.

Increased life expectancy means that governments and local authorities in North America, Western Europe and Japan need to make provision for more elderly people.

The types of provision they need to make include the following:
- Housing that is affordable and easily managed by older people.
- Building services such as electricians, plumbers and handymen to deal with emergencies, fit burglar alarms, fit security lighting, change bulbs, adapt the shower and bath for the elderly and disabled, fix the central heating, etc.
- Garden maintenance, landscaping, lawn mowing and tree surgery.
- Health provision to meet the needs of the elderly including specialist cancer and heart units.
- Car parking and shopping facilities that are suited to people who are less steady on their feet.
- Access to social and religious services, which will include more home visits and day-care centres.
- Libraries and other leisure facilities.
- Encouraging employers to give jobs to older people, e.g. craftsmen as advisers in DIY stores.

One of the key issues is who pays for these services. Some elderly people...
- have the money to buy help from private specialist companies
- have to rely on welfare services (paid for by the tax-payer)
- may move in with their sons / daughters.

PROGRESS CHECK

1. State two advantages for an area losing population through migration.
2. Define life expectancy and explain why it is increasing.
3. Name a group of refugees and explain why they wish to move to another country.

1. **Accept any two of the following:** Lower population pressure; Reduced unemployment; Fewer people to feed; Birth rate falls; Money comes back from migrants; Farm size increases.
2. It is the average life span of population and is increasing due to better social and economic conditions (health, nutrition, work, water and sanitation).
3. **Examples could include the following:** Turks to Germany; Ethiopians to Somalia; Zimbabwean to South Africa; Mexicans to USA. They are pulled by better lives at their destination or pushed by poor conditions at home.

10.1 The location and function of settlements

LEARNING SUMMARY

After studying this section you should be able to understand:

- how to describe the site and situation of rural and urban settlements
- how to recognise the functions of settlements and the services they offer

The location of settlements

AQA A	✗
AQA B	✗
EDEXCEL A	✓
EDEXCEL B	✗
OCR A	✗
OCR B	✗
WJEC A	✗
WJEC B	✗
CCEA	✓

The location of settlements involves the study of both **site** and **situation** of different settlement types.

Different types of settlement

There are two types of settlement:
- **Rural** (e.g. a village or scattered farms)
- **Urban** (e.g. a city or small town).

Residents in **rural settlements** are mainly farmers, workers from urban settlements or retired people. Rural settlements are smaller in size, population and population density. **Urban settlements** are involved in industry, commerce or administration. They include towns, cities, conurbations and megalopolises.

> **KEY POINT**
>
> **Rural** settlements consist of a small number of buildings in the countryside, which have an agricultural or dormitory function, a low population density, a close community and a small number of services.
>
> **Urban** settlements consist of a continuous built-up area, with industry and commerce. There is a high population density, acquaintances rather than friends and many services.

The siting and situation of settlements

Check whether a question asks for a site or situation. If it asks for location it means both.

> **KEY POINT**
>
> **Site** describes the features of the place where the settlement is located. **Situation** describes the features of the area in which the settlement functions.

There are several factors that influence the **site and situation** of settlements:

- Dry point in an area of poor drainage (e.g. Ely) and wet point in an area where water supply is good (e.g. Gretton in Gloucestershire)
- Spring line, e.g. Princes Risborough.
- Shelter and defence, e.g. Durham, Edinburgh and Conwy.
- Resources such as minerals, e.g. coal.
- Communications, e.g. gap towns (e.g. Dorking), route centres (e.g. Crewe) and bridging points (e.g. Worcester).
- Planned, e.g. new towns and cities (e.g. Harlow and Milton Keynes), expanded towns (e.g. Swindon).
- Resorts (e.g. Bournemouth) or spas (e.g. Buxton).
- Ports, e.g. Grimsby and Southampton.
- Religious centres, e.g. Canterbury.
- Market centres, e.g. Norwich.

These factors were important when the settlement was founded, but are less so today.

Figure 10.1 A spring line village

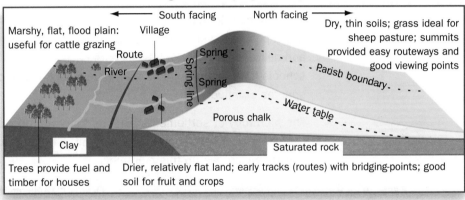

The function of settlements

AQA A	✗
AQA B	✗
EDEXCEL A	✓
EDEXCEL B	✗
OCR A	✗
OCR B	✓
WJEC A	✓
WJEC B	✓
CCEA	✓

> **KEY POINT**
>
> **Settlement function** describes the main economic activity of the settlement and the jobs of the people working there.

Settlements can be **classified** according to their main function:

- Manufacturing, e.g. Sheffield.
- Hi-tech industry, e.g. Reading.
- Administrative centre, e.g. Cardiff and Norwich.
- Car manufacturing, e.g. Swindon and Sunderland.
- Container and ferry port, e.g. Harwich.
- Aerospace, e.g. Bristol.
- Holiday resort, e.g. Blackpool and Bournemouth.
- Educational, e.g. Oxford and Cambridge.

All larger settlements also act as centres for administration for the area around them.

> You need to know the names and functions of towns in your area.

Services in settlements

Settlements provide housing, administration, industry, commerce and services. The services include local government offices, shopping centres, schools and hospitals. Settlements can be arranged into a **hierarchy** according to their population size, range of services and distance apart.

Central Place Theory attempts to explain the size and spacing of settlements and the services they offer using the following ideas: **goods, range of goods, threshold population, sphere of influence** and **hierarchy**.

Goods purchased regularly, such as bread and newspapers, are called low-order or convenience goods. They are usually available in the village or corner shop. Goods purchased irregularly are called high-order or comparison goods, e.g. televisions, clothing and furniture. People compare prices on these goods; they want choice and are prepared to travel further to city centres or retail parks.

The **range of a good** is the maximum distance that people are willing to travel for a service. They travel further for high-order, comparison goods.

The **threshold population** is the minimum number of customers needed to maintain a service. Small local shops need a small threshold population that buy low-order goods regularly. Comparison good shops need a larger threshold population because goods are bought infrequently. Very specialist shops, e.g. jewellers, need a very high threshold population and are usually only found in large settlements.

The **sphere of influence** is the area served by the settlement. It is the area from which people travel to use the settlement, or the area to which bus services run and deliveries are made. Newsagents have small spheres of influence, secondary schools have larger spheres than primary schools and hospitals have very large spheres of influence.

The **hierarchy** of settlements extends from metropolitan areas, through cities, towns and villages to hamlets. The number of services offered and the sphere of influence increase up this hierarchy.

Figure 10.2A Hierarchy of settlements

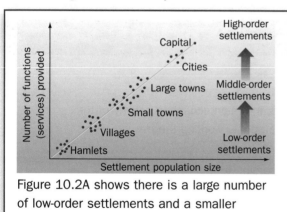

Figure 10.2A shows there is a large number of low-order settlements and a smaller number of high-order settlements.

Figure 10.2B Hierarchy of shops and services

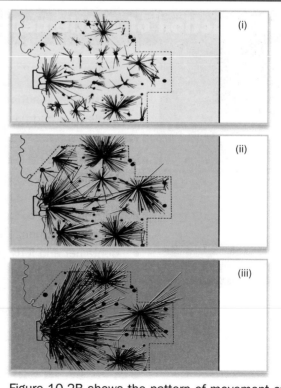

Figure 10.2B shows the pattern of movement of people to settlements for (i) food, (ii) solicitors and (iii) hospitals.

Figure 10.2C Sphere of influence

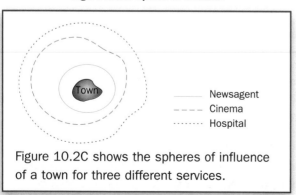

——— Newsagent
– – – Cinema
········ Hospital

Figure 10.2C shows the spheres of influence of a town for three different services.

10.2 Land use in settlements

After studying this section you should be able to understand:

● about urban land use and zones within settlements

Patterns of land use in settlements

AQA A	✓
AQA B	✗
EDEXCEL A	✓
EDEXCEL B	✗
OCR A	✗
OCR B	✓
WJEC A	✓
WJEC B	✓
CCEA	✓

KEY POINT

Every settlement has its own land use pattern. The pattern reflects factors that may have acted recently or over a longer period of time.

Factors in a land use pattern can include the following:

● Available transport, speed and frequency.
● Competition between users.
● Relief, slopes, rivers and coastlines.
● Railways, airports and motorways.
● Town planners, zoning and Green Belts.
● Social, ethnic and racial differences.
● Tradition, values and culture.
● History.
● Land ownership.
● Types of employment.
● Housing types.
● Local climate.

Surveys of land use in settlements show areas with similar land use. These are called land-use zones. For example, a zone of lower-quality terraced housing can often be found near to the CBD.

Settlement Patterns

To simplify and explain the complex pattern of land use in settlements, a number of patterns have been recognised. The three main patterns are the **concentric zone**, the **sector** and the **multiple nuclei**.

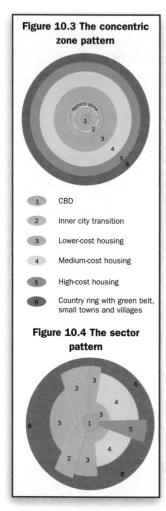

Figure 10.3 The concentric zone pattern

1. CBD
2. Inner city transition
3. Lower-cost housing
4. Medium-cost housing
5. High-cost housing
6. Country ring with green belt, small towns and villages

Figure 10.4 The sector pattern

No settlement fits exactly to any of the patterns. Hills, rivers and historic buildings (e.g. a cathedral, castle or large house) may distort the concentric rings. Matching a settlement to the standard pattern helps increase understanding of the special features of that place.

The concentric zone pattern

The concentric zone pattern was based on American cities, particularly Chicago in the 1920s. The Central Business District (CBD) is at its centre.

The CBD shown in Figure 10.3 is mainly made up of shops and offices. Around the CBD is the zone of transition, twilight zone or inner city. This is an area of older housing, declining industry and derelict land. Outside this are three housing zones, which increase in quality away from the centre. The settlement expands by 'invasion and succession' (or ripple effect) where an inner zone moves outwards.

The sector pattern

In the sector pattern, lines of transport to the centre are given more emphasis. Industry (in zone 2) and lower cost housing develop along the line of main roads or railways. Land use zones look like wedges. The settlement expands by 'filtering', i.e. when new housing is built on the edge, more affluent people move out.

The multiple nuclei pattern

The multiple nuclei pattern shows different land uses clustered with several centres, which are nearly as important as the CBD. The nuclei or centres may be for shopping, industry or entertainment.

N.B. No settlements fit these patterns perfectly. However, many settlements do show aspects of these patterns very clearly.

Think of ways to find the edge of the CBD.

Figure 10.5 The multiple nuclei pattern

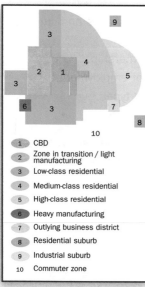

1. CBD
2. Zone in transition / light manufacturing
3. Low-class residential
4. Medium-class residential
5. High-class residential
6. Heavy manufacturing
7. Outlying business district
8. Residential suburb
9. Industrial suburb
10. Commuter zone

Census data for urban wards can help to identify the inner city.

Land use in the Central Business District

Competition makes land prices high in the CBD. The CBD contains the main retail and commercial premises, covered shopping arcades, pedestrianised areas, major public buildings and administrative headquarters. Shops sell high-order goods, and high-rise buildings are present. There is a high daytime population, but few people live there. Land use and buildings are continually changing in the CBD. The congested CBD faces competition from out-of-town centres. The CBD is known as '**downtown**' in the United States.

> **KEY POINT**
>
> Greenfield sites are undeveloped open land. Brownfield sites are vacant or under-used land that has been built on and is ready for redevelopment.

Land use in the inner city

The land around the CBD is called '**the inner city**', the 'twilight zone' or 'zone of transition'. In this zone there are derelict old factories and poor terraced housing, often built in the 19th Century. Some of these 'brownfield' sites are being replaced by CBD buildings, large warehouses or new housing, roads and railways. During the period of redevelopment they become temporary car parks.

Many people living in the inner city suffer deprivation (unemployment, overcrowding, crime, and pollution). Government policies have tried to redevelop, renew, rehabilitate and gentrify these problem areas, e.g. Hulme in Manchester and Toxteth in Liverpool.

Land use in the suburbs

Housing is expensive in the suburbs, but much of it was built over 60 years ago and is now deteriorating.

Away from the CBD, land prices fall. Houses (mainly detached and semi-detached) and gardens become bigger and people there can use their car or public transport to get to work or the city centre.

As population and mobility increased, cities sprawled, initially along the main roads and railways, over the surrounding countryside. Factories and offices have moved from the inner urban area to 'greenfield' sites in the suburbs near to motorways or ring roads.

Many local authorities moved people from the inner areas to large council estates in the suburbs. Some of these have become problem areas. People living in the suburbs tend to segregate into areas of similar class, income or ethnic background.

The country ring

> **KEY POINT**
>
> **Counter-urbanisation** is the movement of people and economic activity out of larger settlements into the surrounding countryside and towns.

Land values are lower in these areas. Since the 1970s, housing, commerce and industry have moved out of the urban area to the settlements in the countryside. This is called **counter-urbanisation**. Quality of life is better in these areas as there is more space and less congestion, crime, vandalism and pollution.

Land use in settlements in LEDCs

The concentric zone and sector models were developed from studies of settlements in North America. They have been changed for cities in LEDCs.

The function of the CBD remains the same as in the MEDC city. However, much of the area will be redeveloped with modern high-rise blocks, shopping malls, hotels and apartments. The area is very busy and at times chaotic with heavy traffic and street sellers crowding the pavements.

The area may contain one or two older buildings in an unusual style that are relics of a colonial past. A central square may contain an impressive former colonial administrative building including the law courts, a large church or cathedral and the apartments of former colonial administrators.

The **inner zone** contains middle-class and high-class housing. There will also be blocks of flats for the working class. Some self-built housing will be found in this area. The **outer zone** includes large houses and bungalows for the rich as well as squatter settlements. To increase security some people live in walled suburbs with a guard at the gate.

Industry is to be found along transport routes into or around the urban area. This may be in new large factories or rundown former houses that have become workshops.

Figure 10.6 The pattern of land use in an LEDC urban area

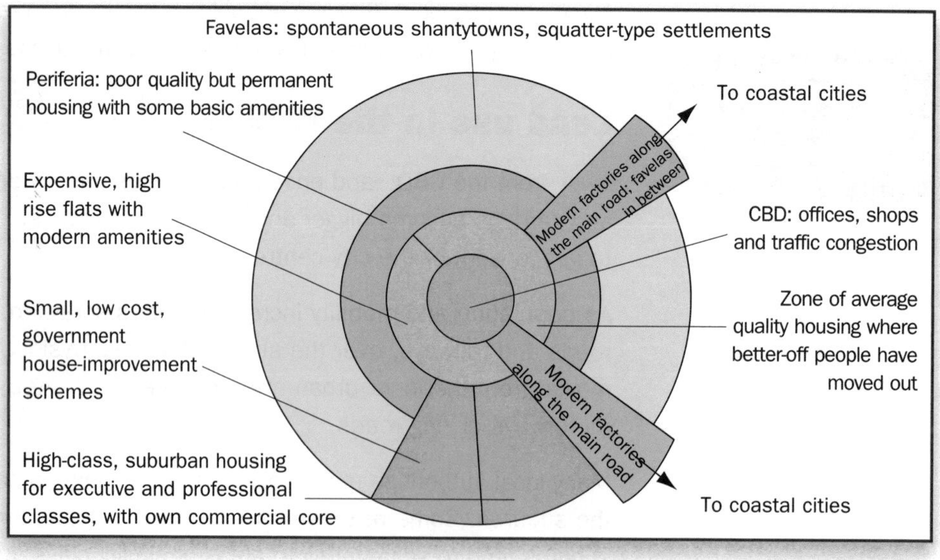

Favelas: spontaneous shantytowns, squatter-type settlements

Periferia: poor quality but permanent housing with some basic amenities

To coastal cities

Expensive, high rise flats with modern amenities

CBD: offices, shops and traffic congestion

Modern factories along the main road, favelas in between

Small, low cost, government house-improvement schemes

Zone of average quality housing where better-off people have moved out

Modern factories along the main road

High-class, suburban housing for executive and professional classes, with own commercial core

To coastal cities

Shanty towns (called squatter settlements in some countries or *favelas* in Sao Paulo in Brazil) are found around larger settlements in LEDCs. They are illegal and house the poor, with other poor people arriving from rural areas. The residents are squatters who have no legal rights.

Housing is primitive, made of plywood and scrap metal, sometimes with only one room where a whole family eats and sleeps. Few houses have electricity, toilets or running water. Rubbish collection is unreliable and disease and crime are frequently found there. Many of the streets are alleyways lined with informal businesses, workshops and houses.

Factors affecting land use in settlements

AQA A	✓
AQA B	✗
EDEXCEL A	✓
EDEXCEL B	✗
OCR A	✓
OCR B	✓
WJEC A	✗
WJEC B	✓
CCEA	✓

What factors influence the arrangements of **land-use zones** in a settlement? An answer to this question allows planners to rearrange the land use in an attempt to improve the quality of life of the people.

The factors influencing land use in settlements include...
- accessibility
- competition for land
- the mixing of land uses
- the specialised needs of certain land uses.

Access

The location of transport routes makes some places in the settlement more accessible than others. For example, bus and tram routes allowed the countryside to become accessible because people no longer had to walk to work and the suburbs developed.

Shops are located in very accessible places. This means the CBD, at ground floor level, is dominated by shops. However, as congestion has increased, larger shops have moved to the edges of settlements to retain their accessibility and provide space for car travellers to park.

Another example of **accessibility** is housing that was built next to factories. This still happens in some countries, e.g. Singapore. In the UK, industry has moved to more accessible locations on ring roads and motorways where it is closer to settlements. People travel to these industrial estates by car.

> Remember examples of these factors and mention that they can change. For example, the London Docklands became redundant, but has been revived as a financial services and newspaper printing area.

Competition for land

Competition for land is at its highest in the CBD due to the good accessibility. Access is high because the centre is often the focus of rail and bus routes. As a result, land prices rise. **High rents** mean that only national chain stores, financial services, hotels and offices can afford the rents. Oxford Street and Regent Street in London and Fifth Avenue in New York are good examples.

A sign of the competition for each piece of land is the presence of **high-rise office blocks**. This means each piece of land can be used several times. Further from the town centre rents fall and residential users are able to compete. At the edge of the settlement, where land prices are lower, people can afford larger plots of land for their detached houses.

> **KEY POINT**
>
> In some CBDs, the competition for land has fallen because of out-of-town centres. This has caused a decline of the CBD; shops have become empty or occupied by temporary bargain stores or charity shops.

Mixing of land uses

Some land uses do not mix. It is unlikely that high-income residential areas will be found close to heavy industry or airports. On the other hand industries that need a large labour force, such as the clothing industry, which requires large amounts of female labour, tend to locate near to large housing estates. Pressure on land means that some new developments do mix unsuitable land uses. For example, new housing is built alongside new bypass roads, but the houses have double-glazing and high fences to deflect the noise.

Specialised needs

Good examples of specialised needs include…
- shipyards on deep-water estuaries
- airports on extensive areas of flatter land
- warehouses and distribution depots near to motorway interchanges.

Industry and employment

In the UK, manufacturing industry has declined whilst service industries have grown to become the main employer. Service industries tend to locate either in the CBD or on Business Parks at the edge of the settlement. These new locations have high quality environments, large areas of parkland and fountains as well as air-conditioned premises.

> **PROGRESS CHECK**
>
> 1. No settlements ever match an urban land use pattern perfectly. Why is it useful to study these urban land use patterns?
> 2. How can census data for small areas in a settlement be helpful to town planners?
> 3. Why is housing so expensive in the suburbs when land values are lower there?
>
> 1. Matching the pattern suggests a general explanation. Variations from the pattern suggest local factors. 2. The data shows areas of deprivation and other groups with special needs. It also assesses housing quality. 3. Tends to be on larger plots of land with bigger houses. Demand is high, especially from families with more than one wage earner.

11 Urbanisation

The following topics are covered in this chapter:

- **Urban growth and urbanisation**
- **Urban problems and planned solutions**

11.1 Urban growth and urbanisation

LEARNING SUMMARY

After studying this section you should be able to understand:

- the causes of urban growth

Urban growth

AQA A	✓
AQA B	✓
EDEXCEL A	✓
EDEXCEL B	✓
OCR A	✓
OCR B	✓
WJEC A	✓
WJEC B	✓
CCEA	✓

In the last 150 years, urban areas have grown rapidly in both population and size through **natural increase** and the **migration** of people from the countryside. Some recent examples of urban population growth are shown in the table below.

City	Population in 1970 (millions)	Population in 2008 (millions)
Greater Mexico City	8.6	19.2
Sao Paulo Metropolitan Area	7.1	19.6
Kolkata (Calcutta)	7.0	13.2

Figure 11.1 Projected urban population growth

Key

1 Africa
2 Asia
3 Europe
4 Latin America
5 North America
6 World
7 MEDC
8 LEDC

N.B. Oceania not included

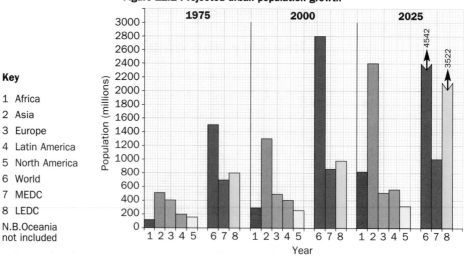

According to UN projections, it was estimated that 50% of the world's population will live in urban areas by the end of 2008 and about 70% will be city dwellers by 2050, with cities and towns in Asia and Africa having the biggest growth.

In 1900, only London and Paris had populations greater than 1 million (called **millionaire cities**). By 2000 there were over 300 millionaire cities.

Megacity	Population (millions)
Beijing	10.7
Buenos Aires	12.6
Cairo	11.1
Delhi	15.0
Dhaka	12.4
Jakarta	13.2
Karachi	11.6
Kolkata (Calcutta)	14.3
Lagos	10.8
Los Angeles	12.3
Manila	10.6
Mexico City	19.4
Moscow	10.7
Mumbai (Bombay)	18.2
New York	18.7
Osaka-Kobe	11.2
Rio de Janeiro	11.4
Sao Paulo	18.2
Shanghai	14.5
Tokyo	35.2

> Finding the total population of a city is difficult because it keeps changing. People come and go and a city boundary changes.

Cities with more than 8 million people used to be called **megacities**. In 1950 there were only 2 megacities – New York and London. By 1990 there were 21 megacities (16 of them were in LEDCs). The definition of a megacity has recently been changed to mean a city that has a population of more than 10 million, and in 2008 there were 19 megacities (14 of them in LEDCs). At current rates of growth there are expected to be 33 megacities by the year 2025, with 27 of them in LEDCs.

The signs are that over the next forty years, cities of 500 000 will grow even faster than the very large cities. At the same time the populations of rural areas are expected to decline. This will occur particularly in Africa and Asia.

Figure 11.2 The world's megacities

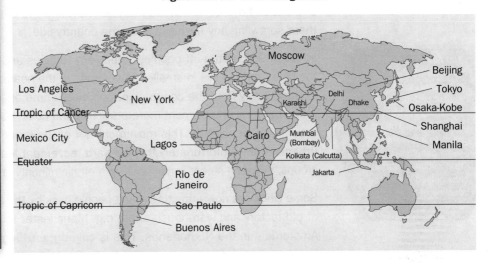

Some countries, especially LEDCs, have one city that is much larger than all the others in the country. This is called a **primate city**. Examples of primate cities, and their second largest cities, include the following:

- Paris has 9.6 million (Marseilles has 1.3 million).
- London has 7 million (Birmingham has 1 million).
- Mexico Central City has 8.6 million (Guadalajara has 1.6 million).
- Bangkok has 7.5 million (Nanthaburi has 481 000).

There are several reasons for the development of primate cities:

- High rural to urban migration.
- The development of a core region containing the main economic activities.
- It is the capital city of a centralised government.
- The capital and a major port are in the same city.

> **KEY POINT**
>
> The words **conurbation** or **megalopolis** are used to describe an urban area where a city has grown to absorb several larger towns, e.g. the Manchester conurbation.

Causes of urban growth

There are three main causes of urbanisation:

- **Rural to urban migration** (see p. 119). This occurred in MEDCs in the past as rural people moved to the new factories, ports and mines found in the urban area. Towns rapidly expanded and became cities. This migration is occurring in LEDCs today as people in rural areas look for jobs, education and health care. Poor harvests, lack of agricultural land and farm mechanisation have also pushed people away from the rural areas.

- **Natural increase** in urban population, which takes place as health care becomes more widely available and medical advances produce a better quality of life and increase life expectancy.
- **The re-drawing of urban boundaries**, which happens as the urban areas expand to house all the people living there.

In the UK, cities spread as public transport was improved. Suburbs of semi-detached houses developed on new housing estates. Light industry provided nearby employment or the new residents could **commute** to the CBD by bus and train. In the 1980s, business parks and out-of-town shopping centres encouraged the sprawl of urban areas. However, since the 1950s, many local authorities have established green belts around the edge of the cities to stop them sprawling any further across the countryside.

> You need to be able to describe suburbanisation, gentrification, green belts and counter-urbanisation. You also need to know why some people suggest that suburbanisation has helped cause the decline of inner city areas.

In the 1990s, better-off people, particularly families and the retired, moved out of the urban area to live in smaller settlements in the nearby countryside. They wanted to move away from the congestion, pollution, crime and noise of urban life. They found the rural environment more attractive and could travel quickly into the urban area if they needed to. This movement out of the urban area is called 'counter-urbanisation'. Unfortunately this outward movement leaves behind lower income groups, including recent in-migrants from ethnic minority groups and the unemployed.

Some cities are now attracting young people back by the imaginative **redevelopment** of old factory and warehouse sites, e.g. Manchester and Leeds in the UK and Amsterdam in the Netherlands. This is called **gentrification**.

> **KEY POINT**
>
> **Urbanisation** is the process that leads to an increased proportion of people living in urban areas. It is taking place in most countries in the world.

Urbanisation

AQA A	✓
AQA B	✓
EDEXCEL A	✓
EDEXCEL B	✓
OCR A	✓
OCR B	✓
WJEC A	✓
WJEC B	✓
CCEA	✓

Urbanisation has been taking place for 200 years, but there has been a dramatic increase in the last 50 years. It began in MEDCs with the Industrial Revolution. Today around 50% of the world's population lives in urban areas.

The table belows shows the proportion of the world's population living in urban areas.

Year	1955	1965	1975	1985	1995	2005	2008	2015
Percentage	30%	34%	37%	40%	44%	48%	50%	52% (estimated)
Number of people (millions)	850	1157	1515	1983	2551	3150	3350	6440 (estimated)

> You need to understand the difference between urban growth (increase in urban area and population) and urbanisation (increased proportion of people living in urban areas).

In MEDCs the rate of urbanisation is slow because the majority of the population already lives in urban areas. In addition, rural areas are more attractive and rates of natural increase in cities are lower. Rates of urbanisation are much higher in LEDCs.

Urbanisation brings advantages and disadvantages. It does mean that more facilities such as education, health care and transport, may develop, but it can also create many problems such as inadequate services and lack of housing and jobs.

11.2 Urban problems and planned solutions

LEARNING SUMMARY	After studying this section you should be able to understand:
	• the problems of urban areas
	• how to recognise some planned solutions to urban problems

Problems caused by rapid urban growth

AQA A	✓
AQA B	✓
EDEXCEL A	✓
EDEXCEL B	✓
OCR A	✓
OCR B	✓
WJEC A	✓
WJEC B	✓
CCEA	✓

KEY POINT

The rapid urban growth of population and city size can cause a whole range of problems.

Housing

Housing is a common problem, because it is often of poor quality, insufficient or too expensive. Where there is not enough housing, prices rise and the poor are forced to live in very low-quality houses. In some LEDC cities, the poor build sub-standard shelters made out of scrap materials, on the edges of urban areas. These **squatter settlements** are called *kampungs* in Jakarta, Indonesia. Land is in short supply and these camps are often built on floodplains (where there is a danger of flooding), steep hillsides (where mudslides occur) or near railways and airports (which can be very noisy).

There are many problems associated with **squatter settlements** including…
- very poor-quality housing
- poor or non-existent water supply
- unreliable electricity, often taken illegally from the mains
- little or no sanitation
- poor drainage for rain and household waste water
- little or no waste collection service and rubbish is dumped on open spaces
- overcrowding and high risk of disease (e.g. tuberculosis)
- little employment because the factories are too far away.

In the UK the lack of affordable housing causes problems. Young people may have to live with their parents or in a poor-quality flat or a damp old terraced house. At its worst people live and sleep in the streets. They cover themselves at night with cardboard and old blankets and on cold, wet nights they sleep in office doorways and hope to get some heat as it escapes from inside the building.

Transport

The M25 motorway around London is sometimes described as the largest car park in the world.

Many urban areas have serious transport problems. Bangkok, in Thailand, is said to have the worst **traffic congestion** in the world. When traffic congestion occurs, average speeds fall and it results in frustration, increasing costs, people being late for work or appointments and falling productivity.

Congestion is mainly the result of...

- the growth of vehicle ownership in recent years, e.g. there has been a 15% annual increase in Indonesia, especially in Jakarta
- poor road layouts especially in rapidly growing LEDCs
- poor public transport with buses and railways unable to keep up with the demand, e.g. trains in Tokyo, Japan and London, and buses in Kolkata (Calcutta), India and Harare (Zimbabwe) are packed during rush hours
- old and worn out rolling stock of public transport (e.g. buses and trains), which breaks down frequently
- breakdowns and accidents, which cause additional delays and congestion as the network reaches capacity.

Unemployment

Many of the people migrating to cities are male. They come to find a job and then ask their families to join them. Many do not have the skills for urban jobs and find themselves unemployed. They join the informal economy and run small businesses providing goods and services. For example, in Beijing, China, they use a bicycle for a delivery business and the pavement as an office. Cheap mobile telephones help.

Pollution

Urban areas suffer problems of **air**, **land**, **water** and **noise pollution**.

Air pollution is caused by **industrial activity** and the **increased numbers** of **vehicles** on roads. These put dust particles and dangerous gases, such as carbon monoxide and sulphur dioxide, into the air. These gases are damaging to health especially for the elderly and those people who have asthma, bronchitis or eye problems. Air pollution increases the dangers of fog and traffic accidents. Los Angeles, Mexico City and Beijing are well known for having high levels of air pollution.

> Make a table with each of these sources of pollution as a row. Then, in two columns, write down a description of the problem and the solution.

Land pollution occurs when domestic and industrial waste is not collected. For example, domestic rubbish is usually collected once a week and its accumulation can cause pollution. In squatter settlements there may be no rubbish collections. Some industrial areas have no way of safely disposing of dangerous wastes, so dump it in open spaces. Official and unofficial landfill sites bring the problem of flies and diseases, e.g. diarrhoea and malaria.

Water pollution can be a problem in urban areas. Rivers and canals can become polluted by domestic and industrial waste. In some LEDCs, only 40% of houses are connected to the sewerage system. Even in some MEDCs, waste material is dumped through long pipes into the sea. This can threaten wildlife and the safe use of tourist beaches.

Noise pollution comes from industry, construction and traffic (including trains, motor vehicles and aircraft). Noise pollution adds to the stress of living in urban areas.

Water Supply

Some urban areas have inadequate water supplies. This is especially true when rainfall is low and the settlement relies on groundwater supplies. Large quantities of water can also be lost through leaking pipes.

The rapid growth of population and industry increases the demand for water, for example in richer areas domestic appliances and swimming pools require more water. It is estimated that water demand increases at three times the rate of population increase.

In the LEDC cities, few people have piped water to their houses. They may have it delivered in water tenders by water sellers or use a communal tap (one tap may serve 500 people and only work for a few hours each day). In the worst cases people have to use polluted wells and open pipes. For example, in some Indian cities clothes are washed in the street from storm water drainage pipes.

The water in many countries may also be of poor quality if water treatment plants cannot cope with demand. Poor water quality brings health threats. In the UK people are buying more bottled water because they dislike the chemical taste of tap water.

Solutions to the problems of urban areas

AQA A	✓
AQA B	✓
EDEXCEL A	✓
EDEXCEL B	✓
OCR A	✓
OCR B	✓
WJEC A	✓
WJEC B	✓
CCEA	✓

KEY POINT

Urban areas have many problems that local and national governments attempt to solve through town and country planning.

Housing

There are **housing problems** in both MEDCs and LEDCs. The solutions in MEDCs have similarities and differences from those in LEDCs.

The main **solutions** to the housing problems in the urban areas of MEDCs include the following:
- Using brownfield sites, e.g. empty houses, former factories, office blocks, flats above shops or railway sidings. This land is often in poor condition and is expensive to restore, but it already has an existing infrastructure and facilities in the town will be within walking distance. It also avoids building on green fields.
- Extending existing towns by adding small suburban estates, often within the line of a newly built bypass.
- Building a small number of houses in several villages by infilling or small developments.
- Building new settlements such as eco-towns and new towns where the entire infrastructure is new and houses can be built to the latest sustainable standards.
- Selecting one key village to be developed to the size of a small town with additional schools, bus routes and all the other services provided.
- Requiring all new developments to have some affordable houses for young people and the less well-off.
- Encouraging groups, such as Housing Associations, to manage properties they have improved for rent.

When a local authority plans to develop housing in an area it consults the people living there and asks for their suggestions. These schemes for housing estates in villages and rural areas usually attract opposition from local people. They are called NIMBYs (Not In My Back Yard) by some people.

The reasons given for opposition can include the following:
- Lack of employment locally.
- Increase in cars travelling on narrow village roads.

- Children travelling to school will cause congestion twice a day.
- The small amount of public transport will not be able to cope.
- The houses will spoil the views and newcomers will not fit socially into the community.

In LEDCs the solutions are different and include the following:

- Discouraging rural to urban migration by improving conditions in rural areas by developing growth poles with jobs, housing, schools and health care. In Indonesia, rural people are supposed to get a permit before moving to an urban area.
- Improving living conditions in squatter settlements by building paved roads and pavements, laying drainage, improving water and electricity supply, building schools, clinics and community facilities. Unfortunately, improvements attract even more people.
- Building subsidised public housing, which may be low-rise, medium-rise or walk-up (e.g. Kuala Lumpur in Malaysia) and high-rise (e.g. Hong Kong and Singapore).
- Encouraging self-help housing through cooperation between the government, local authorities and people. Cheap sites are provided with the basic infrastructure of roads, drainage, water pipes and sewerage systems. People then buy cheap materials to build their own houses under supervision, e.g. South Africa, Zimbabwe and Indonesia.

Find a case study of a planned new housing development in your local area and one in an LEDC, for example, the self-help scheme in Sao Paulo, Brazil (see www.geography-help.co.uk)

Transport

There is a wide range of solutions to the problems created by transport:

- **Building** new roads, widening existing ones or building flyovers, tunnels and bypasses, e.g. in Birmingham, Leeds, Kuala Lumpur (Malaysia), Bangkok (Thailand) and Los Angeles.
- **Maintaining** roads and improving crash barriers, street lighting and coordinated traffic lights.
- **Controlling** the increase in vehicles, by increasing the costs to motorists through taxes on petrol, road taxes, tolls on busy roads and congestion charges (e.g. London). These actions can be very unpopular with voters though.
- **Encouraging** the use of public transport as it is a more efficient use of the available road space. This can be done by subsidising fares or building new and faster transit systems, e.g. the MRT in Singapore, the MTR in Hong Kong, the new tube lines in London, tram systems in Manchester and Sheffield and BART (Bay Area Rapid Transit) in San Francisco.
- **Discouraging** unnecessary travel by making it more expensive, e.g. high costs of parking, taxes to enter restricted zones (Singapore), and encouraging the use of faxes, telephones and electronic mail.

Employment

Service industries have replaced manufacturing as the largest employers in urban areas in MEDC. Jobs are in offices, shops and entertainment. The financial services sector has been a big employer with jobs in banks and building societies. Local authorities, health services and education are also present in urban areas.

In LEDCs tourism is one of the keys to increased employment. Tourists bring foreign currency and demand many services. Many city authorities are allowing the informal sector to grow. Jobs include shoe shiners, street vendors, newspaper sellers, guides, food and drink sellers, taxi drivers, and makers of pottery and crafts, soaps and ornaments.

Pollution

There are several **solutions** that governments can use to counter pollution:

- **Fines** for breakers of environmental laws, e.g. if factories or cars emit more than the allowed level of gases or people litter the streets or discharge chemicals into water sources.
- **Public education** about the causes and consequences of pollution and encouraging people to be more thoughtful, e.g. limited hours for construction working called 'making pollution an individual matter'.
- Improving **waste disposal**, e.g. better sewerage pipes, twice-daily refuse collection in busy cities, provision of plastic sacks and 'wheelie bins'.

Water Supply

The main solutions are...

- investing in the repair and renewal of the existing leaking system of water pipes
- agreeing contracts for supply from areas that have plenty of water
- building more reservoirs to store water
- investing in costly desalinization plants to convert seawater into fresh water
- stopping water pollution at source
- building more water treatment plants
- installing piped water into older housing and replacing lead and steel pipes
- conserving water through education programmes
- saving water by its re-use, e.g. using clothes-washing water to flush toilets
- improving industrial technology in order to recycle water.

A stable government is also able to help reduce the problems. They are able to reduce corruption and unrest, which in turn attracts foreign investors who are attracted by the low wages and lack of trade union activity. Stable governments are also able to obtain foreign aid to repair the infrastructure and provide skills training for the local people. Some city governments have found that when they involve local people in decision making their schemes are more successful.

Urban change in the UK: problems and planned solutions

AQA A	✓
AQA B	✓
EDEXCEL A	✓
EDEXCEL B	✓
OCR A	✓
OCR B	✓
WJEC A	✓
WJEC B	✓
CCEA	✓

> **KEY POINT**
>
> In the UK there are very strong planning laws and controls that help solve the urban problems.

The regeneration of cities

In the 1960s, the areas around the centres of cities in the UK had many problems, e.g. cramped and poor-quality housing, growing unemployment and deprived inner cities.

The first round of plans to solve the problems, called **comprehensive redevelopment**, involved urban **redevelopment** or **renewal**. Slum clearance took place and many terraced houses were demolished. Clearance spread beyond the inner city to include the older suburbs. The people living in these areas were re-housed in new estates on the outskirts or in tower blocks in the inner city. Sheffield, Birmingham and Newcastle build this type of estate. However, these new inner city estates became problem areas as the blocks were poorly built,

The census of population measures deprivation including overcrowding, single parent families, people living alone, unemployment, lack of basic housing facilities and no car.

A good case study is Hulme in Manchester where the 1970s blocks of the 'Crescents' have been replaced by low-rise family housing. People are now moving to live in Hulme. Gardens flourish, schools are doing well, and people owning their houses here can work in the nearby city.

communities were disrupted and crime grew. The tower blocks did not have any sense of community, they were noisy, insecure with dangerous dark corners in stairwells and the lifts and communal central heating frequently did not work.

Later schemes **rehabilitated** older properties by including damp-proofing, central heating, bathrooms, new doors and window frames, spaces for parking and parks. Some of the tower blocks were demolished and low-rise blocks turned into houses with gardens.

Several governments have introduced other schemes to help the people still living in the **inner city**. These include taking the views of local people and having more provision for job creation and community activities.

Governments have noted that there are large areas of unused and derelict land in cities (**brownfield land**). Developers are encouraged to redevelop this land rather than use greenfield sites.

By the 21st century the efforts of planners from 1960 to 1990 to improve inner city areas needed to start again as the repaired and new buildings reached the ends of their lives. Landlords and people living temporarily in these areas had not spent money on their properties. There was still a demand for housing and employment near to the city centre, but crime and problems in the ethnic communities living in these areas was growing. The cities of Manchester, Glasgow, Birmingham and Leicester all made massive efforts to renew these areas.

One famous scheme is the **London Docklands**. This was a government scheme that regenerated the area back to effective use. The scheme included...
* reclaiming derelict land
* building new roads, the Docklands Light Railway and London City Airport
* new water, gas and electricity services
* building office blocks, e.g. Canary Wharf
* creating many new jobs
* building new homes and refurbishing older ones to increase the resident population
* constructing new shopping facilities and a technology college
* planting over 100 000 trees.

The scheme has been criticised for failing to meet the needs of the local people. The homes provided were expensive and the jobs were in financial services and high-tech industries and so were unsuited to local low-skilled people. But, the Docklands has become a major tourist attraction with its mixture of very modern high-rise architecture, restored warehouses, old public houses and restaurants, art galleries, guided walks, hotels, a major sports centre that will be part of the Olympics and waterside views.

Since the 1990s, some run-down areas of cities have become fashionable places to live. The old houses have been bought cheaply and renovated by a wealthier middle class. This is called **gentrification**. The areas chosen usually have good access to office jobs in the CBD.

> **KEY POINT**
>
> **Sustainability** is a new term in many GCSE courses. It means acting today so that the lives of future generations will not be disadvantaged by your actions.

Sustainability and urban planning

The sustainable management of urban areas needs careful planning. It means balancing the demands on the environment, the lives of people and the economy.

Planners for sustainable urban areas have to think about the following:
- New housing needs (every area of England has a target set by the government).
- Reusing derelict and disused sites in urban areas to regenerate the area.
- Planning for public transport to reduce car use, e.g. reducing car parking spaces in urban areas (Cambridge), allowing space for Park and Ride Schemes (Stratford upon Avon), congestion charging (London), urban tramways (Manchester) and bus-only lanes (Birmingham).
- Designing new buildings that demand less energy.
- Making more green spaces with parks and green areas near houses and industry (Sheffield and Ashford).
- Selecting sites that are not environmentally vulnerable, e.g. checking local geology, heritage sites, areas of flood risk, made ground or old refuse tips that are unstable.

Some governments (e.g. the UK, China, New Zealand, Canada and Sweden) are planning **eco-cities** that are environmentally friendly and sustainable.

Government planning for urban areas in LEDCs

AQA A	✓
AQA B	✓
EDEXCEL A	✗
EDEXCEL B	✗
OCR A	✓
OCR B	✓
WJEC A	✓
WJEC B	✓
CCEA	✓

A number of LEDC governments have planned schemes to ease the problems they have in cities. These schemes include the following:
- **Brasilia**, the new capital city of Brazil completed in the 1960s, to act as a growth pole to pull development away from the cities of Rio de Janeiro and São Paulo in the south-east of the country. Whilst the city has had some success, there is still heavy pressure on the older cities.
- **New towns** have been built in Singapore and Egypt to divert growth from Singapore City and Cairo. They have been successful in re-housing people from the overcrowded areas in the main city.
- **Eco-cities** are planned for Dongtan (China), Curitiba (Brazil) and near Kampala in Uganda.
- **Growth poles** have been established in rural areas to reduce the push factors driving people into the cities. This strategy has been used in LEDCs such as Brazil, Venezuela and Madagascar.

Despite these efforts, the problems of large cities in LEDCs continue to grow. Successes are overtaken by more people arriving in the urban area.

PROGRESS CHECK

1. Describe the pattern of megacities.
2. Define suburbanisation and counter-urbanisation.
3. How do planned eco-cities deliver sustainability?

1. Many in S.E. Asia, coastal areas of the USA, only 1 in Africa, scattered in Europe and none in Australia. 2. Suburbanisation describes the movement of people outwards from the centre of settlements to the surrounding residential areas within the urban area. Counter-urbanisation involves people moving away from urban areas to smaller towns, a new estate, a commuter town or a village. 3. They must balance the demands on the environment, the lives of people and the economy today without damaging the needs of people tomorrow. This includes planning for housing and employment, reusing derelict land, reducing private car use, less waste, providing green spaces and recognising special local features.

12 The management of energy and resources

The following topics are covered in this chapter:

- Resources and energy
- Alternative sources of energy

12.1 Resources and energy

LEARNING SUMMARY

After studying this section you should be able to understand:

- how to define renewable and non-renewable resources
- the main sources of energy and their alternatives
- how pollution and global warming are caused
- how to define sustainable development

What resources are

AQA A	✗
AQA B	✗
EDEXCEL A	✓
EDEXCEL B	✓
OCR A	✗
OCR B	✗
WJEC A	✓
WJEC B	✓
CCEA	✓

When something is used from the Earth it becomes a **resource**. For example, petroleum and uranium only became resources when mankind started to use them.

Just as materials become resources, so the process is reversible as they are replaced by some new resource. Coal has been replaced in many uses by oil.

Resources, energy and fuel

AQA A	✓
AQA B	✗
EDEXCEL A	✓
EDEXCEL B	✓
OCR A	✗
OCR B	✗
WJEC A	✓
WJEC B	✓
CCEA	✓

Energy is used to run machinery and to provide heat and light. Energy is stored in fuels (e.g. oil and coal) or in moving water and wind. Coal and oil are also raw material resources for the chemical industry. Today the main form of energy is electricity, which can be obtained from all of these fuels.

World consumption is growing at a rate equivalent to the UK's entire energy market each year. This adds the equivalent of an entire USA market (currently the world's largest energy consumer) every ten years. However, 2 billion people are still without access to modern energy. As populations and cities grow, access to traditional energy forms becomes difficult, and local environments may be degraded.

The growing demand for resources and energy

AQA A	✓
AQA B	✓
EDEXCEL A	✓
EDEXCEL B	✓
OCR A	✗
OCR B	✗
WJEC A	✓
WJEC B	✓
CCEA	✓

The demand for energy grows as population increases and economic development spreads to more countries. The demand for resources and energy is not evenly spread across the world. MEDCs have only 25% of the world's population, but they consume 80% of the energy produced. Some MEDCs are trying to reduce their energy demand through more efficient motor vehicles, machines and better insulation.

Most LEDCs do not have significant **reserves of energy** of their own, so they get their energy from the efforts of people or animals or through imported fuels. Demand for energy in LEDCs is set to rise as these countries industrialise and more people own cars.

The following are issues relating to increased energy demand:
- Increased demand means that prices rise and this causes the cost of living to increase.
- Countries need to feel that their overseas sources of energy are secure and will not be interrupted by local disputes, civil wars, terrorist action or political actions against them.
- Poor use of existing energy supplies means that some resources could become exhausted.
- Campaigners believe that the oil companies are protecting their businesses by not investing in alternative sources (the oil companies deny this).
- Policies relating to energy use should include planning for the future.
- Some developing countries need more energy if they are to provide a standard of living that matches that of people living in the western world (e.g. 1.6 billion people in LEDCs lack electricity).

The International Energy Agency estimates that by 2030 the world energy demand will increase by 45%. That equates to an equivalent of 100 million barrels of oil a day – on top of the 240 million barrels of oil equivalent a day currently consumed.

> Make a list of renewable and non-renewable resources. Be clear in your mind which resources could fit in either group.

Renewable and non-renewable resources and energy

Renewable resources include trees, fish, oxygen, fresh water, biomass, hydro-electric, solar, wind, wave, geothermal and tidal power. These resources do not become exhausted if managed in the right way.

Non-renewable resources include coal, oil, gas and minerals. Some were formed millions of years ago and are known as fossil fuels. These resources can become exhausted and currently about 95% of the world's energy supply comes from non-renewable sources.

Some resources can be thought of as renewable and non-renewable.
- Wood can be used for fuel and trees can be replanted, but in reality the LEDCs cut trees for fuel but do not replant them, so the resource becomes non-renewable.
- Soil is renewable if it is farmed properly, but poor management can cause it to become infertile.
- Nuclear power is non-renewable, but the current levels of reserves will last at least 1000 years.

> **KEY POINT**
>
> Energy resources are vital to the development of a country.

Energy, resources and their management

AQA A	✓
AQA B	✓
EDEXCEL A	✓
EDEXCEL B	✓
OCR A	✗
OCR B	✗
WJEC A	✓
WJEC B	✗
CCEA	✓

> UK coal production is less than consumption and about one third of the coal used is imported. The UK has large coal reserves in Yorkshire, Derbyshire, Nottinghamshire and Scotland. Large reserves and production are found in China, the USA, South Africa, Australia and India.

Coal

Coal is a sedimentary rock formed by the compression of trees and plants millions of years ago. It used to be the main fuel for industry, especially for iron and steel making and for heating homes. Today it's mainly used in power stations to produce electricity. It contributes about 25% of the world's energy supplies.

All the continents (except South America) have large coal reserves. China is the fastest growing area for the use of coal. Coal is not normally transported between countries. There are over 150 years of coal reserves left, but the cost of mining makes many areas uneconomic at the moment.

The main features of the **coal mining** industry include the following:
- It can be mined underground (shaft mining) or on the surface (open-cast).
- There are still at least 150 years of reserves for this relatively efficient fuel.
- Coal mines create pollution (visual, noise and air).
- Mining can be dangerous and accidents do occur.
- Coal is bulky and costly to transport.
- Burning coal can create acid rain and adds to global warming through the release of carbon dioxide and methane.

Figure 12.1 An oil field

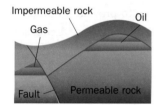

Oil and Natural Gas

Oil and natural gas are found in pockets beneath a layer of impermeable rock. They were formed from tiny sea creatures buried millions of years ago. Major oil fields are found in the Middle East (e.g. Saudi Arabia and Kuwait), Alaska, Iraq, Iran and Russia. Natural gas is found in Russia, the USA and Canada, and in smaller amounts in Venezuela, Chile, Australia, Mexico and many countries of S.E. Asia.

The main features of the **oil** and **gas industry** include the following:
- The industry is run by global companies, e.g. Mobil, BP and Shell, who explore, extract, refine, transport (often by oil tankers and pipelines), and market petroleum products.
- The Governments of countries where large reserves are found control the production level of oil and natural gas.
- Petroleum, refined from oil, is the raw material for many chemical products, including pharmaceuticals, solvents, fertilizers, pesticides and plastics.
- Oil is the world's major source of energy and is vital to the industries and ways of life in all countries.
- Both fuels can be burned in power stations to produce electricity.
- The fuels are extracted by drilling wells.
- Drilling can be dangerous in difficult environments such as Alaska and the North Sea, e.g. due to explosions and fire.
- Drilling in the North Sea takes place from massive oil rigs.
- Oil and natural gas are transported using pipelines and massive sea-going tankers (i.e. they are easier to transport than coal).
- Burning these fuels produces fewer greenhouse gases than burning coal.
- Serious environmental damage is caused if a pipeline breaks or a tanker is grounded, e.g. the *Exxon Valdez* in 1989.
- Developing an oil or natural gas resource creates wealth in the area.

- Oil has become a political weapon with the oil-producing and oil-exporting countries (OPEC) limiting supplies to maintain higher prices.
- Large reserves of oil are often found in politically unstable areas, e.g. Iraq.

It is difficult to predict when oil supplies will run out because...
- countries are secretive about their reserves
- ways of extraction are improving all the time, so some known sources that cannot be used at the moment may become available in the future
- demand varies greatly and production can be reduced
- new sources are being found.

Current predictions are that oil will be available beyond 2050.

Nuclear energy

Nuclear energy is stored in uranium atoms. It is released as heat, which turns water into steam that drives turbines creating electricity. Energy in a nuclear station is created when neutrons strike uranium 235. Nuclear energy is seen as the source of energy for the future.

Accidents (e.g. Five-Mile Island, Pennsylvania in 1979 and Chernobyl, Russia in 1986) caused many people to question its use. One problem is how to safely decommission a power station at the end of its life.

The UK has 19 nuclear stations including Hinckley in Devon, Sizewell in Suffolk, Hunterston near Glasgow, Dungeness in Kent, Dounreay in the north of Scotland and Wylfa on Anglesey. These stations generate 20% of our energy needs (oil and gas is about 36% and coal 38%).

France has few fossil fuel resources, so has turned to nuclear power. EDF (Electricite de France) produces 87% of the country's electricity and it exports to several European countries including the UK. There are 59 nuclear plants in France and 2 more are planned. Globally, there are about 500 nuclear reactors, which produce nearly 20% of the world's energy supply.

Views are divided on the future for nuclear power. The technology has the ability to create almost unlimited cheap power with relatively low environmental risks. Those against nuclear power point to the accidents, the dangers of military use (e.g. Iran and North Korea), its inflexibility to meet peak demand and the problems of nuclear waste disposal. Current UK policy is for a new generation of reactors to be on line by 2017.

The main characteristics of the nuclear industry include the following:
- Uranium reserves will last for many years.
- Refined uranium is relatively easy to transport.
- Power station sites do not need to be located near to the raw material source.
- Nuclear stations need large amounts of water and so tend to be located near to coasts or estuaries.
- Nuclear power stations do not produce any greenhouse gases.
- It is easier for countries with low fossil fuel reserves to import small amounts of uranium to set up power stations.
- There are public concerns about the safety of nuclear power in terms of the transport of fuel and local radiation effects.
- Nuclear waste remains radioactive and dangerous for many hundreds of years.

China and India as well as some LEDCs are developing nuclear energy sites.

> Make sure you are able to list the advantages and disadvantages of using nuclear power.

12.2 Alternative sources of energy

LEARNING SUMMARY

After studying this section you should be able to understand:

- the need for alternative sources of renewable energy such as hydro-electric, wind, solar, geothermal and wave power
- how pollution and global warming are caused
- how to define sustainable development

Renewable sources of energy

AQA A	✓
AQA B	✓
EDEXCEL A	✓
EDEXCEL B	✓
OCR A	✗
OCR B	✗
WJEC A	✗
WJEC B	✗
CCEA	✓

Using fossil fuels for energy harms the environment and these fuels will run out. Nuclear energy is an unpopular source of power. For these reasons, governments and non-governmental organisations (NGOs) are developing alternative sources of power. They aim to find and harness efficient, cleaner and more permanent sources of power. The main alternative sources of energy are hydro-electricity, wind, sun (solar power), waves and tides.

Hydro-electric power (HEP)

Hydro-electric power comes from moving water as it passes over a waterfall (e.g. Niagara Falls) or is released from behind a dam (Kariba Dam, Zambia). The water drives turbines that generate electricity. Good sites for HEP stations are steep-sided valleys or gorges cut in strong impermeable rock in areas of reliable rainfall. The huge dam on the Yangtse (China) in its gorge section has been criticised for the environmental damage it caused because so many people had to lose their homes.

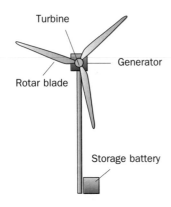

Figure 12.2 Cross-section of an HEP station

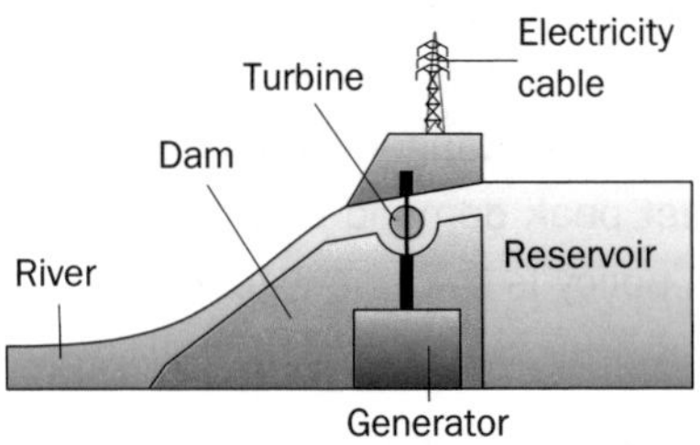

Figure 12.3 A wind turbine

The main characteristics of hydro-electric power include the following:
- No greenhouse gases are produced.
- Once the dam is constructed, it provides relatively cheap electricity.
- The dam controls the flow of water and can be used to prevent flooding downstream.
- Lakes behind the dam can be used for recreation and wildlife sanctuaries.
- The dam is expensive to build and often difficult to access.
- A large area of land may be flooded and people displaced (e.g. the Volta Dam in Ghana).
- The reservoir lake behind the dam can slowly silt up.

Wind Power

Electricity-generating **wind turbines** are found along the Dutch, Danish and German North Sea Coasts. UK wind turbines are mainly located in North Wales and the Lake District. Objectors to wind power say wind turbines create visual and noise pollution and are a danger to birds. Offshore **wind farms** are being built where the winds are stronger and noise is not a problem. Wind is unreliable so wind farms have to be supported by a regular source of electricity.

The main characteristics of wind power include the following:

- The electricity produced is cheap and does not cause air pollution.
- Sites can take a small number of turbines, which may serve a few houses or several hundred (individual houses can have their own turbine).
- Windy sites are unfortunately often in attractive upland areas.
- Turbines are noisy for people living nearby.
- Large numbers of turbines would be needed to generate enough electricity to make any major impact on the demand for electricity (fossil fuels produce far greater energy).

Solar Power

Greenhouses and conservatories are examples of where **solar power** is used to create warmth. To produce solar power, a panel containing light-sensitive cells is exposed to **sunlight**. The cells can be used to heat water or to convert the sunlight into electricity.

The main features of solar power include the following:

- It is mobile and is used to power electronic equipment.
- Satellites and other space stations use solar power to extend their effective lives.
- Its use is limited by night and by clouds.
- The technology is only 15% efficient at converting sunlight into energy although every day the Earth receives about 20 000 times more energy from the sun than it needs.
- Solar power is being used in the UK to heat radiators and water in individual houses, to power roadside warning signs and to monitor pipelines for oil, gas and water.

Power can also be generated from the tides and geothermal sources.

Managing resources to help sustainability

AQA A	✓
AQA B	✓
EDEXCEL A	✓
EDEXCEL B	✓
OCR A	✓
OCR B	✓
WJEC A	✓
WJEC B	✓
CCEA	✓

Demand for energy and resources continue to grow. A growing population and higher standards of living add to the demand. Some energy sources and resources are being depleted. For the long term future, **sustainable management** needs to take place.

The consequences of increased resource use

Social consequences:
- Increased gap between rich and poor.
- Growing dangers to health.
- Demand for energy rises in order to run 'essentials' such as cars and air conditioning.

Economic consequences:
- Increases in prices as energy resources are depleted.
- Increases in costs for exploration, development and production.
- Need to find finance to develop renewable sources.

Environmental consequences:
- Global warming.
- More pollution, danger of more accidents.
- Fragile vegetation areas under threat, e.g. ice caps and forests.

Political consequences:
- Need for international co-operation.
- Changing power structure as energy-rich nations emerge.
- Public protests and lost votes when fuel prices rise.

Sustainable development

Sustainable development meets the needs of the present generation whilst retaining our ability to meet the needs of future generations.

Sustainable development takes place through...
- conservation
- resource substitution
- recycling
- use of appropriate technology
- pollution control
- using renewable energy sources
- international action by groups of countries
- lower consumption of energy through better insulation
- using fluorescent light tubes
- using smaller cars, cycling and using public transport.

Some planners in the UK include actions to ensure a settlement survives and is sustained. For example, they want to build affordable houses for families with children of school age in a village where the school is threatened with closure.

Ways of using energy and managing development in a more sustainable way

Examples of **sustainable development**:
- The use of brownfield land rather than green fields for new housing, factories and business parks.
- Building house and flats that include wall and roof insulation, solar panel and recycled materials.
- The farming of forests so that more trees are planted than are being removed.
- The imposition of quotas on sea fishing.
- The provision of cycle tracks in urban areas.
- Improvements in electrically-driven public transport.
- Park-and-ride schemes (this is disputed by some who feel they encourage car use).
- Organic farming using manure rather than chemical fertilisers.
- The use of alternative energy sources instead of fossil fuels.

PROGRESS CHECK

1. What is the difference between renewable and non-renewable resources?
2. Suggest reasons for the lack of popularity for the development of nuclear power.
3. Describe and explain what is meant by sustainable development.

1. A natural resource is called a **renewable resource** if it is replaced by natural processes as quickly as it is used by humans and other natural processes. Solar radiation, tides, winds and hydro-electricity are **renewable resources**. Wood and paper are renewable resources if replanting keeps pace with harvesting. A non-renewable resource is a natural resource that is not produced at a rate equal to that at which it is used. Coal, petroleum and natural gas are examples. 2. Accidents, difficulties with disposal of waste, dangers in transporting fuel, possible health risks near nuclear power stations. 3. Sustainable development meets the needs of the present generation and retains our ability to meet the needs of future generations.

13.1 Understanding farming

LEARNING SUMMARY

After studying this section you should be able to understand:

● farming as a system
● how to locate the different types of farming in the UK
● the factors affecting farming
● how to describe different types of farming

Farming as a system

AQA A	✗
AQA B	✗
EDEXCEL A	✓
EDEXCEL B	✗
OCR A	✗
OCR B	✗
WJEC A	✓
WJEC B	✗
CCEA	✗

Agriculture is part of **primary industry** that also includes fishing, mining and forestry.

Each type of farming can be described as a system with inputs, processes and outputs (see Figure 13.1).

Figure 13.1 Systems diagram of agricultural activity

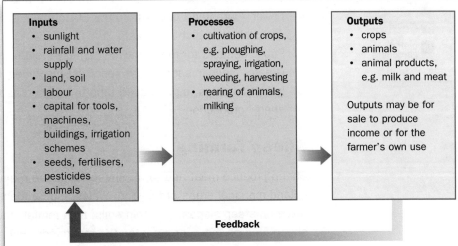

Feedback from the system:

● Outputs produce profit for use on the farm
● Experience determines next year's decisions
● News from the government (NFU and DEFRA) and media suggests changes
● Some output is retained as animal feed

Distribution of the main farming types in the UK

> **KEY POINT**
>
> Each area of the UK has several types of farm, though one type will tend to be dominant.

It will be helpful if you know case studies of two of these types of farming.

Figure 13.2 The main farming types in the UK

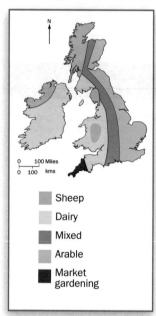

- Sheep
- Dairy
- Mixed
- Arable
- Market gardening

Dairy farming

Dairy farming involves the rearing or purchase of cattle for milk. This farming is found in south-western England, lowland areas of Wales and Lancashire. Dairy farmers prefer fertile, well-drained soils that produce high quality grass. Dairy farms supply dairies for the production of milk products. Milk production has been subsidised since 1945, but quotas restrict the amount.

Since 1960 the number of dairy farms has decreased by 80%, but the remaining farms are bigger. Milk production has not fallen because...

- farmers use silage as winter feed rather than hay
- milking machinery has become more efficient
- larger farms are more efficient (the average is 65 hectares with 70 cows)
- new barns are drier and help the cattle to stay healthy.

Arable farming

Arable farmers produce crops such as wheat and barley, vegetables and oil seed rape for cash. They are mainly found in eastern England, including Norfolk and Lincolnshire, and eastern Scotland. They use large machinery and prefer flatter land.

There have been several changes on arable farms:

- The end of set aside payments from the EU and more organic farms.
- Lower guaranteed prices from the EU to make arable farmers more competitive in global markets.
- Public demand for more environmentally friendly farming practices.
- Greater mechanisation, with specialist machinery that is often hired.
- Industrial crops, e.g. oil seed rape to be used as fuel for alternative energy production.

Sheep farming

Sheep produce meat and wool. Sheep farms are mainly family-run and found in upland marginal areas of England, Wales and Scotland. Sheep farming can take place on steep slopes, with thin soils, high rainfall and low temperatures. The sheep feed on the poor grass on the moorlands. Hill sheep farmers receive subsidies from the EU and some farmers earn income from tourists. The lambs produced each spring go to lowland farms for fattening for meat.

The main characteristics of sheep farming:

- Prices for the sale of sheep (especially lambs) are very low.
- Costs of labour and feed are rising.
- Outbreaks of disease have undermined confidence in the industry.
- Sheep farmers are being urged to change, e.g. to encourage tourists.

Market Gardening

Market gardening is **intensive** farming. It produces high quality crops of fruit, salad, vegetables and flowers for sale to supermarkets, smaller greengrocers and the public. Market gardens are found in Cornwall and Devon, the Isles of Scilly, the Vale of Evesham and the Fens. Farms may be very small and use heated glasshouses, artificial soils and irrigation to obtain a high quality output, which is taken to markets in refrigerated lorries.

Market gardening originated close to urban areas in order to quickly supply perishable food to people living in the cities who did not have gardens. A recent trend has been towards producing more organic crops.

Factors affecting farming

AQA A	✓
AQA B	✗
EDEXCEL A	✓
EDEXCEL B	✓
OCR A	✗
OCR B	✓
WJEC A	✗
WJEC B	✗
CCEA	✗

Farmers decide what to grow, what animals to keep, the level and type of inputs and the methods they will use. Their decisions are based upon social, economic and environmental factors. Their attitudes and level of knowledge are also important.

Social and economic factors

Social and economic factors are **human factors**. They include labour, capital, technology, markets and political factors.

> The importance each factor carries varies from farm to farm. Try to find out how each one influences a farm near you.

Labour:
- In MEDCs, labour is skilled but expensive, e.g. in the UK, Japan and Canada. Farmers buy or hire machinery to save labour costs.
- In the UK, part-time employment on farms is increasing, the proportion of farmers over 65 is increasing and wages are below national averages.
- In LEDCs, labour is cheap and plentiful and many farms are labour intensive, e.g. India, China and Java. Today, more farmers in LEDCs are using machinery. This creates rural unemployment and the workers migrate to cities to find work.

Capital (finance):
- Capital, the money the farmer has to invest in the farm, can be used to increase the amount of inputs into the farm, e.g. machinery, fences, seeds, fertiliser and renewing buildings.
- If a farmer can afford to invest capital, yields will rise, which will create greater profits that can be used for more investment.
- Sources of capital are available from the government and EU.

Technology:
- Machines (e.g. stronger horse-powered tractors) and irrigation are two types of technology that can increase yields.
- Glasshouses, with computer-controlled technology, provide ideal conditions for growing high quality crops.
- Genetic engineering has allowed new plants to be bred that are drought and disease-resistant and give higher yields.
- In LEDCs the majority of farm output is by labourers.
- Machines replace labour and can work longer at peak times such as harvest, do the dirty and heavy jobs and help keep a smaller number of skilled farm staff.

Markets:

- Farmers grow crops that are in demand and they change to meet new demands, e.g. rubber plantation farmers in Malaysia have switched to oil palm as the demand for rubber has fallen.
- Markets vary throughout the year and farmers change to suit them.
- Some producers run their own Farmers Market in order to cut out the middle man, improve prices, be in contact with the public eating their produce, reduce transport and packaging costs and help small producers.
- Farming is in crisis in the UK because the costs of production are higher than the prices consumers want to pay.
- Farmers need a thriving mix of food-purchasing outlets (e.g. local shops, farm shops, farmers markets and supermarkets). One route should never dominate the market.

Government:

- Governments influence the crops farmers grow through regulations, subsidies and quotas. In the UK the Common Agricultural Policy of the EU is important.
- Governments offer advice, training and finance to farmers. In new farming areas they may build the infrastructure of roads and drainage, e.g. Amazonia.
- In some countries, e.g. Kenya and Malaysia, the government is trying to help nomadic farmers to settle in one place.
- Some governments plan and fund land reclamation and improvement schemes. For example, in the UK farmers receive payments if they maintain hedgerows and land around their fields so that wildlife is encouraged.

Environmental factors

Environmental factors are **physical factors**. They include climate, relief and soil.

Climate:

- Temperature (minimum 6°C for crops to grow) and rainfall (at least 250 to 500mm) influences the types of crops that can be grown, e.g. hot, wet tropical areas favour rice, while cooler, drier areas favour wheat.
- The length of the **growing season** also influences the crops grown, e.g. wheat needs 90 days. Some rice-growing areas have two or three crops per year.
- Climate change is affecting agriculture, the crops, livestock, weeds and pests as well as pressing farmers to reduce their output of greenhouse gases.
- The demand for alternative energy sources is influencing the crops being grown, e.g. cereals and oil seed rape for fuel.

Relief:

- Lowlands, such as floodplains, are good for crops.
- Steep slopes hinder machinery and have thinner soils; lower, more gentle slopes are less prone to soil erosion. For example, Hill sheep farms are found on the upland areas of Wales and the Lake District.
- Tea and coffee crops prefer the well-drained soil on hill slopes.
- Temperature decreases by 6.5°C for every 1000 metres gained in height.
- South-facing slopes receive more sunlight.

Soil:

- Soil fertility is improved by using fertilisers, but too much causes damage to the soil and rivers.
- Alluvial soils are often found on the floodplains and, given the right climate, are good for rice cultivation.

PROGRESS CHECK

PROGRESS CHECK

1. Name four types of farming in the UK.
2. What types of factors influence farmers' decisions?
3. Describe how governments can affect farming in MEDCs.

1. **Any four from:** Sheep; Dairy; Mixed; Arable; Market gardening. 2. Social, economic, and environmental factors. 3. Through regulations, subsidies, quotas, training, grants and reclamation schemes.

13.2 Factors influencing changes in farming

LEARNING SUMMARY

After studying this section you should be able to understand:
- how to recognise the ways in which farming is changing
- farming in the future

Agricultural change

AQA A	✓
AQA B	✗
EDEXCEL A	✓
EDEXCEL B	✓
OCR A	✗
OCR B	✗
WJEC A	✗
WJEC B	✗
CCEA	✗

KEY POINT

Farmers and other agriculture workers have to be aware of changes that are taking place in the environment, people's demands and local and global markets.

Changes in UK farming

Changes in UK farming include the following:
- The number of people employed full-time in farming is falling, whilst part-time and temporary working has increased.
- Supermarkets and food processing firms offer contracts to farmers to grow crops to specific dimensions and quality.
- There is more organic farming as the public demands greater health security from their food and less environmental damage.
- Farmers are selling more produce from the farm to consumers and local markets.
- Farmers are recognising competition from overseas.
- Farmers are diversifying their sources of income through links to tourism, e.g. holiday cottages, farm parks, golf courses, farm shops and adventure playgrounds.

Changes in farming in LEDCs

During the 1960s, as world population grew, there was concern in many countries about providing an adequate **food supply**. The main plan to increase food supply was called the **Green Revolution**. Countries such as India and Indonesia made efforts to increase the supply of rice and wheat using irrigation, new seeds and fertilisers.

The following are the main aspects of the **Green Revolution**:
- Use of new high-yielding varieties (HYVs) of seed. The first successful HYV was IR-8, the 'miracle rice' that doubled yields.

- Larger amounts of fertiliser and adequate controlled water supplies are needed by the HYVs.
- Newer HYVs have reduced the growing period from 180 to 100 days.
- Scientists are developing varieties that need less irrigation, resist disease and taste good.
- Governments offer loans, advice, storage and transport facilities to poorer farmers.

Benefits of the Green Revolution:
- Total production doubled, especially in China.
- Better living as farmers sold their surplus, e.g. Punjab in India.
- Increased sales of chemicals for crops on a global scale.

Problems of the Green Revolution:
- Irrigation is essential for the best results from HYVs.
- HYVs are costly to grow, needing more fertiliser and irrigation.
- Farmers affording to grow HYVs get richer, but the gap between them and poorer farmers, who cannot purchase the fertilisers, increases.

Farming in the future

AQA A	✓
AQA B	✗
EDEXCEL A	✓
EDEXCEL B	✓
OCR A	✗
OCR B	✗
WJEC A	✓
WJEC B	✓
CCEA	✗

Stewardship and sustainable agriculture

Environmental stewardship encourages farmers to apply their skills to improve their farm environments for people and wildlife. The schemes address several areas including...
- using organic farming methods such as natural fertilisers and free-range livestock to sustain and improve the soil, landscape and environment
- reducing pollution – improving water quality by reducing soil erosion and nutrient leakage
- improving biodiversity conditions – addressing issues such as the decline of farm birds, mammals and insects
- better landscape character – helping to maintain traditional landscape features, such as field boundaries.

The EU and Common Agricultural Police (CAP)

There are about 11 million farmers in the EU. The CAP has been in action for member states, including the UK, since 1962. Its objectives are...
- to increase productivity, promote technical progress and ensure best methods of production including labour
- to ensure a fair standard of living for the agricultural community
- to stabilise markets and to secure supplies of seeds and agricultural materials
- to provide consumers with food at reasonable prices.

Criticisms of the CAP include the following:
- It restricts global trade in farm products and gives unfair protection to farmers in the EU.
- It keeps prices high for food in the EU.
- It promotes large farming estates at the expense of small family farms.
- The amount of subsidy received by member countries is very uneven, e.g. France gains more than Germany.

14 Industry

The following topics are covered in this chapter:

- Economic development and industry
- Industrial location
- Economic activity in MEDCs and LEDCs
- Economic change at a global scale
- Economic change: growth and decline

14.1 Economic development and industry

LEARNING SUMMARY	After studying this section you should understand: • how to define primary, secondary and tertiary industry • industry as a system

Different types of industry

AQA A	✗
AQA B	✗
EDEXCEL A	✓
EDEXCEL B	✗
OCR A	✗
OCR B	✓
WJEC A	✓
WJEC B	✓
CCEA	✗

Industry can be divided into three main types: **primary**, **secondary** (manufacturing) and **tertiary** (services). Recently, tertiary industry has been sub-divided to give a fourth type: quaternary industry.

> **KEY POINT**
>
> An **occupation** is the job that someone does; **employment** is the industry in which they work. A person can have the occupation of accountant and be employed in the car industry.

Figure 14.1 Employment structure in countries at different levels of development

> A pie chart is a useful way of showing the balance of primary, secondary and tertiary industry in a country.

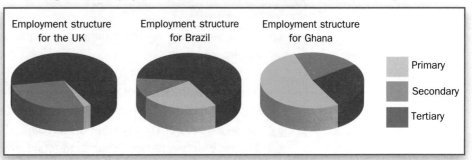

Employment structure for the UK · Employment structure for Brazil · Employment structure for Ghana

Primary
Secondary
Tertiary

Primary industry involves extracting resources from the sea or land. It is located where the raw material is available and includes farming, fishing, forestry, coal mining, oil drilling and hunting. Primary industries are dependent on factors such as climate and geology as well as government intervention, e.g. the Common Agricultural Policy of the EU.

Secondary or manufacturing industry makes products by processing raw materials or assembling components. The raw materials may be obtained from primary industry or could be products of other secondary industries, e.g. a tin of fruit or a motor car is manufactured by secondary industry using the products of primary and manufacturing industries. This type of employment is in decline in the UK and USA, because cheaper labour can be found in S.E. Asia.

Tertiary industry provides a service, e.g. health, administration, retailing and transport are called service industries. Most working people in the UK are employed in tertiary industries, including doctors, teachers, shop assistants, entertainers and lawyers.

Quaternary industry involves research and development as well as information and communications technology, which help companies to function.

Industry as a system

AQA A	✓
AQA B	✓
EDEXCEL A	✓
EDEXCEL B	✓
OCR A	✓
OCR B	✗
WJEC A	✓
WJEC B	✗
CCEA	✗

The manufacturing industry can be seen as a system with inputs, processes and outputs (see Figure 14.2).

Figure 14.2 Systems diagram of manufacturing industry

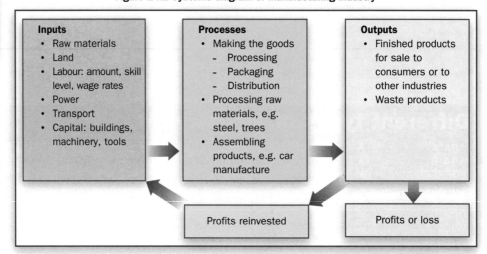

> Notice the similarity of this systems diagram with that for a farm (Figure 13.1, p.151). The diagram provides a helpful guide when studying an industry.

Manufacturing systems are called 'open systems' because only part of the income from sales is used for inputs and reinvestment. Some is taken by the owners or shareholders as profit.

PROGRESS CHECK

1. Divide the following occupations into primary, secondary and tertiary industry:
   A Coal miner **B** Dairy farmer **C** Taxi Driver **D** Doctor **E** Comedian **F** Teacher **G** Bricklayer **H** Garden designer **I** Tax collector **J** Cabinet maker **K** Hairdresser **L** Laboratory technician **M** Waiter
2. For an industry or factory you have studied, draw a systems diagram.
3. Give an example of one occupation found in your local area for each of the three main types of industry.

1. Primary: A, B; Secondary: G, J, L; Tertiary: C, D, E, F, H, I, K, M. 2. **Accept any suitable answer, e.g.:** the inputs of a car manufacturing plant would include pressed body parts, engines, tyres, paints and seats; processing would be on the assembly line and the output would be vehicles to a range of specifications. 3. **Accept any suitable answers, e.g.:** primary – farmer, secondary – furniture maker, tertiary – bank manager, teacher.

14.2 Industrial location

Factors affecting the location of industry

AQA A	✓
AQA B	✓
EDEXCEL A	✓
EDEXCEL B	✓
OCR A	✓
OCR B	✓
WJEC A	✓
WJEC B	✓
CCEA	✓

> You should be able to list at least five factors that influence the location of industry.

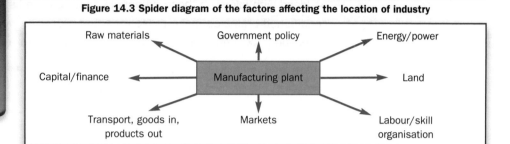

Figure 14.3 Spider diagram of the factors affecting the location of industry

Raw Materials

Raw materials are essential for the production of goods. In the past they have been very important factors in the location of industry because some raw materials were often bulky or heavy, expensive to transport and needed to be used in large quantities. So, factories tended to be located **near** to the **raw material**.

For example, in the iron and steel industry the costs were reduced if the iron and steel plants were located near to iron ore and coal deposits (the bulky raw materials). The steel produced, though heavy, was less bulky and easier to transport than the raw materials. China and India have large iron and steel industries. Another example is the cement manufacturing industry in the Peak District, Derbyshire. Several tons of limestone is needed to manufacture one ton of cement, so the manufacturing plant is next to the limestone quarry. These industries can be described as 'weight losing'.

Some products **gain weight** or **bulk** during manufacture, for example, baking, brewing and soft drink manufacture. A bag of flour is compact and produces a much greater volume of bread. Beer and soft drinks contain large quantities of water. These 'weight-gaining' industries used to be located **near** to their **markets** in order to reduce transport costs.

As transport has become more efficient, the influence of the raw materials on an industry's location has been reduced.

Energy or power

Industries need **power** to operate their machinery. Industries used to rely on steam power, so tended to be located near to coalfields. Today they use **electricity**, which is generated in power stations and transmitted over long distances using the **National Electricity Grid**. This means that, in theory, most industries no longer need to be located close to a source of power, but there are still some benefits to being near a power source.

The manufacture of aluminium uses large amounts of power, so some aluminium manufacturing plants have located close to sources of hydro-electricity power in order to reduce their energy costs. Rising energy costs affect industry, both in increased production costs and higher transport charges. Therefore, locations close to sources of energy or ports for access to cheaper energy are likely to be favoured.

Land

The amount of land needed varies from small workshops the size of a domestic garage to large areas of flat land for steel works and car assembly plants. Industries can build on brownfield sites where houses, old factories and disused railway yards have been demolished to provide space or on greenfield sites on the edges of urban area. Science, business and retail parks can be found in parkland with lakes on these greenfield sites. Car parks, regular buses and air-conditioned premises make these attractive places to work. To encourage new firms some local authorities provide small factories for rent.

Where land is limited, e.g. the City of London and other large city centres, high-rise office blocks increase the floor area.

Capital or Finance

It takes large amounts of money to set up, run and improve industries. Even small factories need capital to get started. Industries purchase raw materials, machines, premises and transport equipment. Banks, finance houses and governments offer loans to people developing a business (**entrepreneurs**). These investors demand a plan and expect some return for their money. The capital may come from abroad.

For an industry in your area, list the factors influencing its location.

Labour

The **availability**, **skill level**, **cost** and **working practices** of the workforce are factors in industrial location.

Some industries need educated and skilled labour that can be trained for new technologies. For example, many computer industries in Silicon Valley, California, have moved to newly industrialised countries like South Korea and Taiwan. Highly skilled labour can often be found around university towns, e.g. Cambridge and Reading, where Science Parks have been built. Cheaper, less skilled labour can be found in S.E. Asia. As part of globalisation, companies have moved manufacturing from the UK into China and India.

Productivity and worker attitudes are important factors to employers. Areas known for stoppages, strikes and poor workmanship will not attract employers. Workers in some industries had very strong trade unions, e.g. mining, car assembly and newspapers. Trade unions protect their members, but they can have a negative influence.

Factories and offices need managers. When choosing a site, the views of the owners and managers are important. They consider the environment in which they wish to live and work, the quality of education for their families and leisure facilities, e.g. golf courses.

Transport

Firms try to keep transport costs to a minimum (**least cost location**). Transport may be needed to bring raw materials or the products of other industries to the factory and deliver finished products to the market or other factories.

A good transport network helps move products quickly. A site near motorway, rail

Note the changing importance of location factors, e.g. cheaper transport means firms can search the globe for cheaper labour.

or airport connections will be attractive for an industrial estate. Sites in remote regions have higher transport costs. In Japan, where many raw materials are imported, firms move to port locations. As transport becomes more efficient its importance is reduced compared to labour costs.

Markets

The goods produced in factories and workshops are sold to meet the demand of the market. Consumers may order goods from a factory or a salesman may have to go into the market to persuade people to buy the product.

Industries that produce perishable goods will tend to locate near to the market, although developments such as refrigeration have made this less necessary.

The people living in an area or country provide a domestic market. If they are affluent, their spending will encourage the growth of industry. In poorer LEDCs there is only a small domestic market, which hinders economic growth.

Where a factory sells nearly all its product to a small group of factories, it is usual for the factories to group together. This is said to create an **agglomeration** and is an example of **industrial linkage**.

Government policy

Governments try to influence industrial location for several reasons:
- To move industrial activity out of congested urban areas into less prosperous areas, e.g. Mumbai and Kolkata in India.
- To move industry onto derelict brownfield sites in the inner parts of urban areas, e.g. the urban development corporations set up in London Docklands and Cardiff Tiger Bay.
- To create jobs by setting aside plots of land for industrial estates with good road, air, sea or rail access and other services.
- To improve air quality by banning industries that create pollution from locating near to residential areas.
- To develop an area by offering loans, subsidies and tax exemptions to companies.
- To attract industry by providing stable government, without corruption.

Industrial inertia

A study of an established factory or industry might show little obvious reason for its location. This may be because the original location factors no longer apply. Despite the disappearance of these original advantages a factory might still be successful due to its reputation, locally skilled labour or because there have been no moving costs. Therefore, there is no need for the factory to relocate. This is **industrial inertia**. For example 'Lakeland' crayons are still made in the Lake District, although they no longer use the local graphite. If the factory did choose to relocate, another site with modern advantages would be chosen.

The special case of the footloose industries

Footloose industries are industries that are free to locate in many places. These industries are increasing in number and include many of the growing industries in finance, information technology, road transport and administration.

14.3 Economic activity in MEDCs and LEDCs

LEARNING SUMMARY	**After studying this section you should understand:**
	• how to describe industry in LEDCs and MEDCs

Case studies of economic activity in MEDCs and LEDCs

AQA A	✓
AQA B	✓
EDEXCEL A	✓
EDEXCEL B	✓
OCR A	✓
OCR B	✓
WJEC A	✓
WJEC B	✓
CCEA	✓

There are large differences in the economic development of MEDCs and LEDCs. In some LEDCs this gap is shrinking as transport and communications make links across the world easier. This is called **globalisation** as MEDCs and LEDCs work together. The management skills and finance in MEDCs are combined with the plentiful, cheap and hardworking labour in some LEDCs.

There may be different levels of economic development within a MEDC, e.g. poor Southern Italy and richer Northern Italy, and North East and South East England.

Industry in LEDCs and MEDCs

Case Study 1: Industry in LEDCs: Industry in Malaysia

Inputs	• The Malaysian government has attracted **transnational companies**, (**TNCs**) sometimes called **multinational companies** (**MNCs**).
	• The TNCs were attracted by lower taxes, freedom from tariffs and generous quotas. Most TNCs in Malaysia are based in Japan so they have headquarters in Japan and factories in Malaysia.
	• The manufacturing was initially low skilled, but has now become more skilled. Spin offs from the main factory include suppliers of small parts and services by local entrepreneurs.
	• TNCs bring foreign exchange (FOREX) to buy machinery for the new factories.
	• TNCs train local people in industrial skills as well as building roads, schools and hospitals.
Outputs	• Originally manufactured agricultural products, then the growth of heavy industry and oil refining.
	• Governments have recently switched to high-tech industries and car assembly (Proton cars).
Physical factors	• Land is available for industry on the Pacific Ocean rim near to other large populations.

Human factors	• Lack of capital to invest in industry. • Investors from MEDCs reluctant to invest in LEDCs because of uncertain conditions. • Shortages of skilled labour and management expertise. • Unstable governments and racial tensions. • TNCs attracted to Malaysia by low labour costs. • Employment of local people created growing domestic market.
Processes	• New purpose-built factories on industrial estates. • Ports and airports expanded to link with the rest of the world. • Unreliable sources of power.

Problems, solutions and environmental impact	• Poor transport systems that are vulnerable to the weather.
	• Limited local markets because of low incomes locally.
	• Unfair trading by MEDCs, including quotas on imports.
	• With the help of TNCs, Malaysia has developed into a **NIC (newly industrialised country)**. South Korea and Taiwan are also NICs and are said to have 'Tiger' economies.
	• TNCs can bring disadvantages:
	  – They pressurise governments to make decisions in their favour, rather than for the country
	  – They transfer profit back to their own country
	  – Many of the jobs created are low skill
	  – Wages can be low and working conditions not good
	  – May cause environmental damage
	  – They have their own plans and may leave the LEDC for an even cheaper location.
	• The Malaysian government has now privatised much of its industry to allow more international support and growth.

You should know why TNCs locate in LEDCs and what advantages and disadvantages they bring.

It will be helpful to know a case study of one TNC in a LEDC and one NIC

Case Study 2: Industry in MEDCs: Car manufacture in Swindon, Wiltshire

Inputs	• Swindon in Wiltshire has changed from a railway town to a motor town. It is the high-tech location of the Japanese car maker Honda. • Honda has 200 global suppliers of components parts that meet the production needs at Swindon. Lorries arrive regularly on site, providing components 2 hours before they are used. This is a 'just-in-time' delivery process.
Outputs	• The Honda site at South Marston is a £1.33 billion, integrated car manufacturing factory, producing finished cars ready for the road. • This site produces around 190 000 cars a year, 75% of which are exported. 180 000 petrol and diesel engines are produced at Swindon every year. • Some engines are exported to the Honda factory in Turkey. Turkish-built cars are sold in Eastern Europe and China.
Physical factors	• The South Marston site used to be an airfield. It covers 1.5 million m² (370 acres). • One of the airfield's runways is used as the on-site test track.

Case Study 2: Industry in MEDCs: Car manufacture in Swindon, Wiltshire (cont.)

Human factors	• Honda is a TNC. It has plants in 29 countries and employs 131 600 people. • Of the 4 000 people employed at the South Marston factory, 3 500 work on the production lines. (About 400 workers are female.) • Honda trains people at the local college, but believes that their work attitude when they leave school is as important as their qualifications.
Processes	• The processes on-site include engine casting and assembly, pressing of body panels, body assembly, painting, final vehicle assembly and test track sign-off. • Honda uses 142 robots to weld body panels together (this system is faster than the previous one, which used manpower and cranes). • Finished cars are moved by transporter lorries to UK dealers or to docks at Southampton, Portbury or Avonmouth (depending on where they are being exported to). • 90% of cars produced at South Marston leave the site within 24 hours of manufacture.
Problems, solutions and environmental impact	**Problems**: • Increased traffic in and out of the factory. A new fly-over has been built to link the factory to the M4 motorway. **Solutions**: • In 2008, 3 000 trucks per year were taken off the roads when a new direct rail link to the factory opened (this will reduce CO_2 emissions). • Two trains per week are planned to take 200 cars to a central depot in Belgium.

Case study 3: New industrial areas in the UK: High-tech industry in the M4 corridor

Figure 14.4 The M4 corridor

Inputs	• Growth of modern factories on new industrial estates stretching from the western edge of London, near Heathrow airport, to Bath and Bristol and including Reading, Maidenhead and Newbury. • Universities in London, Oxford, Reading, Bath and Bristol provide highly educated graduates. • The high-tech industries tend to be the new growth industries (sometimes called the 'sunrise' industries). • Raw materials are small and can be transported easily. • Investors from many countries are ready to invest in the area.
Outputs	• Research and development of new electronic products. • Computers, computer software, telecommunications and media equipment.

Physical factors	• Rapid road communication along the M4 corridor. • Large areas of flat land for new factories, usually on the edge of cities. • Large areas of the industrial estates are covered in grass and trees, with lakes, fountains and car parking making them attractive places to work. • Fast railway service along the corridor. • The environment around the corridor is an attractive, rural place to live.
Human factors	• The companies tend to employ relatively small numbers of highly skilled people. • The workforce is intelligent and inventive; they tend to move around from company to company. • Wages tend to be high and this creates high demand for service industries.
Processes	• Industries are said to be footloose because they are not controlled by the traditional industrial location factors. • Some firms are based on older manufacturing companies, e.g. Rolls Royce and British Aerospace.
Problems, solutions and environmental impact	• Congestion on the main motorways and urban roads. • High house prices. • Drinking and domestic water shortages. • Government has proposed the building of many new houses, but there is much local opposition. • Demand for more houses and factories creates pressure on existing land. • There are dangers of bankruptcy and unemployment in the highly volatile nature of the high-tech industries where changes take place very rapidly.

14.4 Economic change at a global scale

LEARNING SUMMARY

After studying this section you should understand:
• the rise of the Newly Industrialised Countries (NICs)

The decline of manufacturing industry in MEDCs

AQA A	✓
AQA B	✓
EDEXCEL A	✓
EDEXCEL B	✓
OCR A	✓
OCR B	✓
WJEC A	✓
WJEC B	✗
CCEA	✗

The globalisation of industry

The globalisation of industry refers to TNCs that operate in many countries. They use labour, raw materials and parts from different countries to produce desirable goods at the lowest cost for the TNC. They sell all over the world.

The Ford Motor Company is a TNC with headquarters in Detroit, USA. Ford cars are found all over the world, sometimes under different names with small changes in design. They have factories producing parts in at least 20 countries. In 2002, Ford ended car production in the UK. In Europe, Ford assembles the Mondeo range in Genk (Belgium), Fiesta in Valencia (Spain) and Cologne (Germany), Ka in Valencia, and Focus in Valencia, Saarlouis (Germany) and Vsevolozhsk (Russia). Similar examples could be given for Ford in S.E. Asia and South America.

Many other companies, large and small, also find the cheapest source of production for their goods. Much of the clothing, footwear and electrical goods found on the British high street are made in S.E. Asia. The key point is the lower cost of production, especially labour costs.

Supporters of globalisation make the following points:
- The wealth created in the MEDC allows its people to have a good standard of living and buy cheap goods.
- Industrial jobs are created for people in the LEDC, with education and training provided.
- The improved skills for workers in the LEDC allow some to start their own businesses.
- People in the LEDC find an improvement in their standard of living (though not as much as that in the MEDC).

Critics of globalisation make the following points:
- Companies in the UK and USA may exploit the less well-off in countries, e.g. India, Indonesia and Bangladesh, by paying low wages to people working in poor conditions.
- Some MEDCs, e.g. the UK, have lost their manufacturing industry to countries with cheaper labour costs.
- Only small amounts of the profits made by the TNC find their way to the LEDC where the goods are made.
- TNCs may dominate the governments of the countries in which they work. This can cause damage to their society, culture and environment.
- If the government of an LEDC tries to increase taxation in order to pay for education housing and health, the TNC can threatened to take production elsewhere.

Critics suggest that a local strategy for economic activity should be promoted. Other people looking at the emerging economies of India and China are concerned that, in the end, some MEDCs may suffer economically.

14.5 Economic change: growth and decline

LEARNING SUMMARY	**After studying this section you should be able to understand:**
	- the changing structure of industry
	- how to recognise change in the location of shops

The decline of manufacturing industry in MEDCs

AQA A	✓
AQA B	✓
EDEXCEL A	✓
EDEXCEL B	✓
OCR A	X
OCR B	✓
WJEC A	✓
WJEC B	✓
CCEA	✓

Traditional heavy industries, e.g. iron and steel making, have declined in many MEDCs. This is because...
- raw materials have become exhausted, e.g. iron ore in South Wales
- markets have moved to other countries, e.g. ship building from Clydeside to the Far East
- there is competition from countries with cheaper labour, e.g. textiles from Lancashire to India and China, china and earthenware from Stoke-on-Trent to

China and Indonesia, electrical goods (e.g. TVs, washing machines and cookers) from the West Midlands to Taiwan and South Korea
- older companies did not keep up to date by investing in new technology, e.g. car manufacture in the West Midlands moving to China, Turkey and Brazil.

The closure of traditional industries can have devastating effects on an area. Unemployment spreads from the closed plant to affect its suppliers. People in the area have less to spend so the local retail and entertainment industries suffer. People may not be able to continue their mortgage repayments and house prices fall. Unemployed people in the UK receive benefits, but this means there is less money for the government to spend on schools, colleges and hospitals.

The growth of service industries in MEDCs

In many parts of the UK and other MEDCs, the declining traditional manufacturing industries have been replaced by service industries (sometimes called the growing tertiary sector). These growing industries include banks, insurance, IT support, retail, personal services and entertainment employment. The newer industries require a more highly educated workforce with skills, particularly in mathematics, science and English as well as interpersonal skills.

There are several reasons for the growth of the service industries:
- People in work have higher disposable incomes.
- People with savings look to invest.
- New technologies such as mobile phones and computer games.
- The ageing population has 'grey' pounds to spend from their final salary pension schemes.
- There is a demand, especially from women, for beauty salons.
- A higher awareness of health and fitness leading to a growth in gymnasia, swimming pools and health clubs.
- Increased leisure time with hobbies and pastimes.
- More appliances to improve the quality of life at home.
- The use of the Internet for sales.
- The increasing number of very elderly people requiring home care and residential care.
- Demand for entertainment, clubs, casinos and events promotion.
- Increased number of students because more stay on at school or enter higher education.

One advantage of this growth is that the industries are relatively footloose and are able to locate near to their markets. This tends to create a more even spread of economic activity, though large urban areas will still be the main centres of service industries.

Industry in LEDCs

AQA A	✓
AQA B	✓
EDEXCEL A	✓
EDEXCEL B	✓
OCR A	✓
OCR B	✓
WJEC A	✓
WJEC B	✓
CCEA	✓

The **characteristics of LEDCs** are as follows:
- Low average income.
- Poor infrastructure of roads, railways, airports and unreliable water and electricity supplies.
- Low GDP, indicating low production and low income for the people.
- Poor housing, education and health services.
- Many employed as farm labourers or working for themselves on small farms.

- High rates of population growth, but low life expectancy.
- Low energy consumption per head.
- Migration of people from rural areas to the cities.
- More of a focus on primary industries, e.g. farming, fishing and mining.
- Lack of finance to buy machinery in order to increase efficiency of domestic industries, so the country sells its raw materials cheaply to MEDCs.

There are several ways to help LEDCs develop:
- Improving the infrastructure so goods can be brought to market.
- Moving away from low value added economic activity such as agriculture and mining.
- Providing education and training, particularly in health care and technology.
- Supporting regions that have resources, e.g. crops, minerals, timber, to develop their own industries rather than exporting the raw materials.
- Encouraging richer nations to write off any debts that are owed to them by the LEDC.
- Providing finance and expertise to allow the LEDC to start up its own industries.
- Taking advantage of the surplus labour available in the LEDC and begin labour-intensive industries that generate income for the country.
- Encourage the development of rural industry that reduces urban migration, e.g. used in China.
- Reform and invest in agriculture so that production increases and surpluses can be sold.

There is disagreement about the best way to help these countries develop. Some people believe they can be helped through large projects such as building dams to create electricity, irrigation and drinking water or building factories to capitalise on the local cheap labour. Others believe the best way forward is to develop basic technology projects that are more sympathetic to the ways of life of the people, but allow them to improve their standard of living gradually.

There are three sets of examples of LEDCs at different stages of development:

1. Countries whose economies have been growing over a period of time, e.g. China, India, Brazil, South Africa, Costa Rica, Mexico, Turkey, the Philippines, Egypt, much of South America, Malaysia and Thailand.
2. Countries with an uneven record of development, e.g. most countries in Africa, Central America, the Caribbean; the Arab world and some of S.E. Asia (excluding Singapore, Philippines, Brunei, Malaysia and Thailand).
3. Countries with little sign of development, e.g. Haiti, Somalia, Sudan and Myanmar.

Strategies to increase economic activity in MEDCs / LEDCs

AQA A	✓
AQA B	✓
EDEXCEL A	✓
EDEXCEL B	✓
OCR A	✓
OCR B	✓
WJEC A	✓
WJEC B	✓
CCEA	✓

Development areas and growth poles

Some governments recognise the need to develop industry. This could include...
- the **regeneration** of an area where its industry has declined and unemployment has increased, e.g. the decline of iron, steel and pottery in Stoke-on-Trent, the closed coal mines in South Wales, and the reduction of shipbuilding in Tyneside and Belfast
- **encouraging new industry** in an area, e.g. growth poles in Brazil that attract people away from the crowded areas around Rio de Janeiro and São Paulo or rural development grants in more remote parts of Wales and Scotland.

A case study of London Docklands and a local retail park would be useful. Despite their success, government policy restricts development of these centres because they damage town centres, encourage car use and use greenfield land.

Governments can encourage industry by establishing a **development area** or **growth pole** where companies receive benefits including...

- grants for the establishment of new factories
- ready-built premises with low rents
- small premises to allow the growth of new companies
- good road links to motorways and railway container depots
- advertising to promote the advantages of the area.

The changing location of retail industry

The retail industry includes shops that used to be located in the **Central Business District** (**CBD**). Shops were also found in suburban high streets and local centres. Since the 1980s, the UK has copied the US pattern, with shops moving to the edges of the urban area.

There are several types of **out-of-town** shopping centre:

- Superstores containing a large supermarket and often a petrol station and car wash.
- Retail parks with outlets for garden supplies, furniture, carpets, toys, pet food and accessories, DIY stores, sports goods and clothing.
- Regional shopping centres with an undercover shopping centre, with two or three major chain stores acting as anchors and up to 200 other shops, cinema screens, restaurants and huge car parks.
- Outlet villages where chain stores sell discounted lines, often from the previous season's fashions, e.g. Bicester in Oxfordshire, Colne in Lancashire and the Swindon Designer Outlet (built on a former railway works).

These shopping centres have been popular and successful. They have free car parking, good access, a range of shops in warm and dry malls, good levels of safety due to security guards and competitive pricing.

However, they do cause problems at peak times when tailbacks block surrounding roads and motorway slip roads. They are also less accessible to the elderly and those without cars. The **out-of-town** centres have also caused problems for town centres:

- The loss of large shops has made the town centre less attractive to shoppers.
- Smaller local shops have closed because fewer shoppers visit the town centre.
- Vacant premises are often filled with discount and charity shops.

Sustainable Economic Development

AQA A	✓
AQA B	✓
EDEXCEL A	✓
EDEXCEL B	✓
OCR A	✓
OCR B	✓
WJEC A	✓
WJEC B	✓
CCEA	✓

Sustainable economic development aims to meet human needs while preserving the environment so that these needs are met in the present and the indefinite future. The famous definition for sustainability states that activity *'meets the needs of the present without compromising the ability of future generations to meet their own needs'.*

Economic activity that threatens sustainability

Economic activities that threaten sustainability include the following:

- **Illegal logging**: the cutting, transport, purchase or sale of timber in violation of national laws, e.g. logging of protected trees in the national parks of Korindo (Indonesia) and Peru, South America.

- **Poaching** (wild animals and plants) and illegal fishing, e.g. some protected animals and plants are said to have good medicinal uses.
- **Building housing estates** on green land and floodplains to meet the demand for affordable houses, but decreasing the amount of open land and increasing the flood risk.
- **Use of fossil fuels** that contribute to global warming.
- **Building new roads**, motorways and airport runways that encourage travel.

Strategies for sustainable economic development

The following are strategies for sustainable economic development:
- Use of brownfield sites by reclaiming land that has become derelict or unproductive. This can be expensive as the soil may be polluted with dangerous chemicals and the owners may not wish to release their land. (This policy is being used in the UK, Australia and the USA.)
- Introducing more rangers and game wardens to protect forests and endangered animals.
- Managing tourism to protect fragile environments, e.g. barrier reefs.
- Taking pressure off 'honeypot' sites by managing the numbers of visitors.
- Developing renewable energies for industry and transport that are less damaging to the environment.
- Agreeing targets for the reduction in greenhouse gases (this can face opposition because it might threaten standards of living in some MEDCs).
- Building houses that help to reduce global warming, e.g. better insulation of walls, windows and roofs.
- Thinking locally to reduce the number of miles over which food is transported.
- Encouraging the use of public transport.
- Increasing the cost of air fares in order to reduce travel, and encouraging businesses to use IT methods of communication rather than physically travelling.
- Promoting home-based resorts, and travel by train.
- Providing jobs near to where people live in order to reduce commuting.
- Recycling products to reduce the demand for resources.
- Better national and international laws to enforce sustainable activity.
- Introducing ecotaxes on the use of fossil fuels, increasing import duties on goods that are not environmentally friendly, and taxes on materials sent to land fill sites, introducing charges for those producing hazardous waste materials and pollutants and taxes on land that is not being used sustainably. (Not all of these are practical ideas but some countries have introduced taxes on new cars that use large amounts of fuel.)

15 Development, trade and aid

The following topics are covered in this chapter:

- **Understanding development**
- **Understanding trade and aid**

15.1 Understanding development

LEARNING SUMMARY	After studying this section you should be able to understand:
	• how to describe different levels of development
	• plans to aid development

Development

AQA A	✗
AQA B	✗
EDEXCEL A	✗
EDEXCEL B	✓
OCR A	✓
OCR B	✗
WJEC A	✗
WJEC B	✓
CCEA	✗

Every country strives for development in order to be able to improve its economy and raise the quality of life of its people.

> **KEY POINT**
>
> **Development** is the use of resources and technology to create wealth, which is used to improve quality of life (economic, social and cultural).

What is development?

AQA A	✓
AQA B	✓
EDEXCEL A	✓
EDEXCEL B	✓
OCR A	✓
OCR B	✓
WJEC A	✓
WJEC B	✓
CCEA	✓

Development is a change that improves the well-being of people in terms of material wealth and quality of life.

Development includes...

- better food supply (more regular and of a better quality)
- improved health care, especially for the young, the pregnant and the elderly
- decreased infant mortality through education, pre- and post-natal care
- longer life expectancy through health care and nutrition
- secure employment (allows material provision for later years)
- better working conditions, fewer accidents and less physical damage
- access to education, especially secondary level and for females
- security in old age
- warm, dry housing
- safe water supply and sanitation.

There are four aspects that summarise development:

- **Economic** development including greater income and wealth through industrial growth.
- **Social** development with better standards of living, access to education, health, housing and leisure.
- **Environmental** development that brings improvements and restoration of the natural environment.
- **Political** development with progress to effective representative government.

> You need to be able to list these 'quality of life' features. If you are asked how the quality of life in an area can be improved, you can use these four aspects as headings.

Different types of development

AQA A	✗
AQA B	✗
EDEXCEL A	✓
EDEXCEL B	✓
OCR A	✓
OCR B	✓
WJEC A	✓
WJEC B	✓
CCEA	✓

Development can begin with economic growth, but it also includes literacy rates, life expectancy, poverty rates, leisure time, environmental quality, freedom or social justice.

Examples of three different types of development:

1 **Development in Brazil:** As the country develops its timber and mineral ores, some parts of the Amazon rainforest have been cleared for housing, agriculture and the Trans-Amazonian Highway. This development is raising the quality of lives of the people living there.

2 **Development in India:** The Green Revolution has been applied to agriculture in the Punjab. Income and living standards have improved for many people. Manufacturing (e.g. textiles and IT assembly) and service industries (e.g. call centres) have also developed to provide paid employment and a higher standard of living.

3 **Development in the Caribbean:** Tourism has been introduced to replace declining sugar cane and banana industries. Beach resorts, roads and power supplies have been provided and the jobs available are improving people's lives.

> You need to be clear about what development means in Geography (the word can have a different meaning in English, Psychology or Town and Country Planning).

Measuring the level of development

AQA A	✓
AQA B	✓
EDEXCEL A	✓
EDEXCEL B	✗
OCR A	✗
OCR B	✓
WJEC A	✓
WJEC B	✓
CCEA	✓

There are a number of ways of measuring a country's level of development:

- The changing percentage of labour in primary, secondary and tertiary jobs.
- Birth and death rates, and the rate of population growth.
- Infant mortality and life expectancy at birth.
- Adult literacy (being able to read and write) and access to secondary education.
- The **Gross National Product** (GNP).
- Health measures, e.g. the number of people per doctor and access to clean water.
- **Human Development Index**, which was created by the UN in 1990 to provide international comparisons. The index varies from 0 to 1 (1 being the most developed), and includes life expectancy, literacy, years in education and income per person.

Measuring development in this way has been criticised, because it is difficult to measure. For example...

- GNP does not include subsistence production for the person's own use.
- National figures may not be accurate and could be distorted by corrupt governments.
- Within a country there will be variations from the average national figure, e.g. between northern and southern Italy, south-east Brazil and Amazonia, and between cities and rural areas.

> **KEY POINT**
>
> **Gross National Product** is the total value of all goods and services produced by a country in one year, divided by the population total to give an average amount per head.

Figure 15.1 Measures of development for selected countries

Country	GNP (US$)	Birth rate per 1000	Death rate per 1000	Life expectancy (years)	Adult literacy (%)	People per doctor	HDI (World Rank Value)
Ethiopia	100	38.2	11.8	51.8	35.9	34 000	(169) 0.406
Ghana	452	29.2	9.39	59.4	64.2	25 000	(142) 0.533
Brazil	4400	19.2	6.4	71.7	88.6	900	(70) 0.800
Japan	40 940	8.3	9.3	82.3	99.0	500	(8) 0.953
UK	19 600	12.0	10.0	79.0	99.0	440	(16) 0.946
India	380	23.0	6.4	63.7	61.0	1700	(128) 0.619
China	750	13.1	7.0	72.5	90.9	950	(81) 0.777

You may be presented with a table of data about different levels of development. Read the data and units used carefully. If you have to make comparisons they can be between rows or columns.

The main **development characteristics** of LEDCs are the following:

- Birth rates are high and death rates are falling, which leads to population increase and a strain on resources.
- High infant mortality rates (due to poor health services, inadequate diet and poor housing) mean people have more children in the hope that some live.
- Lack of protection against killer diseases, e.g. malaria and AIDS.
- Lack of finance to provide enough homes and remove some of the squatter camps / shanty towns.
- Higher life expectancy increases the non-economically active population and puts a further strain on resources.
- Low levels of literacy because education is not available (especially for females) or is expensive. This leads to an unskilled workforce.
- Lack of food or poor quality food leads to low work output.
- Shortage of clean water allows spread of diseases and infections, e.g. cholera, dysentery and diarrhoea.
- GDP, GNP and HDI are low.
- Little industry (and often only based upon primary products) so little, if any, profits.
- Poor infrastructure (roads fail in poor weather and railways unreliable), which makes it difficult to set up industry.
- High percentage of the population live in rural areas and survive on poor agriculture.
- Poor or corrupt governments, slow development, and any available money is spent on prestige projects or the army.
- In debt to richer countries.

Case study of development issues in Ghana

Ghana is in West Africa. The word *Ghana* means *Warrior King*. Ghana traded with the Portuguese in the 15th Century, before it was colonised by the British. The British established a crown colony, Gold Coast, in 1874. Ghana achieved independence from the UK in 1957.

Ghana is divided into 10 regions and has good natural resources. Gold, timber, cocoa, diamond, bauxite and manganese exports are major sources of income. Oil exploration has started and the amount of oil produced continues to increase. It has a population of about 23 million at a density of 83 per km².

Although it is one of the richer countries of West Africa, it still relies on international financial and technical aid.

Problems facing Ghana	Some solutions to Ghana's problems
• 50% of the GDP comes from agriculture. • Subsistence agriculture employs 55% of the people, mainly on small farms. • High inflation is making food and other goods expensive. • Tribal disputes can lead to violence. • One in ten of the working population is unemployed. • Drought, deforestation, overgrazing and soil erosion damage agriculture in the north. • Poaching and habitat destruction threaten wildlife. • Supplies of drinking water are inadequate and polluted. • The telephone system is outdated and does not cover all of the country. • Refugees arrive from neighbouring countries. • Illegal drug abuse is a problem in parts of the country. • Lower life expectancy (59 years) because of the spread of AIDS. • High risk of disease, especially malaria. • Loss of well-trained people who look for work in Europe.	• The International Monetary Fund gave loans for the reorganisation of agriculture. • Ghana invested in education so that everyone can attend primary and secondary schools (though there is a shortage of places in the senior years of secondary education). • Offshore oil drilling is proving successful and earning much needed FOREX. • High prices for two exports, gold and cocoa, are helping the economy to grow. • Stable government and low levels of corruption. • Ensuring a safe environment that will encourage tourists, e.g. to the National Parks, and the development of Lake Volta for cruising. • Funding of projects like the Akosombo Dam on the River Volta, in order to produce hydro-electricity for the aluminium industry.

Millennium development goals (MDG)

The millennium development goals of the UN for all are...

- an end to poverty
- an end to hunger
- sustainability
- universal education
- equality
- health
- partnerships.

Solutions to the problems of development

The solutions to the problems of development include the following:
- Free and fair trade and aid.
- Greater use of appropriate technology.
- Planned sustainable development.
- Responsible positive role for TNCs.
- Development projects in LEDCs.
- Regional development plans.

PROGRESS CHECK

1. How could you measure the difference in development between LEDCs and MEDCs?
2. List five development characteristics of a LEDC.
3. Identify some solutions to the problems of underdevelopment in LEDCs.

1. Useful measures include GDP, GNP and HDI. 2. **Any five from:** High birth rates; Falling death rates; High infant mortality; Poor housing; Poor health care; Poverty; Poor education; Malnutrition; Lack of clean water. 3. Trade and aid from MEDCs, appropriate development projects, stable governments and inward investment by TNCs.

15.2 Understanding trade and aid

Trade

AQA A	✓
AQA B	✓
EDEXCEL A	✗
EDEXCEL B	✗
OCR A	✓
OCR B	✓
WJEC A	✗
WJEC B	✓
CCEA	✗

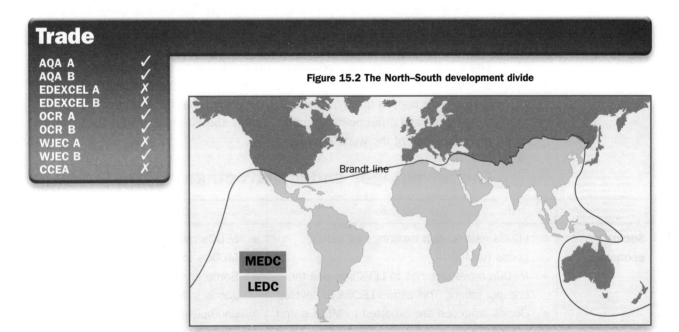

Figure 15.2 The North–South development divide

Brandt line

MEDC

LEDC

Figure 15.2 shows a map drawn in 1980 by an international committee chaired by former German Chancellor, **Willy Brandt**.

The map shows the world divided into two areas. To the north of the line are the richer MEDCs while to the south are the 'Third World' LEDCs. Since 1980 the gap between many MEDCs and LEDCs has increased, although some LEDCs that are to the south of the line (e.g. China, India, Brazil, Malaysia, Indonesia and South Korea) have developed considerably.

Trade

KEY POINT

Imports are goods purchased from abroad and brought into a country. **Exports** are goods purchased by other countries and sent out to them. Exports can include expertise and financial services. The **balance of trade** is the difference between the money earned from exports and the money spent on imports.

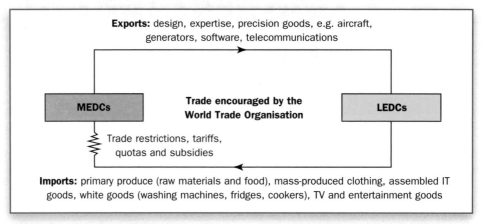

Figure 15.3 Trade relationships between MEDCs and LEDCs

Pattern of trade

Trade is the movement of goods and services between producers and consumers. Governments and companies aim to purchase the cheapest goods available for a given quality. However, their choice also depends on trade agreements and other political factors. Japan, the EU and the USA account for more than half of the world's trade.

The advantages and disadvantages of trade

	Advantages	Disadvantages
Socio-economic	• LEDCs gain foreign exchange by selling goods to MEDCs. • MEDCs move factories to LEDCs to use the cheaper labour. This allows LEDCs to develop. • Goods produced are exported to MEDCs and other LEDCs. • MEDCs gain cheap imports of raw materials and finished goods, and export specialist manufactured goods, expertise, financial, design and planning services. • LEDCs have ready markets for their exports and develop a market at home as people earn more money	• LEDCs remain dependent on MEDCs to buy their products. • Some emerging LEDCs dump cheap goods in MEDCs, which can lead to unemployment in the MEDCs. • There is a danger of unequal financial outcomes, e.g. trade deficits. • International companies may move from one LEDC to another if wages rise or workers make demands.
Environmental	• LEDCs learn ways to develop their resources without damaging their environment. • Money from trade can be used to improve life in the LEDC, e.g. roads, water supply, electricity, housing, working conditions and open spaces.	• MEDCs exploit resources in LEDCs and, with little sustainable provision, damage fragile environments. • Factories in LEDCs that produce goods for trade with MEDCs may give less attention to health and safety.
Political	• MEDCs help governments in LEDCs to improve stability. • MEDCs can exert pressure on LEDC government policies, e.g. humanitarian and environmental matters. • Trade with MEDCs may lead to more aid given.	• LEDCs become dependent on purchases from one or more MEDCs. • MEDCs may place conditions on LEDCs governments if they wish to trade.

Trade and interdependence

Every country trades. One country may have the resources and the expertise to produce the goods that another country needs. Trade is important for the development of countries. Some LEDCs see trade as their way to earn the money they need to develop. When countries trade with each other they are said to be interdependent.

For example, **Japan** has a large population and is economically well developed. But, it has little flat land, few natural resources and limited sources of energy. Japan imports machinery, food, oil, chemicals and textiles, mainly from the USA, Pacific Rim countries, China, India and the EU. In return, Japan exports motor vehicles, office machinery, scientific and optical equipment, semi-conductors and other electronic components. In an average year the value of Japan's exports is greater than imports when foreign investments are included.

In contrast, **Kenya** is an LEDC that has areas of rich soil where crops such as tea, coffee and fruit can be grown for export, but the country struggles to grow enough food for its people. Government reforms to help exports are ignored by farmers who are growing food for local markets. There is great potential here for industries based upon crops. Attempts to introduce textiles and clothing industries have not been successful.

The Kenyan government has offered incentives to foreign firms (including tax holidays and lower duties on imports) to locate in Kenya, but overseas companies lack confidence to invest. The greatest possibilities are in the tourist industry, but the country lacks the money to develop its potential. Kenya mainly imports machinery, transport equipment and oil products. The EU remains Kenya's largest trading partner, both as a source of imports and a destination for exports, but growth has been slow. Each year the value of the imports is greater than exports.

Fair Trade

> Think of the positive and negative aspects of making trade fairer for MEDCs and LEDCs.

In the past, powerful MEDCs have exploited LEDCs by purchasing cheap raw materials from the LEDC but then selling them expensive machinery. This has left the people of the LEDC with low wages, little purchasing power and a poor quality of life. Today some organisations in MEDCs have recognised how unfair this trade can be and the MEDCs are now paying a 'fair' price for the goods. This allows people in the LEDCs to have more money with which to raise their standard of living and purchase goods from MEDCs. Fair Trade goods include tea, coffee and clothes and can be found in many UK shops.

Aid

AQA A	✓
AQA B	✓
EDEXCEL A	✗
EDEXCEL B	✗
OCR A	✓
OCR B	✗
WJEC A	✗
WJEC B	✗
CCEA	✗

Why is aid needed?

Aid is the movement of resources from a MEDC to a LEDC. It can include money, equipment, food, training, expertise and loans. The UN encourages countries to spend 0.7% of their GNP on aid (but few countries do this). Aid is intended to help LEDCs continue their development and improve the quality of life of their people. Aid can be given to help with a sudden short-term problem or a longer-term project.

Questions on aid will appear on exam papers, so make sure you revise this topic thoroughly. Draw up a table of the advantages and disadvantages of the different types of aid for the giver and receiver.

Type of Aid	Advantages	Disadvantages
Emergency (short-term) To areas hit by earthquakes, floods, hurricanes, tsunamis, drought and volcanic eruptions	• Immediately provides food, clothing, shelter and medical assistance • Delivered directly to those in need (less chance of corruption)	• Creates dependency • Treats the problem rather than the cause
Political (governmental or conditional or tied) Often bilateral when a rich country donates money or goods to a country, but with strings attached	• Training and education available in MEDCs for people from LEDCs • Helps stability in LEDCs • Raises standard of living and educational level • Experts go from one country to help another, e.g. from the UK to Turkey to help build dams	• LEDCs have to buy from 'partner' MEDC, e.g. arms and manufactured goods • The aid often has to be spent on prestige projects and contractors have to come from the MEDC that has given the aid
Charitable (voluntary) Non-governmental organisations (NGOs), e.g. Oxfam, Save the Children Fund and Comic Relief collect money in MEDCs to help people in LEDCs.	• Money goes directly to the people in need • Also used for emergencies • Linked to low cost self-help schemes • Used to train farmers and reduce soil erosion	• Many demands on charitable funds • Lottery prizes attract funds away from charities • Dangerous conditions for helpers in some unstable countries
Long-term (sustainable) Where organisations commit for a long-term programme, e.g. the Intermediate Technology Group	• Develops local skills to run and maintain equipment • Uses local raw materials in a sustainable way • Trains local people	• Economic activity remains at a low level • Trained local people migrate abroad for higher wages
International organisations (multilateral) The World Bank, United Nations and the International Monetary Fund	• Helps to train local people (e.g. farmers) and increases food production • Massive resources to help with large problems, e.g. disease	• May not be available to countries with hostile regimes • Danger of LEDCs becoming dependent on the aid • Used for prestige projects that do not help the rural poor

Appropriate technology and sustainable development

AQA A	✓
AQA B	✓
EDEXCEL A	✓
EDEXCEL B	✓
OCR A	✓
OCR B	✓
WJEC A	✓
WJEC B	✓
CCEA	✓

> **KEY POINT**
>
> **Appropriate technology** and **sustainable development** are ways of reducing the gap between rich and poor people today and in the future.

Appropriate technology

Some aid has been criticised as being too high-tech for LEDCs. The local people lack the expertise to maintain the project and have difficulty sustaining it. Spare parts are expensive or not available in the LEDC.

Appropriate technology schemes are low-tech, cheaper, use local materials and there is less to go wrong. They leave local people in control and there is less bureaucracy. These schemes often use the abundant local labour supply; products are cheap and local people can afford them.

Examples of appropriate technology projects include the following:
- Installing simple bamboo water pumps in villages.
- Providing bicycles for farmers to transport goods to market.
- Using local streams to generate small amounts of hydro-electricity.
- Collecting rainwater in large clay pots.
- Using cement and chicken wire to reinforce walls and roofs.
- Making earth blocks in a wooden press for building projects.
- Installing small windmills to create electricity.

Critics of these schemes say that whilst it helps poor people in rural areas, it does little to bridge the gap between the rich and poor countries. These critics point to failed appropriate technology projects, for example, some biogas converters in rural India have been abandoned, and productivity remains low.

Sustainable development and aid

Sustainable development not only meets people's needs today, but also those of future generations. Some experts believe that the world is moving towards **unsustainable development** as people consume more and more energy by using mobile phones, the Internet, cars, air travel and air conditioning. These experts suggest that if population and energy consumption continue to increase, the future of resources and the environment becomes more uncertain.

The UK government has established a series of principles to guide those involved with sustainable development.
- Living within environmental limits. Water, timber, fish and oil are rapidly being exhausted. The use and disposal of non-renewable resources is altering the environment and pollution is increasing. To be sustainable, the UK industry needs to use cleaner technologies, fewer resources (to prevent waste) and to regard environmental care as important as customer care. Examples of recent actions include low energy TV set top boxes, and purchase of energy-efficient products such as refrigerators. The slogan is *'working towards achieving more with less'*.
- Ensuring a strong, healthy and fair society where the needs of everyone are recognised.
- Achieving a sustainable economy.
- Using sound science responsibly.
- Promoting good governance.

Examples of sustainable development in action include the following:
- Using methane gas from landfill sites for power, thus reducing its effects on global warming.
- Changing methods of paper production in Indonesian forests to reduce their carbon footprint.
- Tanzania and Malaysia plan to use ICT more to aid their mutual development.
- Balancing the use of bio-fuels and food production so less fossil fuels are used, but food shortages and food prices do not increase.
- Promotion of international trade to reduce poverty by MEDCs providing financial and technical assistance to LEDCs.

- International businesses to provide employment to LEDCs.
- Companies in MEDCs look for local suppliers in LEDCs as this brings employment and finance to the local area of the LEDC.
- Suppliers in MEDCs could provide materials for water supply, sanitation, energy, housing, healthcare, education and communications in LEDCs whilst increasing their own businesses.
- The UK is working with China to make soil and crop nutrient management more sustainable; expand the use of biomass, biogas and organic fertiliser.

Sustainable fishing

'Give a man a fish and you feed him for a day. Teach a man to fish and you feed him for a lifetime.' This proverb can be updated to ensure fishermen act sustainably. Sea fish stocks are being fished faster than fish are breeding.

Some fishing methods mean that small, young, dying fish are thrown back into the sea. The EU has imposed quotas, regulations on net size, closed seasons and exclusion zones to conserve stock. This has proved a tough policy for politicians, fishermen and consumers. However, it is vital if fishing is to continue in the long term.

Sustainable forestry

Forestry provides income and employment for some countries. It is difficult to stop forest clearance and deny land to poor people who live near to forests, particularly tropical rainforests. The governments of these countries may need the foreign exchange to improve agriculture or education and there is demand worldwide for their hardwoods. Sustainable forestry allows some mature trees to be removed without decreasing biodiversity. The trees are cut, removed carefully and new trees planted. This is hard to supervise in some of the more remote forests.

In the UK, clearance of woodland at the start of the 20th Century resulted in only 5% of the UK being forested. Today it is nearly 12% and through sustainable forestry the aim is to make sure that the quality, size and facilities of the forests are still available for future generations.

In the future, governments will have to keep a watch over their forests. There is a tension between the users of forest products, in particular timber, and environmentalists demanding sustainable action.

PROGRESS CHECK

1. What are the environmental advantages and disadvantages of trade?
2. Identify the different types of aid.
3. What do you understand by the terms 'appropriate technology' and 'sustainable development'?

1. Trade can improve standards of living and provide finance for environmental improvements, but sometimes one of the partners is exploited. This can lead to environmental damage.
2. Emergency; bilateral / multilateral; NGO / charitable / voluntary; tied and long-term aid.
3. Appropriate technology matches the skills and resources of local people. Sustainable development meets the needs of people today without compromising those of future generations.

16 Tourism

The following topics are covered in this chapter:

- **The growing demand for tourism**
- **Types of tourism and tourist models**

16.1 The growing demand for tourism

> **LEARNING SUMMARY**
>
> After studying this section you should be able to understand:
> - how to define tourism and describe the ways in which it is changing
> - how to describe the growth and characteristics of tourism in LEDCs and MEDCs

Leisure and tourism

AQA A	✓
AQA B	✓
EDEXCEL A	✓
EDEXCEL B	✗
OCR A	✓
OCR B	✗
WJEC A	✓
WJEC B	✗
CCEA	✓

Many people in MEDCs have free time for leisure activities after their day at work and any duties they have at home. Most people in MEDCs also have paid annual holiday periods. These trends are also appearing for people in paid employment in many LEDCs.

People use this leisure time for **recreation** and **tourism**. **Recreation** is leisure time that lasts less than 24 hours and includes entertainment, skill improvement, rest and relaxation.

> Recreation becomes tourism when the person spends at least one night away from home.

> **KEY POINT**
>
> **Tourism** is a major earner and source of employment in the UK and many other countries.

What is tourism?

AQA A	✓
AQA B	✓
EDEXCEL A	✓
EDEXCEL B	✗
OCR A	✓
OCR B	✗
WJEC A	✓
WJEC B	✗
CCEA	✓

Tourism is the increasing voluntary movement of people, for a limited number of days (temporary), from their place of residence to visit another place. It involves the locations they pass through, those who make their trip possible and the people living at their destination.

Tourism is a **tertiary** or **service industry** that provides relaxation and enjoyment for one group of people and is a source of income, through a wide range of jobs, for others. Some of the jobs provided will be directly related to the tourists, e.g. waiters and guides. Other jobs will be less directly involved, e.g. doctors and shopkeepers.

People become **tourists** for a number of reasons including...

- recreation
- to play at or attend a sporting event
- to visit friends
- for adventure
- to celebrate
- to meet health needs
- to experience a foreign culture
- to escape daily routine
- for prestige or status
- for education.

Domestic tourists visit places in their own country, while **international tourists** visit other countries.

> Remember that tourism involves an overnight stay and should not be confused with recreation. Most questions on examination papers will be about tourism rather than recreation.

The growth of tourism

AQA A	✓
AQA B	✓
EDEXCEL A	✓
EDEXCEL B	✗
OCR A	✗
OCR B	✗
WJEC A	✓
WJEC B	✗
CCEA	✓

Tourism is the **largest** and **fastest-growing industry** in the world today. It is estimated that 10% of the people in paid employment work in the tourist industry and that there are over 900 million tourist arrivals worldwide (see Figure 16.1).

Figure 16.1 International tourist arrivals worldwide and by region

Region	World share in 2000 (%)	World share in 2007 (%)	Annual growth 2000–2007 (%)
World	100	100	4.5
Europe	58	54	3.2
Asia and Pacific	16	20	9.8
Americas	18	16	1.6
Africa	4	5	8.1
Middle East	4	5	13.6

> Many factors account for the growth of tourism. They can be divided into two groups as demand factors and supply factors.

Despite this growth, the international tourist industry is worried about its future because of...

- the growth in international terrorism aimed at tourists
- the increasing cost of travelling, partly due to the high price of oil
- the environmental impact of tourist flights
- growing concerns about the security of jobs and the value of money
- health scares in some popular destinations, e.g. SARS, AIDS and swine flu.

Demand factors are factors increasing the number of people wanting to be tourists. **Supply factors** are factors encouraging the development of tourism.

> Be ready to account for the growth of tourism in some places but not in others. Be ready to suggest how each of these factors could be applied to places you know.

Figure 16.2 Demand and supply factors in tourism

Demand factors	Supply factors
<ul><li>People have increased amounts of income available for holidays (greater affluence).</li><li>Jobs provide paid holidays.</li><li>The length of the working week has been reduced.</li><li>It is easier to travel.</li><li>Cheaper package holidays are available.</li><li>Advertising increases awareness.</li><li>Hectic urban lifestyles.</li><li>Modern telecommunications, including telephones, fax machines and the Internet make international booking more efficient.</li><li>Early retirement and a longer life expectancy mean that more people over 60 are tourists.</li></ul>	<ul><li>Attractive climates, including warm to hot temperatures, little rain, or snow in winter for skiing.</li><li>Culture, including buildings, museums, art galleries and festivals, distinctive food and traditional music.</li><li>The combination of sun, sea and sand.</li><li>Safety and stable governments.</li><li>Special festivals or sporting events.</li><li>Nostalgia or adventure.</li><li>Scenery such as mountains, gorges, waterfalls, coasts and caves.</li><li>Ecology including interesting trees, plants, birds and marine life.</li><li>Famous sites of historic events.</li><li>Sports facilities and nightlife.</li></ul>

16.2 Types of tourism and tourist models

After studying this section you should be able to understand:
- the factors contributing to changes in tourism
- how to recognise the impacts that tourism is having on places.

Types of tourist break

There are many options available to tourists:
- **Package holidays**, which include flights, accommodation, food and a guide.
- **Weekend breaks** at hotels that are mainly used by business people during the week.
- **Family holidays** designed particularly for children with organised events, childminding facilities and evening entertainment,
- **Age-specific holidays**, e.g. for those aged 18–30 or the over-55s.
- **Self-catering** in an apartment, small cottage or house where holiday makers cook most of their meals.
- **Fly-drive**, which involves flights and rental car and where hotels and itinerary may be arranged in advance.
- **Individual, independent or group holidays**, which may be on a low budget or for an extended period, e.g. backpacking.
- **Specialist breaks** that develop a skill, e.g. sailing, painting, gardening and photography.

The advantages and disadvantages of tourism in MEDCs

AQA A	✓
AQA B	✓
EDEXCEL A	✓
EDEXCEL B	✗
OCR A	✗
OCR B	✗
WJEC A	✓
WJEC B	✗
CCEA	✓

Advantages	Disadvantages
• The growing numbers of tourists bring money into the area. • Visitors provide jobs and allow shops and other services to thrive. • Roads and railways are maintained. • Communities stay alive as people can work locally. • A rich cultural life survives as audiences are swelled by visitors on holiday. • Local artists and crafts people can sell their work in galleries. • Local people can use the facilities provided for tourists. • Farmers can increase their income with farmers' markets, holiday cottages, adventure experiences and bed and breakfasts.	• Traffic congested as poor local roads become too busy at peak times. • Car parks fill up and grass verges are damaged by parked cars. • Footpaths are eroded by large numbers of walkers. • Bridleways become muddy from the increased number of mountain bikers and horse riders. • 'Honeypot' sites become overcrowded, to the point where their original attractiveness is threatened. • House prices rise as second-home buyers out-bid local young people. • Farmers have their working land invaded by visitors who cause damage to fences, crops and animals.

Managing the problems created by tourists

Methods used to manage the problem include...
- providing park-and-ride schemes on the edges of the sensitive areas
- reinforcing footpaths and providing alternative routes

- focusing demand on one or two honeypot sites and accepting that they will be sacrificed for the sake of other areas
- ensuring that affordable new housing is built for local people
- demanding that quarrying is landscaped during and after use to make areas more attractive for tourists.

The growth of tourism in LEDCs

AQA A	✓
AQA B	✓
EDEXCEL A	✓
EDEXCEL B	✗
OCR A	✗
OCR B	✗
WJEC A	✓
WJEC B	✗
CCEA	✓

KEY POINT

Some LEDCs have tourist industries, e.g. the Caribbean, China, Kenya, Thailand, Malaysia, Mexico and Egypt. They see the tourist industry as a way of improving their economies and quality of life for their people.

Many LEDCs see tourism as a way of getting development started. They need to have a stable government if they are to succeed in the long term.

The reasons for tourism growth in LEDCs include the following:
- Governments build new airports, roads and hotels supported by investment from MEDCs.
- Costs are lower in LEDCs and they become cheap places for people to visit.
- Companies promoting tourism have advertised holidays in LEDCs.
- Traditional holiday resorts, e.g. the Mediterranean, have become crowded with noise, pollution and high costs.
- People are looking for new experiences and reliable weather.
- Long-haul flights are cheaper (larger aircraft can carry more passengers).

For example, **Egypt** has a large tourist industry based upon the ancient Pyramids and the Sphinx, museums of antiquity and cruises on the River Nile. **China** has promoted its heritage with tours to the Forbidden City, Tiananmen Square, the Great Wall of China and the dam on the River Yangtze. Tourists to such countries bring foreign currency as well as jobs in construction, hospitality, transport and tourism.

The advantages and disadvantages of tourism for LEDCs

AQA A	✓
AQA B	✓
EDEXCEL A	✓
EDEXCEL B	✗
OCR A	✗
OCR B	✗
WJEC A	✓
WJEC B	✗
CCEA	✓

Advantages	Disadvantages
• Tourists spend money on hotels, trips, meals and gifts.	• Weak planning controls in many LEDCs and uncontrolled development, especially of hotels, can make coastal areas and islands unattractive.
• The money that tourists bring can be used to develop the country; its jobs, roads, hospitals and schools.	• Fishermen and other traditional activities can be displaced by coastal development.
• Hotels, shops and transport provide new jobs serving the tourists.	• Many tourist activities are owned by foreign firms and much of their earnings leave the LEDC.
• Other industries grow, including taxi driving, gift making, travel guides, entertainment and security.	• Farming may change to grow the types of food liked by tourists, or food is imported to the disadvantage of local markets.
• Religious buildings, monuments, parks, famous streets and squares are preserved for the benefit of the tourists and the locals.	• Local culture may become modified to suit the daily shows for tourists.
• New industries start up due to tourist demand, e.g. telecommunications, beauty salons and gift shops.	• Crime, prostitution and drug use may increase. • Tourists may have little respect for local traditions and religions.
• Locals learn new ways to do things from tourists and the tourist industry.	• The jobs created are casual and poorly paid. • Valuable water resources are used for swimming pools and showers. • Damage may be caused to the ecosystem.

Examples of the development of tourism

AQA A	✓
AQA B	✓
EDEXCEL A	✓
EDEXCEL B	✗
OCR A	✗
OCR B	✗
WJEC A	✓
WJEC B	✗
CCEA	✓

Resort development and the Butler Model

The coastline and islands of the Mediterranean provide many tourist sites for people living in the cooler and less sunny parts of Europe including the UK, Scandinavia and Germany. The eastern coast of Spain, the French Riviera, and the southern coast of Greece, as well as islands such as Majorca, Cyprus and Crete, are the main tourist areas.

The main holiday season is from April to October and during this period the population of such coastal areas can double. This causes problems for local services, e.g. water and sewerage, but it boosts employment in the hotel and other service industries. The coast of the Mediterranean is some distance from the industrialised core of Europe. Before the growth of tourism, the Mediterranean coast was part of the poorer periphery of Europe.

In 1980 a Geographer named Butler studied the way holiday resorts grow and found similarities between them. The following table shows the stages in Butler's model.

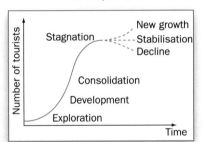

Figure 16.3 Butler's model of resort development

You should know about one resort that has gone through some of the stages of this model, e.g. Blackpool, Brighton, Benidorm and Mallorca.

Exploration	Few visitors, authentic local activity, some locals stop what they were doing and start to serve the tourists.
Development	More people find out about the place from brochures and TV programmes. Tourist companies advertise the site, hotels are built, roads become busier.
Success	The resort becomes very busy, people move to the area for work, local people focus on tourism for income, many hotels are built and local buildings demolished, farmland turned into tourist attractions, roads are very busy and hotels are full in peak season.
Consolidation	The place becomes too crowded and some people stop going there. Local people feel pushed out by visitors and tourist companies, and shops are not as busy as before.
Stagnation	Place gets a reputation as being 'rundown'. Hotels are empty out-of-season and take in homeless people on benefits. Shops start to close and more charity shops appear. The busiest time is only a few weeks per year.
Stabilisation	The resort reinvents itself with conference facilities, heritage trails and competitions.
New growth	New investment comes to meet changing fashions in tourism. Shops reopen and restaurants appear. The site has a busy feel again, jobs become available in construction and tourism, travel programmes start to mention the resort again.
Decline	The resort declines or finds an alternative purpose.

Case study: Tourism in an LEDC

The island of Jamaica, situated in the Caribbean Sea, is 234km in length and up to 80km wide. Jamaica includes the Blue Mountains, and is surrounded by a narrow coastal plain, with many beaches, where the main towns of Kingston and Montego Bay are found. Jamaica is visited by 1 million tourists every year and has an international airport.

Jamaica's climate is tropical (25°C–27°C), with hot and humid weather. It lies in the hurricane belt of the Atlantic Ocean and so sometimes experiences significant storm damage.

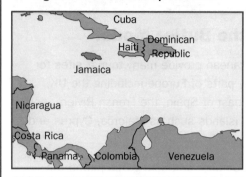

Figure 16.4 Locational map of Jamaica

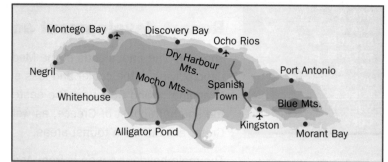

Figure 16.5 Features of Jamaica

Advantages for tourists	Disadvantages for tourists
<ul><li>Warm sunny climate and beaches.</li><li>Good facilities for water sports.</li><li>Plenty of wildlife, especially for bird watchers.</li><li>Local people are well known for their hospitality.</li><li>There are many hotels with a range of prices and facilities.</li><li>A great variety of holidays is available including adventure, golf, family and weddings.</li></ul>	<ul><li>Some parts of the island are dangerous for visitors because of thieves and violence.</li><li>Beaches can become crowded with local traders who pester the tourists.</li><li>Drugs are openly sold on some beaches.</li><li>Some parts of the island are very poor and unattractive to visitors.</li><li>Visitors eating at local restaurants can become ill.</li></ul>
Advantages of tourism for local Jamaicans	**Disadvantages of tourism for local Jamaicans**
<ul><li>Food eaten in hotels and restaurants is grown by local farmers.</li><li>Local artists and crafts people sell their products in the tourist markets.</li><li>Foreign investors bring money to develop tourist attractions.</li><li>Local culture, music and cooking are preserved because they interest the tourist.</li><li>Jamaican products can be purchased on the Internet after people return home.</li></ul>	<ul><li>Profits from tourism may not stay on the island.</li><li>Some areas have been fenced off and are not available to locals.</li><li>Local people may be distracted by the fashions and habits of tourists.</li><li>Gang crime increases as wealthy tourists become targets.</li><li>Drugs intended for the tourists can be used by local people.</li><li>Pollution has increased on the land and in the sea around major tourist sites.</li></ul>

Sustainable tourism

AQA A	✓
AQA B	✓
EDEXCEL A	✓
EDEXCEL B	✗
OCR A	✓
OCR B	✗
WJEC A	✓
WJEC B	✗
CCEA	✓

Increased tourism threatens the places that tourists visit. For example, the erosion caused by people walking across a site will cause damage. The Taj Mahal, Stonehenge, the Lascaux caves in the Dordogne, the Great Barrier Reef in Australia and the Egyptian pyramids are sites where access has been restricted in order to avoid damage.

Visitors to the Cotswolds and Lake District find their peace destroyed by the large number of people. Climbers queue to use the chalk-marked holds as too many people arrive in Snowdonia, North Wales. People that manage tourist sites or plan new ones look at alternative ways to develop them. They want the tourists to bring the revenue, but not at the expense of damaging the attractions of the site.

Sustainable tourism is an important concept in GCSE syllabuses. You need to understand what it is and learn the ways in which it can be managed.

KEY POINT

Sustainable tourism meets the needs of the present tourists and host communities whilst protecting and enhancing the needs in the future. Sustainable tourism minimises the impact of visitors on the environment, local culture and heritage sites, but produces income and jobs for local communities.

Examples of sustainable tourism

Ecotourism is thought to be the fastest growing tourist market. It includes the following:

- An interest in, and concern for, local cultures, heritage sites and ways of life.
- Involvement with wilderness adventures, nature tourism to help with conservation and soft adventures.
- Travelling and learning about flora, fauna and the environment and threats to places from tourism.
- Desire for minimum impact on the area and to protect its ecosystem.
- Supporting local tourism providers in recycling, energy efficiency and water re-use.
- Looking to create jobs and business for local people.
- Managing tourism so that local providers and visitors do not destroy the attractions.

The creation of **honeypot sites** and **wilderness areas** are a strategy that involves identifying popular locations and allowing them to develop. Bigger car parks are built, more public toilets are provided, hotels and restaurants are extended, cycle rides and footpaths are marked, access roads are improved and housing is built. These sites become even more crowded in the summer. Local residents complain, but shopkeepers, hotel and restaurant owners thrive.

Allowing these honeypot sites to attract more people draws demand away from other sites, which protects the site. Around the less popular sites, access isn't improved and car parking is very limited. These areas remain for farming or moorland and, in the more remote parts, as wilderness. In this strategy, some popular sites are sacrificed to protect all the others.

PROGRESS CHECK

1. Why does tourism develop in some places and not in others?
2. Why do both busy and quiet seasons pose problems for holiday resorts?
3. Describe the difference between the demand and supply factors of tourism.
4. List advantages and disadvantages of the growth of tourism for people living in the UK.
5. For a place you have studied, describe the costs and benefits it receives from its tourist industry.
6. What do you understand by ecotourism? How can it be developed in a place you have studied?

1. There are positive features that attract at a particular time plus initiatives by locals and businesses. 2. Pressure in busy seasons, and unemployment and lack of income in quiet seasons. 3. Demand factors are wanted by the tourists whilst supply factors are provided by places and the tourist industry. 4. **Advantages include:** income, jobs, sustain businesses, keep bus and railway services, locals able to continue living in the area and richer cultural life. **Disadvantages include:** congestion, crowding, footpath erosion, higher house prices, damage to land and animals. 5. **Costs could include:** loss of privacy, higher prices and environmental damage. **Benefits could include:** income, better services and opportunities, jobs and sustainable future. 6. Ecotourism involves an interest in, and concern for, local cultures, heritage sites and ways of life. For example, in the remoter areas of the UK it could include environmental protection, information and guidebooks, respect for local culture and crafts, retaining local people, conservation, and profits remaining locally.

Ordnance Survey map

1:50 000 extract Keswick, Lake District

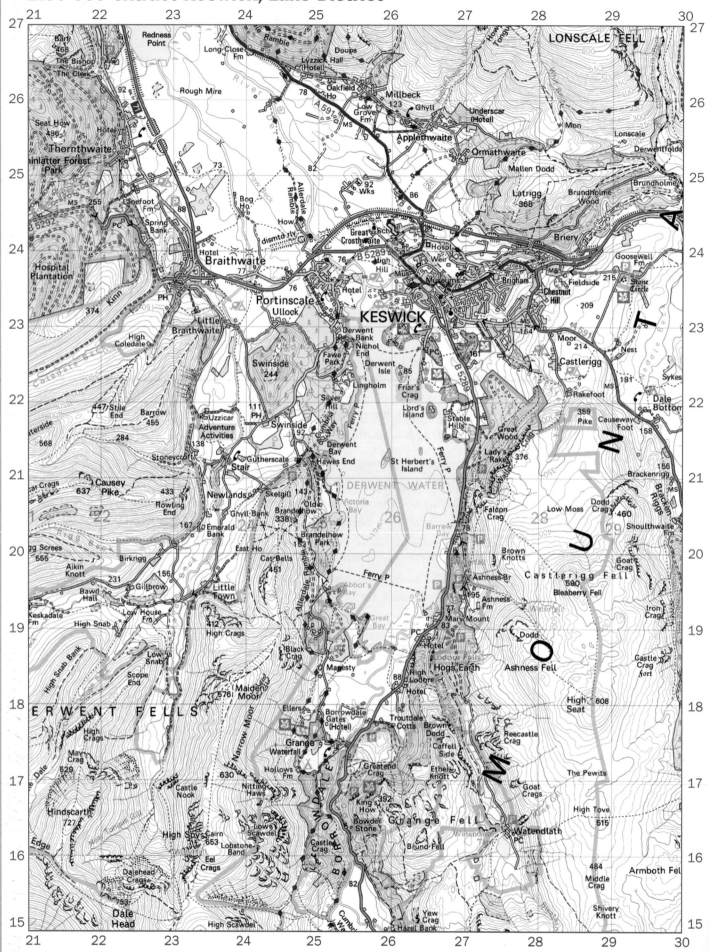

Ordnance Survey key

Communications

ROADS AND PATHS

Unfenced / Dual carriageway — A 470	Primary Route
Footbridge — A 493	Main road
B 4518	Secondary road
A 855 / B 885	Narrow road with passing places
Bridge	Road generally more than 4m wide
	Road generally less than 4m wide
	Other road, drive or track
	Path
	Gradient : steeper than 20% (1 in 5) 14% to 20% (1 in 7 to 1 in 5)
Gates / Road tunnel	

PRIMARY ROUTES

These form a network of recommended through routes which complement the motorway system

PUBLIC RIGHTS OF WAY

··············	Footpath	— — — —	Bridleway
—·—·—·—·—	Road used as a public path	-+-+-+-+-	Byway open to all traffic

OTHER PUBLIC ACCESS

· · ·	Other route with public access {not normally shown in urban areas}	◆ ◆	National Trail, European Long Distance Path, Long Distance Route, selected Recreational Routes
● ● ●	National/Regional Cycle Network	**4**	National Cycle Network number
— — —	Surfaced cycle route	8	Regional Cycle Network number

Tourist Information

TOURIST INFORMATION

⚑	Camp site	PC	Public convenience (in rural areas)
⚐	Caravan site	▨	Selected places of tourist interest
✻	Garden	((	Telephone, public / motoring organisation
⚑	Golf course or links	☀	Viewpoint
i i	Information centre, all year / seasonal	**V**	Visitor centre
🦆	Nature reserve	!	Walks / Trails
P P&R P&R	Parking / Park and ride, all year / seasonal	▲	Youth hostel
⊠	Picnic site		

HOW TO GIVE A NATIONAL GRID REFERENCE TO NEAREST 100 METRES

SAMPLE POINT: Goodcroft

1. Read letters identifying 100 000 metre square in which the point lies ....NY

2. FIRST QUOTE EASTINGS
Locate first VERTICAL grid line to LEFT of point and read LARGE figures labelling the line either in the top or bottom margin or on the line itself 53
Estimate tenths from grid line to point 4

3. AND THEN QUOTE NORTHINGS
Locate first HORIZONTAL grid line BELOW point and read LARGE figures labelling the line either in the left or right margin or on the line itself 16
Estimate tenths from grid line to point 1

SAMPLE REFERENCE NY 534 161
For local referencing grid letters may be omitted

IGNORE the SMALLER figures of the grid number at the corner of the map. These are for finding the full coordinates. Use ONLY the LARGER figure of the grid number. EXAMPLE: 3**17**000m

General Information

LAND FEATURES

⟋⟍⟋⟍	Electricity transmission line (pylons shown at standard spacing)
>--->-->	Pipe line (arrow indicates direction of flow)
ruin	Buildings
	Public building (selected)
⬤	Bus or coach station
⌘ with tower / with spire, minaret or dome / without such additions	Place of Worship
○	Chimney or tower
⬦	Glass Structure
Ⓗ	Heliport
△	Triangulation pillar
↑	Mast
⅄	Wind pump/wind generator
⚡	Windmill with or without sails
┼	Graticule intersection at 5' intervals

	Cutting, embankment
	Quarry
	Spoil heap, refuse tip or dump
	Coniferous wood
	Non-coniferous wood
	Mixed wood
	Orchard
	Park or ornamental ground
	Forestry Commission access land
	National Trust-always open
	National Trust-limited access, observe local signs
	National Trust for Scotland

ABBREVIATIONS

CH	Clubhouse	P	Post office
PC	Public convenience (in rural area)		
TH	Town Hall, Guildhall or equivalent	PH	Public house

ARCHAEOLOGICAL AND HISTORICAL INFORMATION

+	Site of monument	⚔	Battlefield (with date)	VILLA	Roman
· ○	Stone monument	☆····	Visible earthwork	Castle	Non-Roman

HEIGHTS

—50—	Contours are at 10 metres vertical interval
·144	Heights are to the nearest metre above mean sea level

ROCK FEATURES

Outcrop   Cliff   650   600   Scree

KILOMETRES 1   0   1   2   3

Scale 1: 50 000

1: 50 000 scale Second Series

OS map questions

Questions on Ordnance Survey maps appear in all the GCSE geography examinations (in some they are compulsory). You need to practise your map skills – if you do not you are unlikely to do very well. The following questions cover most of the skills you require, but you need to practise on other 1:50 000 and 1:25 000 maps. Keys will be provided for all maps, but it is important that you are familiar with the OS keys at both scales. Use the latest maps – some new symbols have been introduced recently.

For the following questions, refer to the map on p.188

1 **(a)** What feature is shown marking the summit of High Spy GR 234162?

.... **(1)**

(b) If you take the footpath from High Spy to Maiden Moor 237182...

(i) in which direction will you walk? ....

(ii) how far will you walk (in kilometres)? ....

(iii) what landform feature will you walk along? ....

(iv) what are the landforms shown just below the summit on the west side of High Spy?

.... **(4)**

2 Start at the car park at GR 272212.
(a) What type of land use surrounds the car park? .... **(1)**

(b) If you take the footpath to Bleaberry Fell GR 285196 how far will you have to walk (in kilometres)? .... **(1)**

(c) Describe your walk, referring to land use and how steep the climb will be.

....

.... **(4)**

3 The graph shows part of a cross-section drawn between Bleaberry Fell GR 285196 and Cat Bells GR 244198.
(a) Complete the cross-section.

(b) How steep is the gradient of the slope from the summit of Cat Bells (451m) to the lake (70m)?

(i) about 1:2 ☐

(ii) about 1:7 ☐

(iii) about 1:10 ☐

(3)

(1)

Cross-section graph: Cat Bells (451m), Height in metres (axis 100–600), with markers at 70, 100, 200, 300, 400, 500; Lake shown at approximately 70m.

(c) Describe the shape of the valley shown on the cross-section.

....

.... **(3)**

(d) Indicate on the cross-section **two** areas of woodland and **one** area of moorland. **(3)**

OS map questions

4   Refer to grid squares 2825/2826. Describe the valley and course of Whit Beck.

....

.... **(4)**

5   **(a)**   What evidence is there in grid square 2523 that the area is popular with tourists?

.... **(2)**

     (b)   Give the six-figure map reference of the bus station in Keswick.

.... **(2)**

     (c)   What tourist feature is found at grid reference 292238? .... **(1)**

6   **(a)**   Describe the pattern of roads shown on the map extract.

....

.... **(3)**

     (b)   What evidence is there on the map extract to suggest that the building
of a main road around Keswick was difficult?

.... **(2)**

7   If you were travelling along the B5289 from Keswick to Barrow Bay car park (270204),
in which direction would you be heading? .... **(1)**

8   Describe the pattern of settlement shown on the map extract.

....

....

.... **(4)**

9   **(a)**   Describe two pieces of evidence shown on the map that suggest that
Keswick has a problem with traffic congestion.

....

....

.... **(4)**

     (b)   The map shows many public footpaths including the Cumbrian Way along the
west side of Derwent Water (2521). Describe and explain one advantage and
one disadvantage this would have for people living on that side of the lake.

....

....

....

.... **(6)**

(Total 50 marks)

Sample GCSE questions

1 **(a)** Study the map, which shows the global distribution of earthquakes.

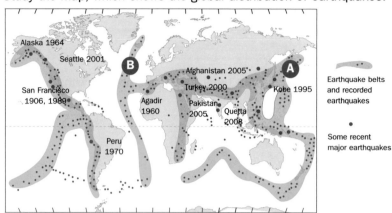

(i) Describe the pattern of earthquake activity shown on the map. **(2)**

> Earthquakes occur in long narrow bands. ✓ There is a
> dense ring around the Pacific Ocean. ✓

Develops the answer by locating a specific pattern and includes a place reference.

(ii) Explain why earthquakes occurring at A are likely to be of a larger magnitude (i.e. stronger) than those occurring at B. **(4)**

> Earthquakes at A are where two plates are converging.
> The oceanic plate is forced under the continental plate
> causing a lot of pressure and friction. ✓ When the
> pressure is suddenly released it can cause a violent
> earthquake. ✓ At B the plates are moving apart. Pressure
> is slowly released ✓ and earthquakes are less violent. ✓

A good answer – carefully applies knowledge of plate margins to explain differences in magnitude of earthquakes.

(b) The figure shows a sketch cross-section of Soufriere Hills volcano, Montserrat (Caribbean).

(i) Describe **three** types of material that may be ejected from the crater when a volcano erupts. **(3)**

> 1. Molten rock called lava. ✓
> 2. Ash is thrown high into the air. ✓

Correct but read the question carefully – it asks for three types of material. A mark has been wasted here.

(II) By referring to **two** different locations of volcanic activity, describe **two** negative and **two** positive effects on human activity. **(6)**

> In Montserrat ash and lava buried the capital city of
> Plymouth ✓ and destroyed the airport and hospital. ✓
> Many people had to be evacuated from the island. ✓
> In some places, volcanic activity is used to make
> electricity. ✓

Well developed first part, but second example lacks a location and the effects are not developed. 4 marks.

(Total 15 marks)

Sample GCSE questions

2 **(a)** **(i)** Name, with examples, two landforms that are formed by longshore drift. **(2)**

1. Spit - Dawlish Warren ✓
2. Bar - Slapton Ley ✓

(ii) Explain the process of longshore drift. **(4)**

When waves approach at an angle to the beach, sand is carried up and across the beach by the swash.✓ The backwash then runs straight down the slope of the beach to the sea.✓ Each wave moves sand a short distance along the beach✓ in the direction of the dominant waves.✓

(b) Explain how beaches are important in reducing cliff erosion. **(4)**

High and wide beaches✓ are good. They prevent waves from reaching the cliffs.✓

(c) Groynes are a type of coastal defence.

(i) Describe how they are used. **(2)**

Groynes are low walls of wood or concrete built at right angles across the beach.✓ They trap sand moved along the beach by longshore drift.✓ This helps to make the beach higher and wider.

(ii) Give one disadvantage that may result from building groynes. **(3)**

Beaches further along the coast will not receive so much sand.✓ They will become lower and thinner ✓which may lead to more erosion of the cliffs or flooding.✓

(Total 15 marks)

Sample GCSE questions

3

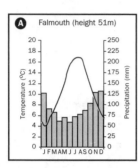
A Falmouth (height 51m)

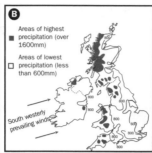
B Areas of highest precipitation (over 1600mm) ■
Areas of lowest precipitation (less than 600mm) □
South westerly prevailing winds

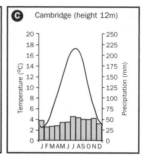
C Cambridge (height 12m)

A: Climate graph for Falmouth

B: Map showing the distribution of precipitation in the UK

C: Climate graph for Cambridge

(a) Study Figures A and C.

    (i) Which place has the highest precipitation in January? **(1)**

       Falmouth ✓

    ← Only single word answers required – no need for sentences.

    (ii) Which place has the greatest annual temperature range? **(1)**

       Cambridge ✓

(b) Study Figure B, a map showing the distribution of precipitation in the UK.

    (i) Describe the pattern of precipitation shown on the map. **(3)**

       Precipitation is highest in western areas. ✓ It decreases to the east. ✓

    ← Two very simple points. Need to give locations for full marks, e.g. East Anglia.

    (ii) Explain the pattern of precipitation shown on the map. **(4)**

       The high areas of rainfall are found in the west of the UK where mountains in areas such as the Lake District make the moist south-west winds rise, ✓ causing heavy relief rainfall. ✓ High rainfall in N.W. Scotland is also caused by depressions. ✓ In S.E. England there is low rainfall because this area is in the rain shadow. ✓

    ← Marks are awarded for explanations. This answer shows good understanding and uses terms correctly.

(c) Use two examples, not from the UK, to explain how the amount of annual precipitation received in an area may affect human activity. **(6)**

    In Switzerland there is a high annual rainfall, with a lot of snow in winter. Winter sports such as skiing attract a lot of visitors. ✓ Many people are employed in the tourist industry in Switzerland. ✓ The high rainfall fills large reservoirs in the mountains, which are used to supply water for HEP. ✓

    ← Well thought out answer, selecting two contrasting examples from outside the UK. Clear focus on the question, applying knowledge and understanding of two case studies.

    In the Sahel the rainfall is low so farmers can only keep small herds of cattle ✓ and crops are difficult to grow. ✓ In some years the rains fail and there is a drought. Cattle will die and farmers will be unable to feed their families. Many children will suffer from malnutrition. ✓

(Total 15 marks)

Sample GCSE questions

4 Study this map that shows the world pattern of population density.

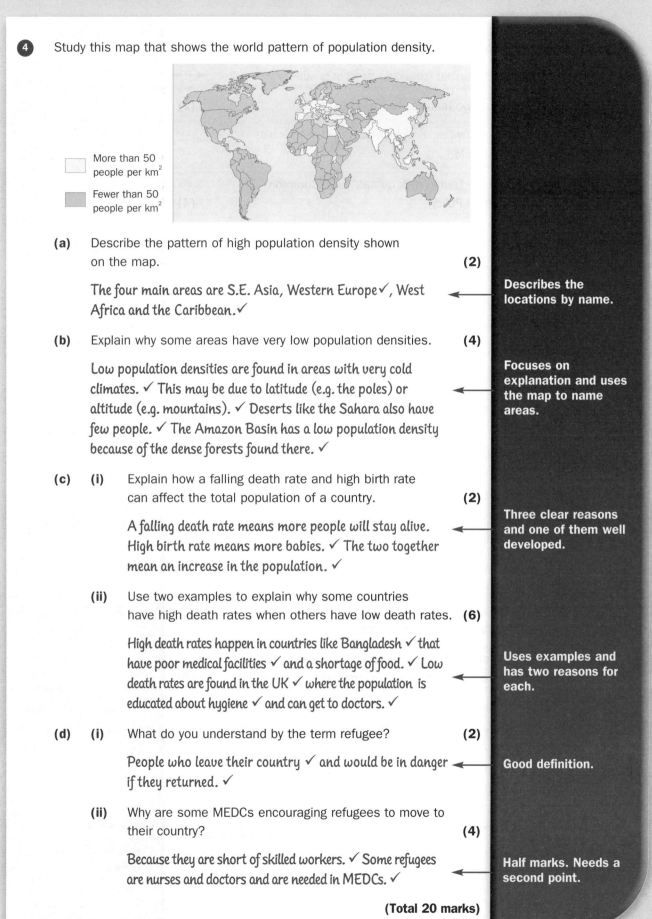

More than 50 people per km²

Fewer than 50 people per km²

(a) Describe the pattern of high population density shown on the map. **(2)**

The four main areas are S.E. Asia, Western Europe✓, West Africa and the Caribbean.✓

→ Describes the locations by name.

(b) Explain why some areas have very low population densities. **(4)**

Low population densities are found in areas with very cold climates. ✓ This may be due to latitude (e.g. the poles) or altitude (e.g. mountains). ✓ Deserts like the Sahara also have few people. ✓ The Amazon Basin has a low population density because of the dense forests found there. ✓

→ Focuses on explanation and uses the map to name areas.

(c) **(i)** Explain how a falling death rate and high birth rate can affect the total population of a country. **(2)**

A falling death rate means more people will stay alive. High birth rate means more babies. ✓ The two together mean an increase in the population. ✓

→ Three clear reasons and one of them well developed.

(ii) Use two examples to explain why some countries have high death rates when others have low death rates. **(6)**

High death rates happen in countries like Bangladesh ✓ that have poor medical facilities ✓ and a shortage of food. ✓ Low death rates are found in the UK ✓ where the population is educated about hygiene ✓ and can get to doctors. ✓

→ Uses examples and has two reasons for each.

(d) **(i)** What do you understand by the term refugee? **(2)**

People who leave their country ✓ and would be in danger if they returned. ✓

→ Good definition.

(ii) Why are some MEDCs encouraging refugees to move to their country? **(4)**

Because they are short of skilled workers. ✓ Some refugees are nurses and doctors and are needed in MEDCs. ✓

→ Half marks. Needs a second point.

(Total 20 marks)

Sample GCSE questions

5 **(a)** **(i)** Name one output from a dairy farm. **(1)**

The main output from a dairy farm is milk. ✓ ← No need for a full sentence – can just write 'milk'.

(ii) Describe two features of a market garden. **(2)**

Intensive farming ✓ of high quality crops such as fruit and salad ✓ ← One mark for each.

(iii) Explain the terms 'milk quotas' and 'Common Agricultural Policy'. **(4)**

A milk quota is the maximum ✓ amount of milk a dairy farmer is allowed to sell. ✓ The CAP is the way in which the EU plans its agriculture. ✓ ← Second mark lost for CAP as explanation is a little vague.

(b) Suggest four reasons for the development of hill sheep farming in North Wales. **(4)** ← Four reasons at a mark each so be brief.

In N. Wales the mountains create slopes that are too steep, ✓ the soils are thin ✓ and the climate too wet and cold ✓ for good crops. ← Climate point could be more specific.

(c) Explain why changes are taking place in arable farming in the UK. **(4)**

Changes are taking place in arable farming because subsidies from the EU are being reduced. ✓ Farmers have to be more efficient by using larger machinery ✓ and growing bio-fuel crops. ✓ ← Three marks for three changes, but none of the explanations were developed.

(d) Farm trails, farm shops and caravan parks are being found on some farms. Suggest two reasons for this. **(4)**

This is because farmers have not been making enough money ✓ and have had to find other sources of income. ✓ Also, people have more leisure time ✓ and look for ways to enjoy the countryside, like walking and caravans. ✓ ← You need to be up-to-date with things that are happening around you.

(e) Describe the efforts that have been made to increase agricultural production in one LEDC that you have studied. **(6)** ← Description needed. Note the switch to LEDC.

The main effort to increase production from farms in LEDCs has been the Green Revolution. ✓ This has used new high yielding varieties of seed ✓ and large amounts of fertiliser. ✓ Some governments have introduced more irrigation ✓ and paid agricultural advisers to talk to farmers. ✓ Governments have also given loans to buy machinery and buildings. ✓ ← A good well-written answer. A pity no LEDC named where the Green Revolution has taken place.

(Total 25 marks)

Sample GCSE questions

6 **(a)** **(i)** What do you understand by the terms 'tertiary industry' and 'quaternary industry'? **(2)**

Tertiary industries are services like shops. ✓
Quaternary industries do research as well as develop communication systems. ✓

(ii) Name one raw material of the steel industry. **(1)**

Iron ore. ✓

(iii) Which of these is an input to a primary industry?
fertiliser   road transport   waste product **(1)**

Fertiliser. ✓

(iv) In which sector of industry does a teacher work? **(1)**

None. They hardly work.

(b) Describe two ways in which governments can influence the location of industry. **(4)**

They can set up industrial estates ✓ *with all the services provided.* ✓
They can give grants ✓ *for industries to go to a depressed area.* ✓

(c) Describe and explain what you understand by the term 'industrial inertia' **(4)**

Industrial inertia is when an industry stays in a place ✓ *after the original reason for it to be there has gone.* ✓ *The reason it stays is because the buildings and machinery are there* ✓ *and the people have the skills needed.* ✓

(d) Define and give an example of a footloose industry. **(3)**

(e) Explain why one LEDC you have studied is having difficulty in developing its manufacturing industry. **(4)**

The country I have studied is Nigeria. They are having difficulties because of political problems ✓ *and the people do not have the right skills.* ✓

(f) Describe the main industrial characteristics of a Newly Industrialised Country (NIC) you have studied. **(5)**

An NIC I have studied is South Korea. The country has developed its manufacturing industry ✓ *by educating its men and women so that they can join the labour force.* ✓ *The government protects new industries by using tariffs on imports.* ✓ *Wages are lower than in more established manufacturing countries.* ✓ *The unions are not strong so there have been few strikes over pay and conditions.* ✓

(Total 25 marks)

It is important to know 2 definitions.

Excellent answer.

Just name one.

Think of a primary industry, e.g. forestry.

No need to say why you selected this one.

Never try to tell jokes in answers.

A very good answer.

Note the command to describe and explain.

Candidate not sure but makes a note to return later if there is time.

Note the need to name the LEDC.

Gains half marks for two points that need expanding.

You just need to give a description.

Full marks but a named manufacturing industry would have been a good extra.

Exam practice questions

1 Explain, with examples, the differences between the processes of weathering and erosion.

....

....

.... **(4)**

2 Study this photograph of a granite tor on Dartmoor, S.W. England.

(a) In the box, draw a sketch of the tor. Add two labels to indicate important characteristics of a tor.

(3)

(b) Granite is an igneous rock. Briefly explain how igneous rocks are formed.

....

....

.... **(4)**

3 Describe how you might use the Internet to discover more information about the physical geography of Dartmoor.

....

....

....

.... **(4)**

(Total 15 marks)

Exam practice questions

1 This diagram shows a cross-section of a river valley in a lowland area.

River

(a) On the diagram, clearly label:

the floodplain   levées   alluvium **(3)**

(b) Explain how man-made levées can prevent flooding.

....

.... **(2)**

2 With the aid of labelled diagrams, show how an **oxbow lake** is formed.

(6)

3 Describe and explain the **human** causes of a flood you have studied in an LEDC.

....

....

.... **(4)**

(Total 15 marks)

Exam practice questions

1　**(a)**　Which two of the following are most likely to be found in the Central Business District?

　　(i) Large department store ☐　　**(ii)** Main bus station ☐

　　(iii) Secondary school ☐　　**(iv)** Football stadium ☐　　**(2)**

(b)　For a CBD you have studied, describe and explain two changes taking place in the area.

....

....　**(4)**

2　Study the diagram of land use in an urban area.

1 CBD

2 Inner city transition zone

3 Lower-cost housing

4 Medium-cost housing

5 High-cost housing

6 Country ring with green belt, small towns and villages

(a)　Compare the housing in zones 3 and 5.

....

....　**(4)**

(b)　Modern factories are moving to zone 6. What are the advantages of this new location?

....

....

....　**(3)**

(c)　Describe two advantages and two disadvantages of having a green belt around an urban area.

....

....

....　**(8)**

3　Give two reasons for the growth of shanty towns around cities in LEDCs.

....

....　**(4)**

(Total 25 marks)

Exam practice questions

1 **(a)** The use of coal for energy production in the UK has fallen in recent years. Suggest two reasons for this.

.... **(2)**

(b) Suggest two reasons for the increased use of natural gas for energy production in the UK in recent years.

.... **(2)**

(c) Describe two advantages and two disadvantages of developing sources of hydroelectric power.

....

.... **(4)**

2 **(a)** Using the OS map on p.188, identify two physical features of the Lake District that attract tourists.

.... **(2)**

(b) Name two types of holiday that older people might enjoy in the Lake District.

.... **(2)**

(c) Describe two advantages and two disadvantages that tourists bring for people living in the Lake District.

....

.... **(4)**

3 Global warming could be worse in 100 years.

(a) Describe how global warming is said to be taking place.

.... **(2)**

(b) Describe two ways in which individuals could help reduce the cause of global warming.

.... **(2)**

4 Some governments have increased their national energy production by using nuclear power. Describe the evidence against this strategy.

....

.... **(5)**

(Total 25 marks)

Exam practice questions

1   Study the table below of data about two countries.

Measures of development			
Country	**Life expectancy (years)**	**Adult literacy rate (%)**	**People per doctor**
Ethiopia	52	36	34 000
Japan	82	99	500

(a)   Explain how the information in the table suggests that Japan is a MEDC.

....

.... **(4)**

(b)   Suggest two other measures of development not shown in the table.

.... **(2)**

2   Describe two problems facing a LEDC that wishes to develop, and a solution to one of these problems.

....

....

....

....

.... **(6)**

3   **(a)**   Describe the difference between imports and exports.

.... **(2)**

(b)   Explain two reasons for some LEDCs having difficulty in increasing their exports.

....

.... **(4)**

4   **(a)**   Describe the different purposes of short-term aid and long-term aid.

....

.... **(4)**

(b)   Describe one way in which aid can help an LEDC achieve sustainable development.

.... **(3)**

(Total 25 marks)

Additional skills questions

1   Look at the data below showing percentage use of rock aggregates in the UK in 2001.

Use	%
Roads	32
Housing	25
Offices and shops	14
Factories and warehouses	13
Other public works	16

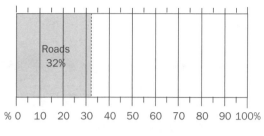

(a)   Complete the graph using the data in the table.   **(4)**

(b)   Name an alternative type of graph that might have been used to show this data

.... **(1)**

2   The table below shows the climate figures for Uaupes, Brazil (latitude: 1°S).

Month	Temp (°C)	Ppt (mm)
January	26.5	252
February	26.8	252
March	26.8	264
April	26.8	262
May	25	314
June	25	248
July	26	246
August	26.4	200
September	27	160
October	27	164
November	26.5	196
December	25.8	264

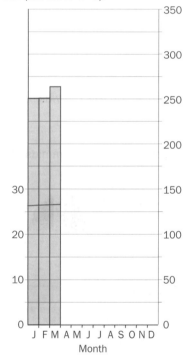

(a)   Complete the graph using the data in the table.   **(4)**

(b)   **(i)**   What is the temperature range?

.... **(1)**

        (ii)   Uaupes receives 2822mm of rain per year. How much greater is this than London's

rainfall? About x2, x5 or x10? .... **(1)**

        (iii)   What name is given to this type of climate?

.... **(1)**

        (iv)   What type of vegetation has adapted to this type of climate?

.... **(1)**

(Total 25 marks)

Additional skills questions

1   Study the two photographs of a honeypot site in the Lake District National Park.

(a)   **(i)**   Explain the meaning of the term 'honeypot site'.

.... **(2)**

      (ii)   Describe two pieces of evidence from each photograph to suggest that the honeypot site is successful.

.... **(4)**

(b)   Describe two problems that face local people living in this honeypot site.

.... **(2)**

(c)   Describe two ways in which the problems you have described can be reduced.

.... **(2)**

2   Study the two population pyramids shown.

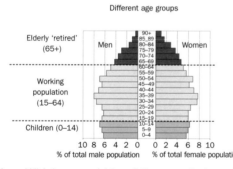 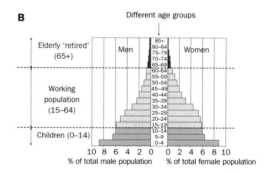

(a)   Which pyramid is of the population of an LEDC? .... **(1)**

(b)   In which pyramid is life expectancy highest? .... **(1)**

(c)   On a population pyramid, which groups form the dependent population?

.... **(2)**

(d)   Describe two reasons for death rates to be falling in most countries.

.... **(2)**

(e)   The populations of MEDCs are often ageing. Describe two problems that may result from this.

....

.... **(4)**

(Total 20 marks)

Answers

Pages 190-191

1. (a) Cairn
   (b) (i) North, 0°–5° (ii) 2km (iii) Ridge (steep sided)
   (iv) Cliffs
   (**Remember – north is always at the top of the map. Use the scale to work out the distance. Some landforms such as (iv) are shown in the key. For others you need to 'read' the contours. Some types of land use are also shown in the key.**)

2. (a) Mixed woodland
   (b) 2.1km (**allow 2.0 to 2.3**)
   (c) Short level walk through the wood, then steeply up following the stream. Leave woods for open moorland – steep climb up to 400m contour. Less steep for just over 0.5km, before slope steepens again with a short, very sharp rise to the summit. Quite a demanding walk! (**1 mark for each change. Reserve 2 marks for changes in land use.**)

3. (a)

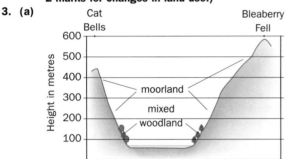

   (**2 marks for accuracy, 1 mark for labelling 'Bleaberry Fell'**)
   (b) About 1:2 (**a very steep slope**) (750/381)
   (**Gradient is measured by dividing horizontal distance/difference in height, i.e. 600/200 = 1:3**)
   (c) Wide, flat valley floor – very steep valley sides rise sharply from the floor. (**Any three points. Credit detailed map evidence, e.g. valley floor is 5km wide.**)
   (d) Woodland on both slopes from the lakeside up to about 150–175m – moorland above both woodland areas. (**1 mark each for 3 clearly labelled land uses – see completed cross section.**)

4. **Answer to include the following:** steep-sided valley v-shape, very narrow valley floor, steep descent, fairly straight. **Give credit for any detail, e.g:** river descends 300m in 600m (1:2). (**1 mark for each point, max. 4 marks**)

5. (a) Caravan park, camping ground, hotel, cycle network, marked path (**any 2, worth 1 mark each**)
   (b) 264236 (**allow 1 either way in 3rd and 6th figures**)
   (c) National Trust Stone Circle (**allow** cycle route)

6. (a) One major E to W route, one N to S route, small number of minor roads, focus on Keswick. (**3 points worth 1 mark each**)
   (b) Railway now dismantled but signs of embankments and cuttings and circuitous route (**1 located piece of evidence = 2 marks**)

7. South

8. One major town, settlement mainly in the valley bottoms, farms in highland valleys.
   (**2 clear points worth 2 marks each**)

9. (a) Bypass built, congested road pattern at centre, roundabouts and T-junctions
   (**2 points worth 2 marks each**)
   (b) **Advantages:** leisure facility, bed and breakfast potential
   Disadvantages: intrusion, noise, litter, crime
   (**1 mark for each description and 1 mark for each explanation plus 2 marks for map evidence**)

Page 198

1. Weathering processes break up (e.g. by freeze-thaw / biological) or decompose (e.g. chemical / biological) rocks *in situ*. (**2 marks**). Erosion processes (e.g. sea, wind, rivers, ice) remove the weathered rocks and transport (carry) them away. (**2 marks**). **You would only receive 1 mark for the following answer:** Weathering weakens the rock structure and makes it easier for erosion to take place.

2. (a) **Your sketch should be large enough to clearly show the narrowing shape of the tor, the rounded rock forms separated by deep joints and the hilltop position. Labels could include:** hilltop location; rounded granite rocks becoming smaller at the top; deeply weathered joints. (**1 mark for adequate sketch, 1 mark each for any two labels**)
   (b) **4 marks given for establishing a sensible sequence:** molten magma in the mantle (**1 mark**) – forced up into the crust (**1 mark**) – intrusive rock (**1 mark**) – cools slowly (**1 mark**) – large crystals form (**1 mark**) – mainly of quartz (**1 mark**) – mica and feldspar (**1 mark**)

3. **Your answer should focus on rocks (granite), tors and river valleys, but could include soils, vegetation and climate (1 mark). Possible sources for locations: GIS (1 mark), Google Earth or 'Aegis' (1 mark), specialist websites for detailed explanations, e.g. Dartmoor National Park (education) (1 mark), British Geological Survey (rocks formations / geological timescale) (1 mark), general websites on physical geography (1 mark). (Credit any 4 sources when linked to physical geography of Dartmoor).**

Page 199

1. (a) **Your labels must clearly identify the 3 features asked for (see p.28 figure 2.12). (1 mark for each label)**
   (b) Levées allow more water to be contained in the river channel (1 mark). Levées can be built high enough to cope with previously known flood levels. (1 mark)

2. (a) **See p. 27 figure 2.10. For full marks your answer needs to show:** an appropriate sequence of events (**1 mark**); the clear formation of an oxbow lake (**1 mark**); an understanding of relevant processes (**2 marks**); the use of some specialist terms (**1 mark**) well presented diagrams and labelling (**1 mark**)

3. **Make sure you select a case study from an LEDC. Link causes clearly to the example you have chosen (e.g. use place names). Human causes of a flood in a LEDC may include:** Deforestation for agriculture, commercial and illegal logging (effects on interception, infiltration, run-off); Over grazing and soil erosion of levées (weakens strength of levée); Flood-prevention schemes upstream (decrease lag times and increase flood discharge downstream); Lack of flood prevention schemes (low GDP – alternative priorities). (**2 marks for each developed cause. Max. 2 marks if LEDC not named. No credit for physical causes**)

Page 200

1. **(a)** large department store; main bus station **(1 mark each)**
   (b) **Description**: Rebuilding brownfield sites with housing, road building schemes, renewal of commercial buildings. (2 changes described)
   Reasons: Changes reflect pressure on the area to stay attractive, alive and up-to-date. (2 reasons given)
2. **(a)** Zone 3 has terraced houses with small gardens or yards. Zone 5 has detached houses with gardens and car parking.
   (2 marks for each comparison)
   (b) New premises (1), more space (1), better access (1), closer to workers (1)
   (c) **Advantages include:** prevents sprawl, green areas near homes, space for recreation.
   Disadvantages include: increases commuting time, increases house prices, constrains good planning schemes.
   (Advantages: 2 at 2 marks = 4; Disadvantages: 2 at 2 marks = 4)
3. Too many people moving into the area, lack of housing, poor people. **(2 marks for each developed reason)**

Page 201

1. **(a)** Causes pollution; reserves depleted; cleaner alternatives; closure of mines; high costs; trade unions **(2 reasons worth 1 mark each)**
   (b) Resource has become available; easier to transport; cleaner than coal **(2 reasons worth 1 mark each)**
   (c) **Advantages:** sustainable, clean, relatively cheap, water areas for recreation
   Disadvantages: costly to build, danger of flooding, loss of river water, attracts malaria, may silt up
   (1 mark for each advantage, 1 mark for each disadvantage)
2. **(a)** Dramatic scenery; beautiful lakes; glaciated valleys; upland tarns **(2 features worth 1 mark each)**
   (b) Painting; walking; guided tours; lake and coach trips; heritage; town shops **(2 types worth 1 mark each)**
   (c) **Advantages:** income, work, keeps shops open, tourist facilities, businesses
   Disadvantages: congestion, higher house prices, noise, fewer homes for locals
   (1 mark for each advantage, 1 mark for each disadvantage)
3. **(a)** Production of greenhouse gases, trapped in the atmosphere, reflect heat back to the earth, raise temperatures **(2 reasons at 1 mark each)**
   (b) Increase recycling, fewer car journeys, holidays taken in the UK, use of recyclable materials and better house insulation **(2 ways at 1 mark each)**
4. Disasters such as Chernobyl and Five Mile Island.
   Problems of disposal of waste.
   Threat of terrorist activity.
   Sustainable alternatives being developed.
   Public concern about safety.
   (1 mark for each well-developed point)

Page 202

1. **(a)** Higher life expectancy shows better quality of life, education available, people have access to doctors **(1 mark for each indicator plus 1 for clear link to MEDC characteristics)**
   (b) Birth rates, death rates, infant mortality, car ownership, industrial structure **(2 indicators worth 1 mark each)**

2. **Problems include**: poor agriculture, tribal disputes, lack of FOREX, outdated infrastructure, crime, disease and unstable government. **Solutions include**: loans, investment in education, working with TNCs, stable government, attracting tourists.
3. **(a)** **Imports:** goods purchased abroad and brought into a country.
   Exports: goods purchased by other countries and sent to them. **(1 mark for each)**
   (b) Poor management, lack of capital, corruption, poor transport services, trade barriers, failed harvests, high local demand **(2 reasons at 2 marks each)**
4. **(a)** Short-term: emergency, follows natural disaster, to meet immediate need
   Long-term: education and training to produce lasting improvements, usually a project. **(2 marks for each)**
   (b) Use of appropriate technology, aimed at local people, not dependent on experts from developed countries to sustain project, low tech, low skill, not bureaucratic, local people in control **(1 way linked to sustainability worth 3 marks)**

Page 203

1. **(a)**

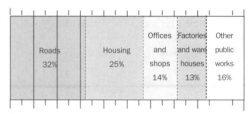

% 0 10 20 30 40 50 60 70 80 90 100%

(3 marks for accuracy of graph plus 1 mark for adding labels correctly)
   (b) Bar graph (individual columns) or pie graph **(1 mark for either)**
2 **(a)** Complete the graph **(4 marks)** and add titles to the correct axes (T($^{\circ}$C), Ppt (mm)) **(2 marks)**. **For completed graph, see p.67 Figure 6.19.**
   (b) (i) 2°C (ii) about x5 (iii) tropical or equatorial **(1 mark for either)** (iv) Tropical rainforest

Page 204

1. **(a)** (i) Popular tourist site, very crowded in summer, facilities managed to meet large demand.
   (ii) Crowds of people, facilities in use, busy street, people in holiday clothes (2 descriptions worth 2 marks each)
   (b) Problems include: difficult parking, increased noise, increased house prices, shops' focus on tourists, unemployment off-season (1 mark for each problem)
   (c) Parking restrictions and permit schemes for locals, affordable housing for locals only, pedestrian-only areas, extension of season with other attractions (2 ways outlined at 1 mark each)
2. **(a)** Pyramid B.
   (b) Pyramid A.
   (c) Young people before working (1 mark), the older retired people (1 mark), others not working not shown.
   (d) Better health care, better diet, cleaner living conditions, improved water supply, access to doctors, more widespread education.
   (2 reasons worth 1 mark each)
   (e) Increased burden on the working population, higher welfare costs, higher state pension costs, more hospitals and doctors needed, larger houses occupied by older couples.
   (2 problems worth 2 marks each)

Index